THE LEADERSHIP
QUESTION

Copublished with the Eagleton Institute of Politics,
Rutgers University

THE LEADERSHIP QUESTION

The Presidency and the American System

Bert A. Rockman

American Political Parties and Elections

general editor:
Gerald M. Pomper

PRAEGER SPECIAL STUDIES • PRAEGER SCIENTIFIC

New York • Philadelphia • Eastbourne, UK
Toronto • Hong Kong • Tokyo • Sydney

Library of Congress Cataloging in Publication Data

Rockman, Bert A.
    The leadership question.

    (American political parties and elections)
    Includes index.
    1. Presidents—United States—History. 2. United
States—Politics and government. 3. Leadership.
I. Title. II. Series.
JK511.R63   1984   353.03'23
ISBN 0-03-058032-3 (alk. paper)

49,863

Published in 1984 by Praeger Publishers
CBS Educational and Professional Publishing
a Division of CBS Inc.
521 Fifth Avenue, New York, NY 10175 USA

© 1984 by Praeger Publishers

456789   052   987654321

Printed in the United States of America
on acid-free paper

To J.R. and A.R.,
My Coauthors

Preface

This book is an outgrowth of a paper I presented a few years ago at an American Political Science Association meeting. It was, I now believe, a simple effort to understand a complex president, Jimmy Carter, and his political standing. But, of course, my real aim was to understand the American presidency as a leadership role and, in fact, the role of leadership itself. This was inevitably a more complex enterprise than I thought, and the book that ensued is more like a first scratching than a final engraving of my still developing thoughts on these perplexing issues.

These thoughts grew into a book at the suggestion of Norman Thomas, who sat on the panel at which my paper was presented, and Gerald Pomper, who, as editor of Praeger's Special Studies in American Political Parties and Elections, waited patiently for the manuscript finally to arrive. Because of their suggestion, I owe them much—a view shared, although somewhat differently, by my family.

Governments stay while presidents come and go, it is said. But presidency book writers stay while editors come and go. So, I owe thanks not to one but to two editors who served me (and I trust the readers of this book) well, and whose patience and good cheer were always appreciated. Betsy Brown, who began as my editor, eventually came to believe that economists must miss fewer deadlines than political scientists. Dottie Breitbart, who saw the book through its final stages, must have wondered if there ever would be a final stage. Thank you both.

A term's leave as a research fellow at the University of Pittsburgh's Center for Social and Urban Research enabled me to complete this project and begin another. I am grateful to the Center's director, Vijai Singh, for his support.

It frequently helps an author to think through a problem by testing it before committing it to paper. Eric Nordlinger, who also read parts of the manuscript, enabled me to set forth some of my thinking by inviting me to talk at a symposium he directed on "The State" at the Center for International Affairs at Harvard. Similarly, George C. Edwards III, to whom I am especially indebted for an extraordinarily conscientious and thoughtful reading of the manuscript, also asked me, along with a number of distinguished scholars of the presidency, to talk on the subject of presidential leadership at a Southwest Social Science Meeting in San Antonio.

Any book benefits in its development from being read at various stages by astute critics. Aside from those mentioned above, a number of other astute, even voracious, critics did their best to make the manuscript better than it was (or now is). Michael S. Margolis, Alberta Sbragia, Joel D. Aberbach, Fred I. Greenstein, and, of course, Gerald Pomper contributed greatly to sharpening my thinking and improving the manuscript. Despite the ritualistic incantations, the discerning reader will understand that I mean to implicate them in the outcome. William J. Keefe, Morris S. Ogul, and Jameson W. Doig all read parts of the manuscript and can be held proportionately culpable.

Melanie Katilius did a truly amazing job deciphering my messages and transpositions and producing from them clearly typed pages. I marvel at her skill, and hope that I have not done permanent damage to her eyesight. Veronica Alzona, Mahmoud El-Warfully, Salwa Gomaa, Philip Johnson, Tim Dodd, and Pamela Deasy all provided excellent research assistance, and I am grateful to them.

To Susan and Robin, I hope this marks my return to your lives.

B.A.R.

Contents

List of Tables

List of Figures

Introduction

A distinguished foreign analyst of political leaders, upon commencing a review of studies of the U.S. presidency, proclaimed that to read most of these studies was to feel as though one was "reading not a number of different books but essentially the same book over and over again."[1] One reason that this is so is that much of the literature on the American presidency unavoidably focuses on the dilemmas of generating leadership in a system not designed to endure much of it. If there is any magnet that draws together the diversity of book titles comprising the presidency literature, it is, I think, precisely this theme. Moreover, much of this literature focuses on the interplay of four elements: (1) the limited capacities for presidential direction of government; (2) the exalted expectations that exist for such direction; (3) the inevitable disappointment of those expectations given the limited capacities; and (4) the residual conditions—structural, situational, and personal—allowing for the exercise of presidential direction. In short, to the as yet unvoiced complaint that this is still another volume devoted to a common, though in my view absolutely central, set of themes, I plead *nolo contendere*. This book is about the dilemmas, conditions, and consequences of generating direction precisely because in any political system few issues are thought to be more important.

The conditions for achieving direction and the leadership that promotes it are analytically puzzling, yet essential to address if we are not to be ensnared by the clichés that discussions of leadership easily generate, or by the inevitable tendencies to assume that these conditions are historically and systemically unique. Nowhere, of course, do the capacities for exercising leadership run unchecked—it is only our illusions that they do that seem to. Everywhere, the process of generating coalitions to develop and sustain courses of action is a struggle. So, the issue is not whether there is such a struggle, but rather under what conditions and forms and through what mechanisms does this struggle to energize government take place.

As analytically puzzling as are the conditions for its achievement, so also are the philosophical dilemmas and political consequences that are evoked by successful leadership. For unless leadership is fueled by overwhelming consensus, great change will also probably mean, for some, great disappointment or loss. How to generate direction and also maintain legitimacy is a dilemma of considerable proportions, challenged perhaps only by the prospect that legitimacy will suffer further in the absence of effective direction.

The capacity to generate direction may be produced through elite consensus, public deference, decisive tools for majority rule, or, potentially, entrepreneurial leaders. American institutions normally make it difficult for substantial direction to be achieved in the absence of elite consensus, but the institutions themselves, by their responsiveness to different constituencies, also reinforce the difficulties of achieving such a consensus.

American political culture, too, interacts with the institutions of government. The values exemplified by this culture emphasize participation and openness, and are inhospitable to deference—a tendency that, to some degree, has now become contagious among a good number of other advanced industrial societies. Yet, despite these factors that discourage leaders, the demand for leadership is high. The paradox of modern society indeed is that there is both increased penetrability of the state and increased dependency on it.

Although the problem of achieving direction is fundamentally a problem of the state, it is almost always the chief executive (and the executive's party) that becomes identified with success or failure in attaining this direction. In the United States, especially, the presidency has come to be considered in contemporary mythology to be the nearest thing to a concrete embodiment of the state. It is in the presidency that we largely have come to see (or hope for) the principal source of policy and programmatic coherence and direction. The successes or failures of the incumbent tend to be identified with the prospects of governance itself. Of course, this view of the presidency is not constitutionally given. It is instead the product of a multitude of factors—technological, social, and political—that place perceived responsibility for national well-being mainly on the president.

The paradox engendered by such a situation can be expressed as follows:
1. the American state is fragmented, splintered, and often divisive;
2. American political norms emphasize responsiveness and maximum access (also induced by institutional characteristics), nonelectoral participation, and thus the representation of diversity;

thus,

3. the culture and the institutions of the state make it especially difficult (but not impossible) to arrive at programmatic expressions of public policy;

yet,

4. in the midst of this splintering, we have focused more and more aspirations on a single officeholder.

In other words, we expect the president to be risk-taker in chief, we weight the odds against his success, and then we excoriate him publicly for his failures.

If we are to see more clearly the circumstances confronting American presidents, the role of leadership and the conditions affecting its exercise need to be more generally conceptualized. We also need to consider carefully the impact of leadership, for its virtues also extract sizeable costs. In Chapter 1, therefore, I focus on elaborating the core dilemma of leadership in constitutional systems, and analyzing proposed solutions to the problem of generating direction. In Chapter 2, the relationship between change—its resistances, definitions, and sources—and leadership is further discussed, leading me finally to connect models of government and of governing to ideas about the role of leadership.

In Chapters 3-6, I examine particular conditions influencing leadership, especially in the U.S. presidency. Chapter 3 emphasizes those features of the American political environment that are more or less constant and which, therefore, ultimately affect all holders of the presidential office. Chapter 4, however, examines cycles of varying duration that narrow at some points while widening at others the openings presidents have to pursue their goals successfully. Despite the bearing of cyclical conditions on presidential leadership possibilities, modern trends nearly everywhere have affected the opportunities for the exercise of central leadership while heightening attentiveness to, and expectations of, central leaders. These trends and their impact are the focus of Chapter 5, which also emphasizes that because of the peculiar characteristics of the American political system and society spelled out in Chapter 3, these modern tendencies have especially powerful effects in the United States. Chapter 6 explores the role of the individual as leader, perspectives surrounding that role, and the skill and stylistic criteria often associated with the idea of successful leadership.

In Chapter 7, I conclude by: distinguishing different ways in which "the leadership question" may be posed, descriptively and normatively; defining conditions under which conflict is variously handled and, thus, direction variously achieved; focusing briefly on problems of directional paralysis in non-American settings; and discussing the persistent problems of, and relationships between, direction, effectiveness, and legitimacy. Finally, I ask whether more "presidentialism" constitutes an adequate answer to "the leadership question" in the United States.

Well over three decades ago, the French sociologist-journalist, Raymond Aron, wrote that "the theory of divided and united elites brings us back to the old idea that freedom depends on a system of checks and balances. . . . A unified elite means the end of freedom. But when the groups of the elite are not only distinct but become a disunity, it means the end of the State."[2] In the American experience, crises of "the state" have been more prominent and deep than threats to personal and political freedoms. The American "state," ironically, was organized to compel the disunity of the elite while simultaneously strengthening its political authority beyond the Articles of Confederation. In view of this institutional disunity, two alternatives are implicitly weighed throughout the book, although neither can be definitively chosen.

The first alternative emphasizes the value of *representativeness* (and implicitly that of freedom). The question it asks is, Does the disunity of the American state merely *reflect* the diversity of its populace, the variety of its interests, and the localized concerns of its citizenry?

The second alternative emphasizes the value of *direction* (and implicitly that of effectiveness). It asks, Does the disunity of the American state, in fact, generate *obstacles* to the attainment of a policy consensus? Does it fortify diversity, and breed veto points to coherent direction?

Although all democratic countries are faced with the dilemma of reconciling representation with direction, the particulars of the American dilemma are that we have glorified the virtues of diversity, variety, and localism, institutionalized them, and then rested our hopes for overall direction on a single source. That is the bargain, for better or worse, that we have arrived at in America. What follows are the conditions and the implications of this bargain.

NOTES

1. Anthony King, "Executives," in *Handbook of Political Science: Governmental Institutions and Processes,* Vol. 5 (Reading, Mass.: Addison and Wesley, 1975), p. 173.

2. Raymond Aron, "Social Structure and the Ruling Class," Part 2, *British Journal of Sociology* 1 (June 1950): 143.

1

Leadership and Constitutionalism

THE CORE DILEMMA

"Politics," Max Weber observed, "is a strong and slow boring of hard boards," requiring "both passion and perspective."[1] What Weber observed of the vocation of politics is true too of the practice of constitutional government. For the arts of constitutional government reside, just as Weber saw the craft of politics, in the balancing of passion with perspective. As politicians who are true to their calling must be steadfast in spirit, they must also be discerning of mind and aware of the ethical paradoxes that inevitably lie in store for those committed to political action. And as politicians who are true to their calling must then reconcile temperament with responsibility, a constitutional system true to its nature ought to promote the reconciliation of a multiplicity of values.

If constitutional government is based upon the reconciliation of potentially contradictory objectives, what then are some of the most obvious paradoxes with which such governments are confronted? Several immediately come to mind. Like aircraft, political systems need not only rudders but stabilizers. They need leadership, but if they are to remain constitutionalist they also need limits on leadership. They require direction, but also consent. And while there are demands for effectiveness, there also is insistence on accountability and responsiveness. These are the central paradoxes of constitutional government. Inevitably, they form the background against which any discussion of leadership in constitutional systems can take place.

In its most direct sense, this book focuses on one institutional source of leadership in one country: the American presidency. In a broader if undoubtedly less direct sense, however, my concerns are with the problem of governing in constitutional polities. As far as possible, it is my intention to think in generic terms about the issues, problems, and tensions of generating direction. It is helpful to do so, I think, for two reasons. First, it will make obvious that the problem of generating direction is not unique.[2] It will also help us to see that much of what is happening on the American scene in the way of sociopolitical trends is not confined to the western shores of the Atlantic. At the same time, however, I believe that an effort to treat the problem of leadership generically will also help to highlight the uniqueness of the American version of the problem. If the problem itself is not unique, the form it takes shows the persisting idiosyncrasies of the American polity.

The core dilemma, in essence, is the balancing of governability and legitimacy. The irony of this dilemma is that while the needs are symbiotic, the dynamics underlying them—leadership and consensus—are often antagonistic.

Governability

Contemporary constitutional governments are confronted with a bewildering array of policy problems, some the result of their own past commitments. Everywhere in the advanced industrial world, policy agendas look both similar and overcrowded. As an example of their similarity, "increasing numbers of the aged, expanding coverage, and escalating costs, on the one hand, inflation, recession, and the crisis of public expenditure, on the other, threaten to bring to a halt the progressive expansion of pension systems which has been a characteristic feature of modern welfare states."[3] In addition, the problems facing modern constitutional governments are sometimes capsulized by the now fashionable term, "overload," the essential features of which are an excess of demand, an overburdening of governmental responsibilities, and a withered political capacity to impose short term costs.[4] As Anthony King has felicitously put it: "just as the range of responsibilities of Government has increased, so, to a large extent independently, their capacity to exercise their responsibilities has declined.[5] Decision makers, accordingly, are now believed to be scrambling to satisfy the demands of increasingly activist and participant publics. The capacities of governments to address long term issues, according to these suppositions, are continually undermined by the activism and relentless pressures of various publics, and the diversity of the elite itself.

"The governability of a democracy," Samual Huntington asserts, "depends upon the relationship between the authority of its governing institutions and the power of its opposition institutions."[6] Presumably, as the power of opposition institutions grows, governments stall. At best, they respond to long-term problems with short-run patchwork solutions. A breakdown in governing capacity, according to this view, means that the horizons of policy making are always foreshortened. It means that issues whose costs but not benefits are immediately perceived, and whose consequences while perhaps momentous are visible to only a very few, are unlikely to be confronted, or if confronted are unlikely to emerge with a successful resolution. Unless they are dealt with, however, the cumulative impact of their neglect may foster a crisis of effectiveness—a decreasing capacity to ensure security, resources, prosperity, or well-being. The situation, as Huntington sees it, is most dire in the United States because the American political structure strengthens the power of opposition forces. But it is by no means seen to be a problem exclusive to the United States.[7]

How big the governability problem is, to an unnervingly significant degree, depends greatly upon the political lenses through which one sees the problem. Those who are in power are more likely to see the problem as significant than those who are pressing demands.[8] Similarly, how much capacity governments have to respond to formidable problems is analytically distinct from their will to do so, although it may be quite complicated to draw this distinction empirically. Moreover, even granting both capacity and will, a governability problem might well persist simply because some problems remain obdurate to even the best-tooled policy engineers. As often as not, only the face of the problem changes.

To be sure, even if the problem of governability were alleviated by a surcease of demands and a lessening of the power of opposing institutions, there would still be no guarantee that governing authorities would pursue long-term strategies. Only their political capacity to do so would be enhanced, not necessarily their will to do so or their expertise. Nor should it be assumed that long-run developments can follow from "intentions, plans, and consistent decisions. . . ."[9]

Legitimacy

Set against the need to develop long-term problem-solving capabilities that may be necessary to deter crises of effectiveness are the values of representativeness and legitimacy. In some form, constitutional systems subject the governing authorities to the consent of the governed—in the broadest sense through the electoral system, and in more specified forms through the interplay of interest groups, parliamentary bodies, and sectors of the government bureaucracy. The difficulty in creating capacity for dealing with long-term problems (especially those with concentrated short-term costs) is common to all governments but most central to constitutionalist systems precisely because of their inherent legitimacy of participation and limits upon the autonomy of government.

In the presence of widespread and operational consensus, of course, the tension between authoritative capacity and political acceptability is certainly lessened, if not necessarily dissolved. Indeed, one way of thinking about political leadership deals with precisely this capacity to engineer social consent. James MacGregor Burns concludes, for instance, that "*transforming* leadership . . . occurs when one or more persons *engage* with others in such a way that leaders and followers raise one another to higher levels of motivation and morality."[10] Eric Nordlinger also observes that appropriate elite manipulation of broadly shared symbols can help to build an operative consensus and thus enhance the policy autonomy of the state.[11]

In the forging of consensus, whether induced by a problem-solving culture,[12] by institutional adaptations,[13] or by entrepreneurial leadership,[14] lies the synthesis of the constitutionalist dilemma: the marriage of direction and legitimacy. The creation of such a consensus, like a lasting work of art, requires genius. But genius, by definition, is uncommon. If it cannot be facilitated by institutions or norms, it must be continually recreated by individual leaders, placing upon them a burden of enormous weight.

Can a Synthesis Be Achieved?

Providing direction and sustaining its impetus is assisted by a fundamental consensus about ends and rough agreement as to means. Without political acceptance and agreement, direction lacks legitimacy. Yet if overburdened with the product of compromise, direction may be either ambiguous or lacking in technical rationality. If by its lack of capacity to provide problem-solving direction, government becomes party to a crisis of effectiveness, then by imposing direction in the absence of agreement, government undoubtedly helps to produce a crisis of legitimacy.

Discussions of leadership, when phrased in general terms, often drift like balloons into the stratosphere of cloudy abstraction. We are inclined to think of leadership when phrased in such terms as an unvarnished and costless good. For in the abstract we know that polities need leadership and direction. And the more boldly we speak of these needs, the more we are inclined to believe their presence will inspire movement on behalf of our own preferred goals. If leadership is benign in the abstract, we would nonetheless prefer placing engines only in vehicles whose owners would drive in the direction in which we want to go. But since we cannot assure this, we need to accept that leadership, while a critical element to governing, is but one side of the constitutionalist equation. For every request for leadership and direction, there is, after all, implicitly a request not to be led. While we want government to promote effective responses to problems, we also want it to be responsive to our concerns. Yet while we want government to be responsive to our concerns, we also want it to have the capacity to look beyond them.

If government is not to flounder, leadership and direction are necessary but not costless. In his ultimately favorable analysis of party government, Richard Rose concludes that on balance:

> Those who disagree with the aims of a particular party will not like the idea of its realizing its intentions. This is the price that must be paid for allowing one's own side to be strengthened too. . . . A cynic or a nineteenth century liberal might argue that inaction is the best form of government. But contemporary politicians will not remain inactive, nor can many problems . . . be resolved except through collective choice. When parties fail, then government also falters.[15]

WE ARE NOT ALONE

Generating leadership, policy coherence, and direction in the United States is an especially tall order. Foreign commentators, even those who are admiring, are frequently mystified by just how the society is governed. One comments:

> Most British observers of American government . . . have a real difficulty in adjusting themselves to the huge, sprawling conglomerate that constitutes the governments (in the plural) of the United States. . . .
>
> In the United States government has perpetually to justify itself, to overcome a set of peculiar resistances . . . to maintain . . . its ascendancy over the competing elements in the dynamic life of a diverse and restless people.[16]

American government and American society are both abundantly complex and diverse. One reinforces the diversity of the other. Divided within itself at each level by the separation of powers and divided across levels by federalism, the system is thus fragmented both horizontally and vertically. Lacking a definitive center, but accessible at many points, the system spawns and reinforces a highly diverse set of grassroots movements and interest groups, and thus a highly diverse set of elites. One consequence of this is that whatever problems of leadership exist in the American system, they have little to do with the supply of entrepreneurial leaders. The problem, in fact, may more nearly have to do with their proliferation. Dispersed authority proliferates leaders, both governmental and nongovernmental, because dispersion multiplies both decision-making channels and interests seeking to influence decisions. The multiplication of leaders, however, is inherently inverse to the scope of authority and the writ of influence each possesses.

Issue leadership—that which provokes attention to new issues and new constituencies—is abundant in America, and consistent with an activist (if class biased) public as well as a loosely structured politics. Although such activism is clearly on the upswing in Europe, too, the American political structure is remarkably receptive and open to it.[17] Indeed, one writer, believing that too little attention is expended on these issue leaders while too much is given to the president, warns that:

> One cannot remember any president who provided the vision, who seized the opportunity to be the educator, or who played a significant role as even a consciousness raiser. . . .
>
> If this is so . . . We shall have to look to those interest group leaders, citizen and social movement leaders and those unreasonable and often unelectable types who dream dreams of a more ideal world.[18]

The problem of special importance confronting governability in the American system, therefore, is not the absence of leaders but the generation of integrated policy making and the provision of mechanisms for enhancing it. The abundance of issue leadership in the United States provides remarkably innovative possibilities for public policy making. It promotes attention to new concerns and widens the scope of debate. Yet, however necessary this diverse leadership stratum is to the circulation of ideas, to the promotion of causes, and to the surfacing of grievances, its great diversity also poses significant challenges to the prospects of imparting direction and integration of policy. Leaders are not lacking in the system, yet *the system* is lacking in leadership, that is, in the capacity to impart and sustain direction.

Although the reins of government are hard to find in America, much less to hold, it is easy to overestimate the tautness with which they are held in other political systems. The problem is not exclusively American in kind, even if in its American version it is *in extremis*—perhaps intended that way. The problem of giving direction to government, however, is universal, and it is illuminating to listen to foreign scholars discussing these difficulties in their own countries. To the American listener, the shock of recognition ought to be, if nothing else, therapeutic.

In the Federal Republic of Germany, for instance, Renate Mayntz reports that in the executive:

> The dominant pattern is one of checks and countervailing powers. The need for consensus building and conflict resolution is correspondingly high; the result can be the neutralization of initiatives and a loss in governmental effectiveness. The pattern of executive leadership in the Federal Republic of Germany seems . . . to make more for a stable than for a very powerful government.[19]

Similarly, in Italy, Sabino Cassese claims that:

> The leadership exercised is more the result of mediation among factions, pressure groups, and parties, than the result of elaboration, promotion, and planning by responsible and expert ministry officials. . . . The Italian system is more suited to reaching agreement about problems as they gradually emerge than to ensuring positive guidance and direction.[20]

And in Norway, according to Johan Olson:

> The major response to the problems of capacity, understanding, and authority, has been a political-administrative division of labor. . . . Consultation and anticipated reactions are more important forms of coordination than command. . . . The tendency toward specialization and segmentation and the tendency toward consensus and anticipated reactions partly counteract each other [in that] the system is probably more segmented in its behavioral patterns than in the substantive premises that enter into policy-making processes.[21]

Substantive consensus, as this quotation from Olson's paper suggests, is a powerfully binding glue. It helps to promote a set of role expectations that produce tacit understandings and develop systemwide perspectives among actors otherwise engaged in their specialized tasks. It is a powerful, if not all-compelling, agent for overcoming the parochialism inherent in the specialized tasks that various agencies of government undertake. To turn specialized agendas into commonly shared ones is the great objective of leadership, and the conditions under which this can be done are more uncommon than common. But what is apparent from Olson's discussion is that this task need not rest upon a command model of leadership, nor upon zealous efforts to exercise authority.

Still, political systems that have been based upon some form of segmentation—the consociational systems of the Low Countries and the corporatist ones of the Scandinavian countries—have not been immune from stalemate and paralysis. The increased difficulties of simply forming governments evidenced in both Belgium and the Netherlands within the past decade give pause to ideas about the discovery of simple formulas for producing governmental effectiveness. The squatters' riots in Amsterdam, for example, lend credence to the notion that the forging of elite consensus may come at the price of alienating those who are distant from the consensus that emerges. And in Sweden, the reputed "utopian" democracy of the 1960s, harsher rumblings have been heard in the 1970s and into the 1980s. Strikes, street disturbances, and increasingly rapid turnover of governments are signs that no simple formula exists for effective government. The relative deterioration in the pace of economic growth of most Western economies has had disquieting effects both in hastening social discontents and in lessening the slack that governments require to deal with problems whose solutions are as yet not visible. Consensus will be more necessary, yet harder to obtain.

The generation of political will, therefore, is not a problem of exclusively American origin. Yet coherent leadership is a topic of constant concern in the American system in part because it defies that which the system was structured to prevent. Not surprisingly, therefore, much attention is paid to the prospects for generating effective political leadership—indeed, it is often a passionate obsession.

GENERATING DIRECTION

Four sources of the American leadership problem are identified here—culture, institutions, individuals, and intermediaries. Each represents a somewhat different level of analysis, and each also holds different prospects of being remedied.

The first source lies in the cultural resistances that have a longstanding basis in the American past, but which are reinforced by the localism of American politics and often inflamed by the populist rhetoric of its politicians. The culture does not as such diminish the thirst for leaders and inspired leadership, but it fails to generate respect for authority, institutions, and the public realm.

The second source lies in the lack of supporting tools for generating coherence from the center, the remedy for which is usually proposed in the form of British-style party government.

The third source lies in the difficulty of locating and electing from the pool of potential leaders those who can comprehend the system and the limits it imposes, bring knowledge to the substance of governing, and yet push the system to respond to their priorities. In short, from the standpoint of a president's leadership, "the worse the system's characteristics, the more [they need to be] . . . compensated for by his virtuosity."[22] Leaders, in other words, need to be resourceful entrepreneurs.

The fourth source is thought to lie in the breakdown of strong intermediate organizations and a more coherently organized Congress. Their restoration is sometimes offered as a means of regenerating a politics of bargaining and accommodation—a modulated pluralism of elites, each with something to deliver in a bargain. There would be, accordingly, less need for presidents to heed the call to "greatness" and more need for them to be squared with other institutional and organizational elites who, in turn, could provide political support.[23] The democratization of organizations and institutions, the pervasive penetration of mass media, the mobilization of key publics, and the splintering of interests and institutions apparently have eroded the foundations on which such pillars of support and legitimation could rest.

Cultural Resistances

If, as James MacGregor Burns writes, "great leadership requires great followership,"[24] then the populist roots of the American political culture provide a ready antidote to the emergence of "great leadership." In a seminal essay on the American political culture, the British political scientist, L. J. Sharpe, argues that the American political tradition has paid scant attention to "the importance of functional effectiveness, the public interest, and public trust," and that, to a considerable degree, this results from "the revolutionary tradition from which stems the belief that all authority should derive from the people."[25] Sharpe concludes, in this regard, that these aspects of the American tradition of government are unlikely "to be sympathetic to the idea that government must have some autonomy."[26]

Yet another British social scientist claims that:

> The American liberal tradition is profoundly individualistic and anti-bureaucratic [yet] the effective exercise of public authority depends on a prior capacity to determine the public interest and the maintenance of public respect for government as beneficial: in other words, on a disposition to approve of collective action.[27]

According to still another writer from across the Atlantic, it is the American political class that most keenly promulgates the antistate culture.[28] A more substantial discussion of this liberal, individualistic, and antistate culture awaits us in Chapter 3. For better or worse, the culture tends to deter the development of professionalism in the practice of politics and especially in the art of government. It encourages the emergence of an elite with a distinctly entrepreneurial and individualistic outlook. American attitudes about government and governing—especially because these attitudes are significantly represented among the elite—may be even more unusual than the distinctiveness of American political institutions.

Beliefs that proclaim government a burden and view politicians and bureaucrats as parasites regardless of its (and their) responsiveness are unlikely to be easily manipulated, and thus are unlikely to be easily remedied.[29] Politicians who degrade political institutions and government itself offer scant hope for providing the adhesion necessary to constitute a political community.[30] Governments may be made and altered (though not easily) by men and women, but societies and the values that radiate from them are shaped and transformed by a chain of historical causes that are mostly beyond manipulation. Rearranging the machinery of government requires prescience, but reconstituting the culture that fuels the machinery may require omnipotence.

Better Tools

Structures, however, can affect culture, and in adherence to this proposition lies both faith in the possibilities of great change and the commitment of would-be constitution makers. One would-be constitution maker argues, for instance, that

> The framers of the American Constitution laid the groundwork for political institutions that fragmented the electorate and multiplied "issues with a disparate local impact." *Attitudes supporting heterogeneity were greatly reinforced.* Small wonder that a welter of local interests should form and become politically entrenched.[31]

To rearrange the machinery of government and alter the structural terms of politics is at the very least to implicitly engage in constitution making. If constitutions are to endure, however, they must be based upon considerations larger than yesterday's symptoms. Constitutional designs need to be based upon what it is like to be out of power as well as to be in power. Giving direction to government inevitably sounds more appetizing when the direction is a preferred one. However crass it may sound, stalemate is a more appealing result when one is in opposition. Constitution making (and thus retooling the machinery) is a demanding task that must reconcile the need to govern with the opportunity to oppose.

Whereas cultural modification might predispose to a general strengthening of authority and to some alteration in the organization of politics, it would not necessarily predispose to any particular governmental form. But ideas about retooling the machinery of government, whether in incremental or comprehensive terms, have tended toward a president-centric orientation to the political system and the society. The American presidency, as much by evolution as by constitutional design, has come to represent the expected fulcrum of leadership—the one source of coherent will in a system that institutionalizes the diversity of wills. With the development of such expectations assuredly comes a craving for tools to enhance central authority commensurately with the rise in expectations. Although a broad range of tools has been proposed, most have focused upon producing party majorities with a stake in presidential programs: in other words, a quasi-parliamentary system with a presidential head.

Nearly forty years ago, in an environment of presidential-congressional cooperation (induced by the crisis of full-scale war), Don Price noted that America was a federation in the process of becoming a nation, and that the American constitutional system, unlike a parliamentary one, was far better equipped to "accommodate the interests of diverse areas and populations in a federal republic."[32] Thirty-seven years later, in less crisis filled but domestically more contentious times, Lloyd Cutler, counsel to a president noted for his legendary political troubles, wrote that the issues confronting government now were ones of an allocative nature which the present system with its multiple veto points could not effectively confront. The pressing need, as he saw it, was to alter the political machinery so as "to form a government."[33] The source for such authority lies in the belief that elections confer a special mandate. For this mandate to be effectively conferred, the electoral (and, thus, representational) process must be simplified so as to reduce the babble of tongues generated by the localized election of officials gathered together in Washington to serve different terms across different institutions. The obvious appeal of quasi-parliamentary government, as put forth by its proponents, is to redirect accountability from institutions to electorates. Instead of institutional checkmating, accountability would flow from electoral decisions. Direct accountability, therefore, presumes the power to enact an agenda and to be judged on it. Such straightforward expectations are inevitably followed by complicating considerations.

The principal complication lies in the assumption that in the United States majority governments could easily be formed under new constitutional conditions. It is not self-evident that the reputed incoherence of the existing parties (usually such reference is to the Democrats) would be easily relieved. Depending upon a good many other factors, either the parties might be large and quite factionalized, or there might be a larger number of smaller parties. The main effect, then, simply might be to alter the places where, and the actors with whom, agreements must be concluded. In any case, one can easily imagine tensions emerging as in Britain between members of Parliament and local party organizations, and between parliamentary and extra-parliamentary parties, or between the inner party elite and the legislative rank and file as in West Germany. Accommodations must be arrived at, and the programs that result are as much a reflection of these compromises as they are the will of any one authority. A quasi-parliamentary system might make the enactment of laws and certainly the legislative movement of broad-scoped agendas somewhat easier, but such agendas themselves will not have been the product of a single officeholder's ideas.

Effective government, as Hugh Heclo noted, is the product of political leadership and bureaucratic knowledge.[34] Spurring movement of an agenda through legislative enactments is only one part of the story, even though it is the element that is most visible to the naked eye. To go beyond that means necessarily to relate enactments to administrative operations, though that relationship must be a two-way street. Pushing change beyond existing organizational routines and practices requires more than loyal soldiers in the legislature. At the same time, absorbing lessons from the permanent government requires some recognition of the limits of change. As one study of Britain shows, while different parties have "controlled" the government, the impact of policy upon the performance of macro-economic indicators has not been noticeable.[35] Party government, by itself, does not equal effective control of the implementation of policy, but even effective control of policy operations does not necessarily mean more effective performance.

In this regard, tools that would strengthen political discipline to produce a form of party government also might have the effect of producing political whiplash—sudden starts and stops. The elevation of temporary majorities to a more or less ruling status presents the potential of radically shifting from one direction to another at the cost of continuity.[36]

To join together the fate of congressional majorities with that of the president is a key aspiration of would-be constitutional revisionists. Presumably, this would help generate more adhesiveness within the parties which in turn could provide the basis for successful programmatic direction from the president. There are a number of operational hurdles in the road of this wish—not the least of which is that it is still possible for the White House and Congress to be dominated by different parties. Thus the prospects of such change appear to be limited at least on the immediate horizon. Except among the rapidly growing legion of living ex-presidents, there is, as yet, no substantial social consensus on its behalf, and without this social consensus there can be, in the American system, no political-legal consensus. To would-be reformers, of course, this is the "Catch-22" of the American constitutional system. Assuming that the biases of the existing system thwart, for the foreseeable future, the designs of those who would seek to synchronize the electoral fates of members of Congress with the president, what then can be done to promote effective leadership?

Better Leaders

A short but not necessarily simple answer to the question of how better leadership can be produced is "to elect good men to the presidency."[37] But what qualities does "good" translate into? Where are such prospects for the presidency to be found? And, are they likely to be elected? Is a good president to be defined, as was fashionable in the immediate aftermath of the exposing of excesses in the Nixon administration, merely as someone who would be unlikely to provoke a constitutional crisis? Is "good," in other words, to be an aspect of a president's moral character? Alternatively, is good meant to refer to one's skills at statecraft? This definition of good, as a consequence of its reputed absence seemed especially to come into fashion during the Carter administration. Yet a third conception of good might well refer to a president's intellectual tools; his ability to grasp the policy issues confronting him and to measure carefully the alternatives.

The presidency of Richard Nixon obviously gave rise to concerns about the first definition, which emphasizes apprehending the virtues of constitutionalism. One might suppose that leaders imbued with such virtues are produced through a socialization process that screens out the overreachers, the overzealous, and the corrupt. The underlying assumption here is that the political game that is played must be conducive to moderation in the quest for power, and probity in standards of conduct. A secondary assumption is pyramided onto the first—namely that if the political game is played in the described manner, then presidents should clearly be recruited from among experienced game players.

The central issues seem to lie in the two assumptions stated above. Does the system help to produce leaders of moderate temperament or of outsized ambitions? Does the system generate a politics highly immunized from corruption or one considerably dependent upon the influence of private money? If the answers to the first parts of each of these two questions are yes, then it should be especially important to recruit presidents from among professional politicians. But if serious doubts exist about providing an affirmative answer, then "good" presidents would have to be found (as the Progressives thought) from outside the professional political arena. Moreover, there would still be significant doubt that "good" presidents could overcome a bad system.

The second definition of "good" emphasizes statecraft; in other words, the capacity of presidents to steer the political system toward outcomes that accord with their goals. For twenty years, Richard Neustadt's book, *Presidential Power,* has been the most celebrated rendition of the statecraft definition of "good."[38] Neustadt's is an especially sophisticated analysis precisely because of its conditional nature. It is predicated on the supposition that a system designed to frustrate the exercise of leadership requires exceptional leaders with finely honed political skills. Neustadt is not unmindful of the need for better tools, yet remains skeptical of the likelihood of their appearance.[39] In their absence, the individual selected will have to compensate for the supporting structures that remain to be erected. In 1960, Neustadt concluded that for our presidents to be effective they would have to be selected from among the especially small class of experienced politicians of extraordinary temperament.[40] They would have to be politicians with a nose for power, yet a capacity to avoid overcommitment.

Similar imperatives, somewhat more abstractly stated, are emphasized by James David Barber in his study of presidential character. Only one of four possible mixes of character types, "active-positives," are likely under Barber's formulation to yield "presidents who want most to achieve results."[41] Barber's formulation emphasizes having the right temperament rather than applying the right technique. Perhaps because Barber's theory is somewhat more behaviorally generalized than Neustadt's focus on the proper uses of the levers of influence, Barber gives us clear hints, methodological issues aside, as to how we should search for those presidential prospects whose passion for power is mitigated by their equal passion for the enjoyment of political life. We need to read with care life histories in order to detect clues about character.

For Neustadt, there is more complication. It is essential to find people with the right temperament, but they must also interact with the right techniques. If, however, the scent for power is as critical as ever, the prey being stalked has become more elusive, a fact well appreciated by Neustadt in the twenty-year interregnum between the first and most recent appearance of *Presidential Power*. In short, if the instinct for statecraft necessarily must be constant, the techniques of its application may have to be altered with changes in the political context. To be effective, Neustadt now concludes, the powers of persuasion may have to be beamed over the airwaves, and not just to other elites.[42] All of this comes at a price, however. To the extent that power is put in constructive pursuit of policy, presidents need to know more than how to project themselves through the media. To be president even of a private company, after all, is to be more than vice-president for sales, notwithstanding the importance of the latter officeholder to the survival of the former. As a corporate president must know his company and not just his potential customers, the president of the United States needs to know about the government of which he is a part, and not just the mass audience to which he must ultimately turn. He can, of course, overdo this.[43] But the successful achievement of policy goals requires attention to the less visible, if equally pertinent, side of the equation. Put bluntly by Neustadt: "The intricacies of motivating bureaucrats in complex organizations are likelier than not to have escaped the President with a talent for TV."[44]

The complexity of government itself increasingly bedevils successful statecraft.[45] To successfully master both the arts of governing and those of mass persuasion is surely to achieve a prodigious, and perhaps improbable, feat. The paradoxes of leadership grow as the instincts necessary for statecraft have become increasingly polymorphous. The virtuosity of skills required of prospective presidents to be both persuasive and effective, Neustadt readily concedes, places great demands on would-be presidents.

Even aside from this perplexing dilemma, and the problem of where such virtuosi are to be found, there is a remarkable subjectivity to the standards employed for evaluating presidential statecraft. Though this complication is discussed at greater length in Chapter 6, it is worth for the moment merely to point to the case of Eisenhower, a president whose political savvy has been both ridiculed and revered. In Neustadt's analysis, Eisenhower was portrayed as a political innocent. As rendered by Fred Greenstein, twenty years later, however, Eisenhower is portrayed as an astute, judicious, and worldly political leader.[46] These differences in interpretation, I suspect, are less likely to be found in the data (though, to be sure, Neustadt did not have access to the Eisenhower files available to Greenstein) than in the different models of statecraft held by Neustadt and Greenstein. To the question, where can "good" presidents be found is added the even more fundamental question: who are "good" presidents?

A somewhat different and yet also related answer to this last question of what constitutes "good" has to do with a president's comprehension of policy options, and his capacity to handle with some agility matters of intellectual complexity. This is the third meaning of good. Since policy making involves asking the right questions as well as making the right choices, and since neither is re-ducible to simple aphorisms or political slogans, a president needs to know not only how to keep options open (statecraft), but also what the options consist of (in-tellect). Certainly a president whose only skill is in policy analysis is not apt to be a president for very long, as a recent example suggests. On the other hand, statecraft without policy analysis is government by sheer instinct.

To join constitutional virtue to statecraft and to intellectual ability is surely, by composite, to define "good." To produce such persons for the presidency with any degree of regularity is quite another matter. At the very least, it is much to ask of a political culture that denigrates politics and politicians, abjures pro-fessionalism in government if not, in fact, government itself, and denounces bureaucrats and intellectuals while, ironically, the system becomes increasingly dependent upon each.

Restoring Intermediaries

Generating leadership may require collectivizing it, not by diluting the formal powers of presidents but by recognizing that the power both to make things happen in the system and to legitimize such actions requires bargaining. In contrast to a presidency-centric system, in which a mandate for programmatic leadership is as-sumed to be exclusively given to the president, is a restoration of strong inter-mediate organizations—political parties, peak associations, and congressional leadership. Turning presidential attentions to reaching accommodations with other elites is seen as a means of reducing the potential for demagogic media appeals and, therefore, for rightfully elevating substance over style.[47]

A genuine pluralism of interests, in this view, requires a lessening of the pres-ent hyperpluralism. Effective bargaining requires partners with the capacity to deliver. A system predicated on bargaining, necessitated in large part by the struc-tural features outlined in the American constitution, requires unity among the bar-gaining partners.[48] For stable agreements to be reached, compromise necessitates stability at the top. Intermediate organizations have not disappeared, of course. In many respects, as with interest groups, they have multiplied, meaning that each carries with it a more narrowly focused constituency with less and less willingness to compromise because the focus of concentration is so circumscribed. In other en-vironments, as well as in Congress, there has been internal splintering and diffu-sion of leadership. Party organizations have tended surprisingly to become both more centralized and purposive, while becoming increasingly hollow at the local levels where they must relate to voters.[49] Some of what has happened in recent times to intermediate organizations possibly is reparable by legal changes. And some repair may be caused by the collective realization of the many newly em-powered that the costs and inefficiencies of excessive splintering can be exorbi-tant. But much is likely to be irreversible—a matter that is discussed in Chapter 5.

Whatever the virtues of governing by accommodation and bargaining (there are of course liabilities too), it is simply not clear, as E. E. Schattschneider so ably pointed out, that large interest aggregates could ever deliver as much as they were given credit for.[50] Nor is it clear that presidents could effectively bargain with congressional committee chairmen who were obdurately opposed to presidential proposals, even in, indeed most especially in, the era of powerful committee chairs. And though presidents were once beholden to a few strong local party leaders, a condition very unlikely to be recreated, they are more likely now to have had substituted in their place the mayors who imbibe at the federal trough. The burden of dependence in this regard has been reversed.

In short, the pluralist dance may never have been the stately minuet that it sometimes has been held to be. At the same time, it may not have devolved quite as fully into the frenetic whirling dervish it now sometimes is reputed to have become. Bargaining partners remain, and ad hoc bargains can be reached, in some respects perhaps more easily for presidents now than when committee chairs bottled up legislation. The past was no less full of logjams. It is just that there are more logs now. Bargains are still a necessary part of how the American political system works. But more agreements now have to be reached with more people who, in turn, each represent fewer.

Everywhere, it seems, there are more obstacles to than conduits for the capacity to move government in coherent directions. As compelling as the need for leadership often is, the resisters to its exercise—however variable the form of these resistances—are also powerful. In a constitutionalist system the key question regarding leadership is not simply how it can be imposed—a view at the source of several recent U.S. presidents' troubles—but, more important, how it can be both legitimate and effective, an obviously more complicated question. Like the setting sun on the horizon, then, the question of leadership seems perfectly formed in the distance. But getting a firm grip on it is much like reaching for the sun: in a word, impossible.

Though the resistances to leadership are increasingly inherent in the complexity of both government and society, they still loom larger in the United States—their sources more multiple, intertwining, and deeply rooted. Americans are often enchanted by the rhetoric of leadership, but the American system mostly operates to deny its possibilities.

NOTES

1. Max Weber, "Politics as a Vocation," in *From Max Weber: Essays in Sociology,* ed. H. H. Gerth and C. Wright Mills (New York: Oxford University Press, 1958), p. 128.
2. See, in this regard, Richard Rose, "The Problem Is Not Unique: A European Perspective on Political Leadership." American Enterprise Institute, January, 1980.
3. Gary Freeman and Paul Adams, "The Politics of Retrenchment: Social Security in Comparative Perspective." Paper presented at the 1979 Annual Meeting of the American Political Science Association, Washington, D.C.

4. See, for example, Anthony King, "Overload: Problems of Governing in the 1970s," *Political Studies* 33 (June-September 1975): 284-296; Samuel Brittan, "The Economic Contradictions of Democracy," *British Journal of Political Science* 5 (April 1975): 153-175; Richard Rose and B. Guy Peters, *Can Governments Go Bankrupt?* (New York: Basic Books, 1979); and Lester C. Thurow, *The Zero-Sum Society: Distribution and the Possibilities for Economic Change* (New York: Basic Books, 1980). Dennis Kavanagh rightly notes that since governing was never easy the notion of overload makes sense only when compared to the peculiarly manageable period of the 1950s and 1960s. See his, "Political Leadership: The Labours of Sisyphus," in *Challenge to Governance: Studies in Overloaded Polities,* ed. Richard Rose (Beverly Hills: Sage Publications, 1980), pp. 214-235. For an analysis that challenges the overload thesis, see Eric A. Nordlinger, *On the Autonomy of the Democratic State* (Cambridge, Mass.: Harvard University Press, 1981).

5. King, "Overload," p. 166.

6. Samuel P. Huntington, "The Democratic Distemper," in *the American Commonwealth-1976,* ed. Nathan Glazer and Irving Kristol)New York: Basic Books, 1976), p. 23.

7. For an analysis of the resources of opposition elements in Britain, however, see Norman H. Keehn, "Great Britain: The Illusion of Governmental Authority," *World Politics* 30 (July 1978): 538-562.

8. See William A. Gamson, *Power and Discontent* (Homewood, Ill.: The Dorsey Press, 1968).

9. See James G. March and Johan P. Olson, "What Administrative Reorganization Tells Us About Governing," *American Political Science Review* 77 (June 1983): 292.

10. However, given the instrumentation that Burns prefers—strong, ideologically driven parties at the beck and call of inspired presidents—there is a distinct likelihood that opponents also would be driven to higher levels of motivation, if not morality. See James MacGregor Burns, *Leadership* (New York: Harper and Row, 1978), p. 19. Emphases are in the original.

11. Nordlinger, *On the Autonomy of the Democratic State,* pp. 99-117.

12. As argued in Sweden, for example, by Thomas J. Anton. See his, *Administered Politics: Elite Political Culture in Sweden* (Boston: Martinus Nijhoff, 1980); and also his "Policy Making and Political Culture in Sweden," *Scandinavian Political Studies* 4 (1969): 90-102.

13. As argued in the Netherlands, for instance, by Arend Lijphart. See his, *The Politics of Accommodation: Pluralism and Democracy in the Netherlands,* 2nd ed. rev. (Berkeley: University of California Press, 1975).

14. See, for instance, Richard E. Neustadt, *Presidential Power: The Politics of Leadership from FDR to Carter* (New York: John Wiley, 1980); Thomas E. Cronin, *The State of the Presidency,* 2nd ed. (Boston: Little, Brown, 1980); and Burns, *Leadership.*

15. Richard Rose, *The Problem of Party Government* (New York: The Free Press, 1974), p. 427.

16. H. G. Nicholas, *The Nature of American Politics* (Oxford, England: Oxford University Press, 1980), p. 1.

17. For a comparative study of protest behavior, for example, see Elliot J. Feldman and Jerome Milch, *Technology versus Democracy: The Politics of International Airports* (Boston: Auburn House, 1981). See also Dorothy Nelkin and Michael Pollack, *the Atom Besieged: Extra-Parliamentary Dissent in France and Germany* (Cambridge, Mass.: M.I.T. Press, 1981), and Dorothy Nelkin and Michael Pollack, "Political Parties and the Nuclear Energy Debate in France and Germany," *Comparative Politics* 12 (January, 1980): 127-142. On the class bias of nonelectoral political activism, especially in the United States, see Sidney Verba, Norman H. Nie, and Jae-on Kim, *Participation and Political Equality: A Seven-Nation Comparison* (Cambridge, England: Cambridge University Press, 1978), esp. pp. 290-295.

18. Cronin, *the State of the Presidency,* p. 377. A similar point is made by Bruce Miroff. See his "Presidential Leverage over Social Movements: The Johnson White House and Civil Rights," *Journal of Politics* 43 (February 1981): 2-23.

19. Renate Mayntz, "Executive Leadership in Germany: Dispersion of Power or 'Kanzlerdemokratie'?" in *Presidents and Prime Ministers* ed. Richard Rose and Ezra N. Suleiman (Washington, D.C.: American Enterprise Institute, 1980), pp. 169-170.

20. Sabino Cassese, "Is There a Government in Italy? Politics and Administration at the Top," in Rose and Suleiman, pp. 201-202.

21. Johan P. Olson, "Governing Norway: Segmentation, Anticipation, and Consensus Formation," in Rose and Suleiman, pp. 252-253.

22. The comment was actually made about the situation of higher level civil servants in New York, but it is equally appropriate for presidents. It was originally attributed to Frederick O'R. Hayes, former budget director of New York City, and is quoted in Donald P. Warwick with Marvin Meade and Theodore Reed, *A Theory of Public Bureaucracy: Politics, Personality, and Organization in the State Department* (Cambridge, Mass.: Harvard University Press, 1975), p. 215.

23. For excellent examples of this argument, see James W. Ceaser, "Political Parties and Presidential Ambition," *Journal of Politics* 40 (August 1978): 708-739, and Nelson W. Polsby, "Against Presidential Greatness," in *American Government: Readings and Cases,* 7th ed., ed. Peter Woll (Boston: Little, Brown, 1981), pp. 418-424.

24. James MacGregor Burns, "More than Merely Power: II," *New York Times,* November 17, 1978, p. A29, as quoted in Cronin, *The State of the Presidency,* p. 378.

25. L. J. Sharpe, "American Democracy Reconsidered: Part II and Conclusions," *British Journal of Political Science* 3 (April 1973): 156.

26. *Ibid.,* p. 157.

27. Kenneth Dyson, *The State Tradition in Western Europe* (New York: Oxford University Press, 1980), pp. 271-272.

28. Anthony King, "Ideas, Institutions, and Policies: Part III," *British Journal of Political Science* 3 (October 1973): 409-423. And, for an analysis of why the American business elite holds antistatist views, see David Vogel, "Why Businessmen Distrust Their State: The Political Consciousness of American Business Executives," *British Journal of Political Science* 8 (January 1978): 45-78.

29. One study, for instance, shows that while a substantial majority of persons among those who had had direct experience in dealing with the federal bureaucracy reported favorable experiences, there was virtually no attitude change even among the favorable respondents toward the federal bureaucracy in general. See, Daniel Katz, Barbara A. Gutek, Robert L. Kahn, and Eugenia Barton, *Bureaucratic Encounters: A Pilot Study in the Evaluation of Government Services* (Ann Arbor: Institute for Social Research, University of Michigan, 1975).

30. No president since Lyndon Johnson, for example, has publicly seemed to accept government as being anything other than a burden. The phenomenon of politicians benefiting personally by berating the institution in which they serve (and thus helping to delegitimize it) has been particularly well illustrated by Richard Fenno. See his, "If as Ralph Nader Says, Congress Is 'the Broken Branch,' How Come We Love Our Congressmen So Much?" in *Congress in Change: Evolution and Reform,* ed. Norman J. Ornstein (New York: Praeger, 1975), pp. 277-287.

31. Charles M. Hardin, *Presidential Power and Accountability: Toward a New Constitution* (Chicago: University of Chicago Press, 1974), p. 168. Emphases are in the original. The quote within the quote is from Richard Neustadt.

32. Don K. Price, "The Parliamentary and Presidential Systems," *Public Administration Review* 3 (Autumn 1943): 334.

33. Lloyd N. Cutler, "To Form a Government," *Foreign Affairs* 59 (Fall 1980): 126-143.

34. Hugh Heclo, *A Government of Strangers: Executive Politics in Washington* (Washington, D.C.: The Brookings Institution, 1977), p. 7.

35. Richard Rose, *Do Parties Make a Difference?* Chatham, N.J.: Chatham House Publishers, 1980), pp. 106-140.

36. This, according to Bruce Headey, has helped account for the absence of a continuously effective housing policy in Britain. See his, *Housing Policy in the Developed Economy: The UK, Sweden, and the U.S.* (New York: St. Martin's Press, 1979).

37. William S. Livingston, "Britain and America: The Institutionalization of Accountability," *Journal of Politics* 38 (November 1976): 894.

38. The book first appeared in 1960; it has been added to on three occasions, most recently in 1980. All references, unless otherwise specified, are taken from the 1980 additions.

39. Neustadt, *Presidential Power,* esp. pp. 241-243.

40. *Ibid.,* p. 243.

41. James David Barber, *The Presidential Character: Predicting Performance in the White House* (Englewood Cliffs, N.J.: Prentice-Hall, 1972), p. 13.

42. Neustadt, *Presidential Power,* pp. 236-238.

43. Richard Rose, "The President: A Chief but Not an Executive," *Presidential Studies Quarterly* 7 (Winter 1977): 5-26.

44. Neustadt, *Presidential Power,* p. 240.

45. See, for instance, Lawrence D. Brown, *New Policies, New Politics: Government's Response to Government's Growth* (Washington, D.C.: The Brookings Institution, 1983).

46. Fred I. Greenstein, "Eisenhower as an Activist President," *Political Science Quarterly* 94 (Winter 1979-80): 575-599.

47. For excellent examples of this argument, see Ceaser, "Political Parties and Presidential Ambition," and Polsby, "Against Presidential Greatness."

48. For a succinct statement of this position, see Lawrence C. Dodd, "Cycles of Congressional Power," *Society* 16 (November/December 1978): 65-68.

49. Compelling evidence for the dissolution of party organizations in at least one locale is provided by Margolis and his associates. See Michael Margolis, Lee S. Weinberg, and David F. Ranck, "Local Party Organization: From Disaggregation to Disintegration." Paper presented at the 1980 Annual Meeting of the American Political Science Association, Washington, D.C.

50. E. E. Schattschneider, *The Semi-Sovereign People: A Realist's View of Democracy in America* (New York: Holt, Rinehart and Winston, 1960), esp. pp. 47-61.

2

Leadership and Change

LEADERSHIP AND CHANGE AS CONCEPTS

Leadership bedazzles us, but also befuddles us. If its prospect seems exciting, its analysis seems mystifying. The concept, James MacGregor Burns informs us, "has dissolved into small and discrete meanings."[1] Certainly, chasing after conceptual clarification of the term leadership can lead us into irretrievable quagmires. We know, for example, that the term is closely, but not exactly, related to others about which more ink has been spilled than precise understanding achieved. Purpose, goals, power, and influence, for instance, are concepts usually believed necessary to thinking about leadership. There is also usually thought to be some connection between power and purpose. After all, power without purpose is crass, whereas purpose without power is futile. Leadership has to sound better than that, and so power is usually wedded to purpose in such a way as to seem very elevating indeed. Burns, for example, defines leadership as the process by which leaders induce "followers to act for certain goals that represent the values and the motivations—the wants and needs, the aspirations and expectations—*of both leaders and followers.*"[2] According to social psychologist David Loye, the function of leadership "is to intervene in the social flow to direct change toward ends that are favorable to the leader and his organization or group."[3] Such definitions presume an inherent consonance of interest and values between leaders and followers (which apparently remains only for the leaders to bring to the surface), and an identifiable followership whose aspirations and interests can be clearly and noncontradictorily set forth.

A further reason why the concept of leadership has been analytically dissected into numerous meanings has to do with the many empirical contingencies affecting its exercise. Factors such as the nature of the goals to be attained, the nature of the audience to be persuaded, the strategies undertaken, the structure of the situation and its context are among the considerations that lead to many theories of leadership rather than to one single clarification. Leadership, it seems, is probably always best preceded by an adjective.

A natural way of thinking about leadership is to see it as relevant to the process of producing significant change—that is, intended adaptations meant to lead to a significant alteration in the status quo. Of course, not all (perhaps not much) significant change is intended, and certainly not all (perhaps not even most) intended change is significant. To connect leadership with change, therefore, presents few answers but many questions.

The first set of questions is about change itself. What is its scope? its depth? its reversibility? What is it about? The substance of policy? The processes by which choices are made? Ultimately, the effects on people's lives? A second set of questions has to do with problems of discerning causality. What, in other words, is the connection between policy intentions and outcomes?—not an insignificant query when presidents either take credit for, or seek refuge from, the barrage of economic indicators released by the government. What, finally, is the extent of unintended change (externalities) produced from intended change? To ask these questions is necessary in order to understand the perplexities involved in attributing success or failure, skill or ineptitude to leadership. To assume that there are straightforward answers is yet another matter.

Agents of Influence

The link between intended and produced outcomes is obviously highly complicated. It is easier to say what we cannot assume of it than what we can. Let us look briefly though at this relationship, first from the standpoint of the agent seeking to successfully generate change, and then at the results produced. From the agent's point of view, the first condition required to produce change is an *ideological consensus* among the members of a government or an administration about what changes are desired, and, very roughly, how they ought to be produced. Emphases on tools for strengthening parties as governing instruments are designed to heighten ideological consensus. The rationale for party government, indeed for parties generally, is to bring "like minds" together in the pursuit of agreed upon policies. The importance of ideological consensus is underscored by President Reagan's former national security adviser, Richard Allen, who at the outset of the administration, observed that in the Reagan administration teamwork and harmony would produce more coherence and consistency in foreign policy because "the President's top advisers are so likeminded in their views of the world."[4] The limits of ideological consensus, on the other hand, are underscored by the disarray in foreign policy making that subsequently ensued. Ideological consensus is essential to coherence, but insufficient to guarantee it.

No matter what its breadth, an ideological consensus is not by itself a consensus on operations. Moving from ideological consensus to *operational consensus* is as essential as it is uncertain. Party government is no guarantor that this transition smoothly follows.[5] An important reason why an ideological consensus is necessary but not the equivalent of an operational consensus has to do with the different functional and bureaucratic perspectives that emerge among members of a government or an administration. These perspectives on operational problems are shaped in variable degree by the priorities and past commitments associated with specialized task environments and organizations. Where one stands, so the aphorism goes, depends upon where one sits. Ideological consensus helps to reduce the zone of conflict, no doubt, but it does not, indeed cannot, eliminate it entirely. Aphorisms aside, where one stands is not exclusively (perhaps not even mostly) determined by role alone, and the stronger the ideological thrust, the more it is likely to vitiate the impact of role.[6] Concrete choices, however, are rarely directly coincident with abstract values or symbols. Although such choices are affected and often steered by ideological commitments, they are unlikely to be completely guided by them. Moreover, to transform ideological commitment into operational commitment likely requires skills and temperament of a different sort than those necessary to arouse ideological commitment.

In all governments, the process of moving from words to specific choices is difficult and inimical to consensus. In some coalition governments, specific choices force decisions in areas where no ideological consensus could be reached. Confronting such choices can result in the fall of the government, whereas avoiding them can result in policy failure. In the United States, absent mechanisms of central aggregation and the breakdown of ideological consensus into operational questions often heighten bureaucratic politics and other intramural conflicts within the executive branch. Operational consensus in the United States is often made difficult to reach because governing, even within the executive branch, is not a collective responsibility.

THE PRODUCTS OF CHANGE

The prospects of producing change grow with successfully moving from agreed upon generalities to agreed upon specific proposals. Virtually the obverse is true, however, when it comes to assessing the nature of change itself—that is, how fundamental it is and how deep its hold. Thus, as we move from changes in specific policies to the institutionalization of such changes, and, then, to the acceptance of their ideological assumptions, the more thoroughgoing is the change that has been experienced.

At the first level, then, a discrete change in *operations* may involve either an incremental adjustment to something being done now or a nonincremental change. It can even involve a series of significant innovations. The development of a federal minimum wage standard, for example, is an operational change, as have been its adjustments throughout the years.

Beyond any specific change, however, lies the possibility of its *institutionalization*. The requirement of administrative supervision begets, but also only begins, such a process. Institutionalizing change means that there will be a community of interests with a stake in safeguarding and enriching the change, assuring a regularized base of support. Once institutionalized, inertia operates to solidify change. The process, of course, can work in reverse as well. Some changes may be aimed at deinstitutionalizing previous changes. Efforts of this nature, for example, were pursued during the Nixon administration, and even more vigorously during the Reagan administration.

Beyond institutionalized change lies the *ideological acceptance* of change—the shift in elite or public assumptions that provides a continuing immunity to restorative forces. All leaders who wish to produce significant change want it to be accepted ideologically, for that assures against reversing course. Put somewhat differently, the ultimate success of any past change is to have it taken for granted. While the programs of the New Deal and the Great Society, for example, each had been institutionalized, ideological acceptance for the most part has been stronger for the socioeconomic changes made during the Roosevelt administration than for those undertaken during the Johnson administration.

The ultimate paradox of change is that all change becomes a part of the status quo, and thus the eventual prize for those who have pushed for change is to have the change protected from those who would now reverse it. Generating change involves a process of moving from broad but vague agreements to specific and concrete ones. To produce durable monuments to change, however, means generalizing specific accomplishments. This first requires institutionalization, and, even more deeply, ideological penetration—acceptance of the premises of the changes that have taken place. The more institutionalized policies (or programs) are, the better the insurance coverage. Widespread normative acceptance is a virtual guarantee against restorative change.

But what is change? How can we see it? At any point in time, contemporary observers are usually the least well positioned to see change or to comprehend what it is they do see. Even when change is quite perceptible, they are especially disadvantaged in their ability to analyze its effects.

Three Faces of Change

Obviously, change is ubiquitous, and the pages of numerous scholarly journals have been filled with efforts to define differences in its magnitude and sweep.[7] Here, I seek to outline three forms of change: *accelerative, incremental,* and *innovative.*

Accelerative Change

Although no precise quantitative watershed can be applied as in the physical world, an accelerative change is largely quantitative rather than directional. As we know from the physical world, such changes ultimately evolve into ones of kind. Water gets colder as temperatures decline, and at a certain point it becomes ice. An automobile traveling at 60 miles per hour that collides with a tree is likely to have different consequences for its occupants (and the tree) than one traveling at 25 miles per hour.

Acceleration does not require a change of direction. It is, however, a change in the rate at which something that was done is now being done. In federal fiscal year (FY) 1972, for example, the federal government spent 90.8 billion dollars on payments to individuals and 34.4 billion on aid to state and local governments. In FY 1980, 226.9 billion dollars in individual payments and 88.9 billion in aid to state and local governments were expended. Expressed in constant 1972 dollars, the proportionate changes are 53 and 33 percent, respectively. Such very substantial increases in these broad categories of expenditure for the most part took place in the absence of major new statutes breaking ground previously untouched. In fact, despite the fiscal concerns of the Nixon and Ford administrations, the acceleration of expenditures in the assistance payments and state and local aid categories between FY 1970 and FY 1977, covering the Nixon-Ford budgetary periods, was remarkable. In relatively constant dollar terms, growth in these categories, respectively, was 93 percent and 70 percent.[8] In brief, acceleration is the speeding up of a direction already set. It sometimes results from a failure of administrative control, thus presenting those presidents who have few instincts for comprehending the innards of government with numerous obstacles to retaining their budgetary discretion.

What goes up in public expenditures, contrary to the law of gravity, rarely comes down. But the rate of increase can be slowed, and in real terms expenditures in some categories do go down as professors at most public universities are undoubtedly aware. In other words, if there is acceleration there also can be deceleration. Braking the rate of movement, as automobile drivers know, is a precursor to changing direction. Braking and accelerating do occur across particular categories of government responsibility, and neither the spurts nor (especially) the stops are purely products of inertia.

Incremental Change

Incremental change is the product of a system in an advanced state of equilibrium. As initiatives become established and institutionalized, as they create a structure of interests and a political force field on behalf of their preservation, and as the discretion of central decision makers is diminished, changes are apt to come about only in small doses. The tighter the web of interests that has been spun around the activities of government, the fewer the degrees of freedom. Yet, the prospects for nonincremental change are always likely to be underestimated. The electoral process, for instance, may generate irresistible tidal waves. Even leadership succession itself may spur new leaders to promote agendas "different" from those of their predecessors, leading to nonincremental change.[9] In general, however, an advanced state of interest group-bureaucratic interlock, characteristic of the industrialized democracies, is likely to produce mainly incremental change.

Innovative Change

Innovations are easier to feel and sense than to define. My definition, therefore, is a rough one. An innovative change is an intended change designed to alter significantly the policies of government, the institutions and structures of government and politics, patterns of social behavior, or standards of living. It may involve bringing about new institutional structures and processes in a large-scale way, as with the emergence of the French Fifth Republic. Or, by creating altered patterns of behavior, it may reshape in a less formalized way the politics of a nation or a region, as occurred with the Voting Rights Act of 1965. Innovative changes may be large or small, discrete or part of a sweeping program of change. But their effects should lead to transforming changes in the status quo.

Broad scale politically intended innovative changes may have many points of origin, but they are likely to need centrally directed support to be enacted. While in the American system presidents react far more often than they initiate, it is difficult for major innovative policy changes to occur without active presidential support. By virtue of the president's unique positioning in the American political system, it is very difficult for coherent or programmatic change to occur without a president's active commitment.

It has been said, and rightly so, that the American political system is a system replete with multiple veto points. The other, somewhat less attended to, side of this assertion is that the American system is therefore also a system of multiple points of initiation. Some of these points will now be discussed.

Sources of Leadership

Bureaucrats and Policy Networks

Although bureaucrats are usually associated with continuity and inertia rather than with the promotion of ideas, they help supply the operative ideas needed when political leaders have to match words with facts. Bureaucrats, as Hugh Heclo's study of the emergence of social security policy in Britain and Sweden shows, help to sustain continuity for large programmatic initiatives.[10] While politicians are in the storefront shifting the merchandise and adjusting to more pressing demands, bureaucrats stay in the workshop ultimately shaping the products to be sold.

In the American system especially, bureaucrats become involved in discrete but often overlapping policy networks. In the United States, at one time or another, these networks include policy professionals in organized interest groups, policy analysts in universities and research institutes, officials at other levels of government, congressional members and staffers, and even members of the White House staff.[11] The policy networks provide a fund of ideas and analyses, and potentially a structure of power. Where opportunities avail themselves, as Martha Derthick's analysis of assistance payments spending indicates, bureaucrats usually will seek to push harder in directions they and their principal clienteles prefer. They are often advocates and entrepreneurs because under most circumstances the American system with its multiple sources of authority encourages those traits, as do laws that grant great administrative discretion.[12]

Under structured conditions, bureaucrats are apt to be a source of accelerative leadership.[13] As a source for innovative ideas, however, other elements of the policy network, especially the appointed "in and outers" of the federal executive, may be gaining in influence.[14]

Congress

Always difficult to conceptualize as a unitary entity, Congress has evolved in incredibly complex and sometimes quite diverse ways.[15] Though it has not always done so, Congress now pulsates with the energies of many minds. Accordingly, it has great difficulty acting with a single mind. While this condition has been true for most of this century, both the energies available for, and especially the impediments to, coherent action have taken large leaps forward in recent years. The vast growth in congressional staff has been solidly documented, and in the words of two scholars has operated to transform "a nominally atomistic legislature of 535 individuals into an 'industry' of nearly 1000 'political firms'."[16] If Congress appeared once to be an institution hostile to ideas and direction, it appears more now to be a maelstrom of many ideas and many directions.

Part of the change, as discussed more fully later in this book, results from a change in the membership itself. Much of it derives also from the dispersion of power and the possibilities for entrepreneurship this creates. A good portion of the change stems from the growth of governmental activity and the bureaucratic-interest networks that this spawns, and some of it stems from the staff growth that, in turn, has been generated from these changes. This burgeoning staff plays a diverse set of roles, but some staff members appear to be "idea bird-dogs." "Substantively," as one observer comments, "the interests of these staffs and their members lead them to be looking for 'new ideas'."[17]

The weakening of central leadership (especially in the House since the Senate never had much) that has occurred during most of this century has produced an institution of munificent pluralism—one that mirrors extraordinarily well (more so than a mere 20 years ago) the remarkable diversity of the activist elements in the society it is elected to represent. In addition, it is busily stirring, even aggressively so; it is receptive to new ideas and changing currents of opinion, however undiscriminating some of these may seem in the salons of intellectual fashion. Noting, for example, the role of Congress in pushing legislation relevant to women in the labor market, Gary Orfield claims that:

> New issues that are not highly controversial can sometimes be forced to the floor, where it is difficult for a member to ignore demands of important newly mobilizing groups of constituents. . . . The fact remains that the Congressional process may be a good deal more responsive to certain kinds of social change than the executive branch.[18]

By its unyielding diversity, and by virtue of the transition from an atmosphere of clubbiness to one of entrepreneurial aggressiveness, Congress has become more a conductor of political electricity than an insulator. "It" shows a remarkable capacity to move specific (and often quite important) changes of the type discussed by Orfield. Its diversity, at the same time, presents great obstacles to the development of coherent agendas that involve distributive costs. These obstacles, however, as the early legislative successes of the Reagan administration showed, are not absolute.

Courts

Some of the most spectacular changes affecting American society, and therefore both directly and indirectly the character of American politics, have been brought about by judicial decision making. Probably few changes, for example, have had the sweeping and catalytic effect on American society as did the 1954 school desegregation case, Brown v. Board of Education.

By design, the courts are supposedly agents of preservation rather than of change. The application of law to cases limits innovation, but only at its outermost boundaries. Quite aside from this inhibition, the courts at times have become major sources of leadership because the individualistic character of the American political culture, in combination with its constitutional and common law traditions, has tended to emphasize the assertion of rights within an evolving body of interpreted law. In the absence of the singular supremacy of political institutions (which could be produced only through their constituted unity), and in the absence of parties dominating the organizational channels of the polity, the adversarial nature of the culture is manifested in the pursuit of rights through litigation procedures. While these judicial procedures are frequently criticized on this side of the Atlantic, they are appreciated perhaps more deeply on the other.[19]

The most decisive leadership role played by the courts derives from the inability of the political system to generate either decisive majorities or a consensus in regard to longstanding prickly issues—typically ones involving definitions of rights. At key moments, therefore, the courts have acted to break up the logjam. (Whether or not a flood follows is yet another question.) Notwithstanding the inherently noninitiatory status of the judiciary, the Constitution of the United States invites the courts to play this log clearing role, while the revolution in rights in the context of an adversarial culture nearly compels it. As Congress so frequently rails against a bureaucracy it has done much to create, so too are the courts blamed by politicians who have done much to expand their role.

The courts, of course, do not themselves have an agenda to put forth, but the collective force of their decision making helps to develop political agendas (and counteragendas). Though they cannot put forward a comprehensive plan for society, the cumulative weight of their decision making can have similar effects. In other words, the courts can be a powerful source of political leadership in society even if they are at best only indirectly influenced by political processes.

As for the effects of judicial activism upon presidential power, probably no succinct generalization is safe. Much depends upon the issues at stake, the prevailing concepts guiding the courts, and the ideological thrusts of any particular president. Still, so long as the pursuit of rights through the courts is stimulated by broad statutory grants of individual rights, the courts inevitably will be thrust into the center of administrative decision making. In the view of one critic of judicial activism, when the courts set forth guidelines for the establishment of administrative regulations and closely monitor their implementation, one important consequence is that presidential control over the executive will be reduced—a product less of bureaucratic recalcitrance than of judicial intervention.[20]

Parties

The assumption that political parties provide both the drive and the organization to impel and then consummate change has been called into question even where they are at their most powerful. Still, parties provide the base for the political activists possessed of the most comprehensive visions of society. Studies of political attitudes among party elites in both Europe and the United States indicate that organizational activists are typically more ideologically robust than public officeholders within the same political party. John May refers to this phenomenon as "the law of curvilinear disparity," by which he means that public officeholders, while more ideologically extreme than the rank and file members of the party, nonetheless are less so than the organizational activists within the party.[21] These activists have been labeled (indeed mislabeled) as "amateurs" in the American context. Richard Crossman, the late Labour Government cabinet minister, described their British counterparts as representing "the battering ram of change."[22]

Party enthusiasts bring with them ideological inspiration. But while they bring enthusiasm, they usually fail to bring sufficient numbers for electoral victory. If their victory within party ranks usually means their short-term defeat at the polls, it frequently also provides a launching pad for the long-term realization of their political goals. Such passions rarely go fully unrequited. Eventually, the enthusiasts may come to control their party's agenda, if not necessarily its nominees. Almost always they are at the fringes of the acceptable—in front of the conventional wisdom of the day, and often ahead of what is realistically do-able. Yet without these enthusiasts and the ideological vigor they provide, parties might be likely only to do that which is safe, or to enter into accommodative elite cartels, thus dispossessing more marginal elements in society.[23]

For nearly two decades American party politics has reflected the leadership role of the activists in both parties. While the activists have more visibly transformed the Democratic party, it is in the Republican party that they may have enjoyed their chief success, defining new issues and generating ideological energy. As in the United States, the organizational activists have helped to transform British party politics, pushing the Tories rightward and Labour leftward, and perhaps thus inducing the creation of a new center-left alliance of Liberals and Social Democrats.

In short, party activists, by their energies and drive, by their passionate commitment to ideals, and by their persistence in acquiring control over political organization, readily can change the terms of political debate. In the fullest sense, they play an important role in the agenda-setting process. As leaders such as Lyndon Johnson, Gerald Ford, and Jimmy Carter in the United States, and Edward Heath in Britain, discovered to their sorrow, they are an essential constituency. It is true, as James Ceaser has astutely argued, that a strong party system plays a role that should serve to constrain presidential aggrandizement and unilateral assumptions of prerogative. But it is not necessarily true, as Ceaser also seems to imply, that such restraints necessarily would be moderating ones.[24]

The potential sources of leadership in democratic societies, and most especially in America, are bountiful. To name those above is to name only a few. In the United States, especially, many other sources of leadership are potentially significant. Purposive interest groups, for example, have played major roles in providing the impetus behind regulatory policies (and now deregulatory ones), and in bringing about changes in the political process itself. Local governments and states, in their remarkable variability, have sometimes produced initiatives less likely to have gained consensus in Washington. At the same time, they also have sounded early warnings of popular moods and resentments. Additionally, in America, the news media have been more intimately observing, and their intimacy has sometimes made them participants in the processes they are covering. And perhaps one of the most significant sources of policy making, the Federal Reserve Board, is beyond the direct grasp of any source of political leadership.

What is unique to the American polity is not the plurality of potential sources of leadership, but the absence of a common point of aggregation through the political party system, and thence to a central point of government decision making. Though there are multiple sources of leadership in the American system, the crucial point is that there is no central site except the White House for shaping coherent (one should not necessarily read wise) agendas. Unlike top executives in other Western democracies, the American president arrives at the top of the heap more or less by his own propulsion, and through his own devices. And while the view from the top of the heap is pleasingly aesthetic, a pleasant view is largely all it commands. A British political scientist, thus, concludes:

> Without a firm party base, without an easy or regular dialogue with the legislature, without near-equals in Cabinet, the President is more nearly insulated in the

second half of the twentieth century than at any previous period in American history.[25]

In other words, if American presidents are unbound by the constraints more typically operating on prime ministers, few are bound to him. Politically he stands as a rugged individualist, and, in this, is reflective of the culture that bred him. By evolution, if not necessarily by design, the American president stands at the center of the political universe splendidly alone and perceived as uniquely responsible. Yet power is transmitted through his office manually rather than automatically. The singular responsibility that is given him to shape a program means that he must also shift for himself in seeing it through.

Still, the presidency remains the most visible single source for establishing coherent direction. The president confronts a system that in recent times especially has shown remarkable vibrancy within its various subsystems. Brownian movement, the random movement of particles, seems a more apt descriptor of the policy process in America than does deadlock. There is much infusion of energy, but coherent change is infrequent—perhaps as it was meant to be. The president's problem is to be able to generate sufficient support to push through *his* agenda. At the same time, his agenda is no one thing, indivisible and unchanging. In fact, it is often protean, shaped by crises and unforeseeable events (though, of course, crises themselves are often shaped by presidents), by the changing needs of an administration over the life of its term, and by a limiting sense of the plausible. The political system provides obvious obstacles to presidentially inspired direction—and these are largely what we focus on, for these, after all, are particularly idiosyncratic to America. Still, direction, as it is everywhere, is also influenced by fate (fortuna, as Machiavelli noted, accounted for much), and by the intractability of many problems.

MODELS OF GOVERNMENT AND OF GOVERNING

The fundamental dilemma of constitutional government, it has been argued, is how to marry direction and legitimacy. While some marriages may be made in heaven, this one clearly requires hard work. For would-be authoritatians, legitimacy is in the product, not the process. To be sure, there is some truth in this, for without direction there is little chance of effectively dealing with large-scale problems. For those, on the other hand, who value overwhelming consensus before government acts, process sanctifies legitimacy, yet perhaps also freezes the status quo.

Two fundamental concepts of government, each with a long and rich tradition, derive from the principles of direction on the one hand, and legitimacy on the other. A free association of words with the notion of government as director would produce language that stresses terminology such as *the state, goals, change, effectiveness, energy, leadership, coherence, mandates, programs, steering,* and *decisive choices.* Not all of this terminology comfortably gathers under the same philosophical roof, but that, in turn, reflects the fact that the view of government as a positive, directing force fits a number of disparate ideologies ranging from modernizing conservatism (Gaullism, for instance) to twentieth-century American liberalism and European social democracy.

The legitimacy model of government—the notion of government as reflector—would inspire in free association words such as *representativeness, responsiveness, equilibrium, consent, accountability, pluralistic accommodation, acceptance,* and *Pareto optimality.* These words, too, fit within diverse philosophical housings ranging from organic conservatism to nineteenth-century liberalism, to twentieth-century pluralist and corporatist political structures.

In practice, of course, there is more intermingling. Contemporary American liberals, for instance, are sometimes given to a simultaneous appreciation of pluralistic politics and boldly entrepreneurial leadership. Alternatively, a particularly inspired analysis of the Swedish elite by Thomas Anton notes that while the Swedish system has been compatible with rapid social and governmental change, it also has fostered an emphasis upon developing consensus rather than goal setting, upon coordination rather than direction, and upon negotiation rather than giving orders. In short, Anton observes, the Swedish political system has helped to produce comprehensive change in a relatively brief time span without "heroic leadership."[26]

Despite the ways in which the values of direction and legitimacy may be accommodated, there can be little disputing the fact that they tend more naturally toward contradiction than toward coincidence. Thus, it is useful to think of (but necessary to avoid reifying) two models of government: a directing model and a reflecting (legitimacy) model.

The director model of government emphasizes planning, directed social and technical change, and active intervention in processes of socioeconomic development. It emphasizes the positive state and sufficient concentrations of authority to propel change. Aside from the obvious—which is that even clearly formulated policies may be humbled by the manipulative capacities of any government—the potential dangers deriving from this model are remoteness of authority and resulting crises of legitimacy.[27] Excessive centralization is likely to result in ossification rather than direction.

The reflector model of government largely envisions the state alternatively as a ratifier of the social consensus, a representative of its diversity, or a responder to dominant and intense demands from the society. Such a model of government readily accords with the idea that society is fundamentally self-regulating (though it also accords with Marxian notions of the state as a mere reflector of the dominant structure of interests). This presupposes a minimalist government. However, it also follows that if government is involved in social and economic affairs, as a result of societal demands, it will lack autonomy and directive capability, and will be over-responsive.[28] Therefore, it will produce inchoateness in policy, inefficiency, and an inability to adapt to changes in ways that incur significant costs. The reflector model of government then risks the danger of ratifying stalemate. Ethnic heterogeneity that threatens the disintegration of the state is likely, as it had been in Nigeria for instance, to induce the adoption of a reflector rather than director type of approach to governing. Faced with the grave potential of system threatening divisions, then, a governing model that maximizes consent and legitimacy rather than direction is likely to be produced.[29]

An important distinction now can be drawn between one's model of *government* and one's model of *governing*. The first implies something about what governments do—whether, for instance, they are actively interventionist or not, whereas the second implies something about the process of policy making itself. While there is no necessary relationship between the model of government and the model of governing, a directive or entrepreneurial model of governing typically has been associated with a directive model of government.[30] Because more energy has to be expended on changing the status quo than on preserving it, the coincidence of directional models of government and governing is understandable. Where the impetus for change is initiated by what Aaron Wildavsky has termed "the party of government" (prowelfare or leftist parties), as was generally the case in Western democracies until the 1970s, a directive model of government is expedited by a directing model of governing. In recent times, however, most notably in Britain and the United States, the directing model of governing has been associated with what Wildavsky calls "the party of opposition" (antiwelfare or rightist parties). Facing a status quo now biased toward governmental involvement, "the party of opposition" wishes to vigorously pursue a program of undoing or dramatically reducing that which already has been done.[31]

In the United States from the New Deal through the 1950s and 1960s, the orthodox Republican view was to promote a noninitiatory presidency and a powerfully constraining Congress. This seemed a safe prescription for a party of no bold plans, and in opposition to the interventionist Democrats. The Whig view of the presidency generally held by Republicans was initially transformed by Richard Nixon who claimed, on the basis of his presumed mandate, an unusually wide swath of territory. Ronald Reagan, of course, has been infinitely more charming than his former fellow Californian, but there has been no reticence in his administration about a mandate for imposing great change. If the Republicans have not appropriated the New Deal, they apparently have appropriated the New Deal concept of the presidency. Thus, regardless of the substantive "vision" possessed by the president, regardless of whether his direction is to have the government intervene more in society or less, the notion that the president is the heroic leader pushing great change is at odds with the reflector model of governing.

There is little getting around the fact that how hard one wants to push change in a given direction has a lot to do with one's conception of leadership. One must, however, be equally prepared for gusts blowing in the opposite direction. The extent to which one desires the status quo may produce a commensurate desire to parry forceful leadership. Can we avoid, as one writer has put it, having our constitutional theories follow the party flag?[32] Can we avoid alternating between the poles of full steam ahead and batten down the hatches on the one hand, and rudderless government on the other? Can we, above all, move in directions that are both clear, yet subtle and nuanced, directions that are accepted, legitimized, and thus sustained and continuous?

To the advocates of energetic and bold directing leadership, then, lie the opportunities to shape society according to their desired vision. But, equally, such advocates risk having society reshaped according to the visions of their opponents. How to gain direction and legitimacy together in order to sustain continuity remains the enduring dilemma of constitutional leadership.

No formula of general applicability awaits, unfortunately. "Politics," we are reminded, "arise out of real and not rationally reconcilable conflicts of interest in society." While almost none are solved, some are settled, and yet "these settlements are normally unfair to someone."[33] This alone should chasten us from utopian illusions. Added to this most fundamental conundrum, though, is that the conditions for effective and legitimate governance have everywhere grown more difficult.

Yet, governance in America is usually more problematic than elsewhere—at least in the sense of producing coherent direction.[34] The prospects for the exercise of such leadership provide our analytic focus in succeeding chapters, especially as these prospects have come to be identified with the presidency. It would be appropriate to recall, however, that leadership is but part of a complex of essential values. To what extent it should command priority cannot be answered here, for that is a highly perplexing question in its own right. To what extent the American polity allows coherent direction to be generated is, however, a subject appropriate to both understanding the contemporary role of the American presidency and placing that role in the perspective of governance. That is our topic.

NOTES

1. James MacGregor Burns, *Leadership* (New York: Harper & Row, 1978), p. 2.

2. *Ibid.*, p. 19. Emphases are in the original.

3. David Loye, *The Leadership Passion: A Psychology of Ideology* (San Francisco: Jossey-Bass, 1977), p. 3.

4. Hedrick Smith, "A Scaled Down Version of Security Adviser's Task," *New York Times,* March 4, 1981, p. A2. For evidence of Allen's assertion regarding ideological likemindedness, see John H. Kessel, "The Structures of the Reagan White House," paper presented at the 1983 Annual Meeting of the American Political Science Association, Chicago, Illinois.

5. In general, see here Richard Rose, *The Problem of Party Government* (New York: The Free Press, 1974), and Dennis Kavanagh, "Party Politics in Question," in *New Trends in British Politics: Issues for Research,* ed. Dennis Kavanagh and Richard Rose (London: Sage, 1977), pp. 191-220.

6. For an effort to show both the limits of the aphorism and the special importance of party and ideology, see Graham K. Wilson, *Special Interests and Policymaking: Agricultural Policies and Poli-

tics in Britain and the United States of America, 1956-70 (New York: John Wiley, 1977). See also his, "Are Department Secretaries Really a President's Natural Enemies?," *British Journal of Political Science* 7 (July 1977): 273-299.

7. The literature is far more prolific in regard to magnitude than it is to sweep. For some specimens, see Otto A. Davis, M.A.H. Dempster, and Aaron Wildavsky, "A Theory of the Budgetary Process," *American Political Science Review* 60 (September 1966): 529-547; See also their, "Towards a Predictive Theory of Government Expenditure," *British Journal of Political Science* 4 (October 1974): 419-452; and Peter B. Natchez and Irvin C. Bupp, "Policy and Priority in the Budgetary Process," *American Political Science Review* 67 (September 1973): 951-963.

8. *Statistical Abstract of the United States* (Washington, D.C.: Government Printing Office, 1980). The figures referred to appear on p. 259. For additional relevant discussion, see Martha Derthick, *Uncontrollable Spending for Social Services Grants* (Washington, D.C.: The Brookings Institution, 1975), and Ronald Randall, "Presidential Power versus Bureaucratic Intransigence: The Influence of the Nixon Administration on Welfare Policy," *American Political Science Review* 73 (September 1979): 795-810.

9. Valerie Bunce, "Changing Leaders and Changing Policies: The Impact of Elite Succession on Budgetary Priorities in Democratic Countries," *American Journal of Politics* 24 (August 1980): 373-395. The argument is generalized to communist systems as well. See Valerie Bunce, "Elite Succession, Petrification, and Policy Innovation in Communist Systems: An Empirical Assessment," *Comparative Political Studies* 9 (April 1976): 3-42.

10. Hugh Heclo, *Modern Social Politics in Britain and Sweden* (New Haven: Yale University Press, 1974); also see Martha Derthick, *Policymaking for Social Security* (Washington, D.C.: Brookings Institution, 1979).

11. Hugh Heclo, "Issue Networks and the Executive Establishment," in *The New American Political System,* ed. Anthony King (Washington, D.C.: American Enterprise Institute, 1978): pp. 371-396; also see Hugh Heclo, "The Changing Presidential Office," in *Politics and the Oval Office,* ed. Arnold J. Meltsner (San Francisco: Institute for Contemporary Studies, 1981), pp. 161-184.

12. On the latter point, see Derthick, *Uncontrollable Spending,* esp. pp. 102-115, and Theodore Lowi, *The End of Liberalism: The Second Republic of the United States,* 2nd ed. (New York: W. W. Norton, 1979).

13. For a more formal treatment of this phenomenon, see William A. Niskanen, Jr., *Bureaucracy and Representative Government* (Chicago: Aldine-Atherton, 1971).

14. See here, for example, Nelson W. Polsby, "The Washington Community, 1960-1980," in *The New Congress,* ed. Thomas E. Mann and Norman J. Ornstein (Washington, D.C.: American Enterprise Institute, 1981), pp. 7-31, and Nelson W. Polsby, "Presidential Cabinet-Making," *Political Science Quarterly* 93 (Spring, 1978): 15-26.

15. For an illuminating analysis of this, see Norman J. Ornstein, "The House and the Senate in a New Congress," in Mann and Ornstein, *The New Congress,* pp. 363-383.

16. The quote is from Robert H. Salisbury and Kenneth A. Shepsle, "Congressional Staff Turnover and the Ties-That-Bind," *American Political Science Review* 75 (June 1981), p. 395. For evidence of staff growth, see, for example, Harrison W. Fox, Jr. and Susan Webb Hammond, *Congressional Staffs: The Invisible Force in American Lawmaking* (New York; The Free Press, 1977), and Michael J. Malbin, *Unelected Representatives: Congressional Staff and the Future of Representative Government* (New York: Basic Books, 1980).

17. Michael J. Malbin, "Delegation, Deliberation, and the New Role of Congressional Staff," in Mann and Ornstein, *The New Congress,* p. 155.

18. Gary Orfield, *Congressional Power: Congress and Social Change* (New York: Harcourt Brace Jovanovich, 1975), pp. 305-306.

19. See, for instance, Richard Rose, "On the Priorities of Citizenship in the Deep South and Northern Ireland," *Journal of Politics* 38 (May 1976): 247-291.

20. Martin M. Shapiro, "The Presidency and the Federal Courts," in Meltsner, *Politics and the Oval Office,* pp. 141-157.

21. John D. May, "Opinion Structure of Political Parties: The Special Law of Curvilinear Disparity," *Political Studies* 21 (June 1973): 135-151. See also Edmond Constantini, "Intraparty Attitude Conflict: Democratic Party Leadership in California," *Western Political Quarterly* 16 (December 1963): 956-972.

22. R.H.S. Crossman, *The Myths of Cabinet Government* (Cambridge, Mass.: Harvard University Press, 1972), pp. 80-97.

23. The dangers of this have been noted, for example, by Sidney Tarrow. See his "Italy in 1978: 'Where Everybody Governs, Does Anybody Govern?' " in *Legitimation of Regimes: International Frameworks for Analysis,* ed. Bogdan Denitch (London: Sage Publications, 1979), pp. 229-248. For related arguments, see Philippe C. Schmitter, "Still the Century of Corporatism?," in *the New Corporatism: Social-Political Structures in the Iberian World,* ed. Frederick B. Pike and Thomas Stritch (Notre Dame, Indiana: University of Notre Dame Press, 1974), pp. 85-131, and Peter J. Katzenstein, "Problem or Model? West Germany in the 1980s," *World Politics* 32 (July 1980): 577-599.

24. James W. Ceaser, *Presidential Selection: Theory and Development* (Princeton, N.J.: Princeton University Press, 1979), esp. pp. 339-353.

25. H. G. Nicholas, *The Nature of American Politics* (Oxford: Oxford University Press, 1980), p. 108.

26. Thomas J. Anton, *Administered Politics: Elite Political Culture in Sweden* (Boston: Martinus Nijhoff, 1980), esp. pp. 184-185.

27. Thus, in submitting to the National Assembly a plan to end the prefectural system of local and regional administration, the French Socialist Prime Minister, Pierre Mauroy, proclaimed the need to nurture local responsibility and to rid France of the remnants of "Napoleon's ancient regime." An American in Paris undoubtedly would find the irony delicious. See Frank J. Prial, "France to Loosen Centralized Rule," *New York Times,* July 17, 1981, pp. A1, A9.

28. Such perspectives can be attributed, for example, to Thurow and to Lowi. See Lester C. Thurow, *The Zero-Sum Society: Distribution and the Possibilities for Economic Change* (New York: Basic Books, 1980), and Lowi, *The End of Liberalism.*

29. The Nigerian Constitution of 1979, modeled after the American, is strikingly designed for government to be able to move only when there is strong and widespread consensus. The circumstance, of course, that Nigeria shares with the United States is the history of a highly destructive civil war. For more general discussions of governance in ethnically segmented societies, see Arend Lijphart, *Democracy in Plural Societies: A Comparative Exploration* (New Haven: Yale University Press, 1977), and Milton J. Esman, ed., *Ethnic Conflict in the Western World* (Ithaca, N.Y.: Cornell University Press, 1977).

30. For empirical evidence relating, *inter alia,* beliefs about the activities of government to ones about the process of governing, see Joel D. Aberbach, Robert D. Putnam, and Bert A. Rockman, *Bureaucrats and Politicians in Western Democracies* (Cambridge, Mass.: Harvard University Press, 1981), pp. 141-155.

31. Aaron Wildavsky, "The Three Party System—1980 and After," *The Public Interest* 67 (Summer 1981): 47-57.

32. William G. Andrews, "The Presidency, Congress, and Constitutional Theory," in *The Presidency in Contemporary Context,* ed. Norman C. Thomas (New York: Dodd, Mead, 1975), pp. 11-33.

33. John Higley, Desley Deacon, and Don Smart, *Elites in Australia* (London: Routledge and Kegan Paul, 1979), p. 288.

34. See Richard Rose, "Government Against Sub-Governments: A European Perspective on Washington," in *Presidents and Prime Ministers,* ed. Richard Rose and Ezra Suleiman (Washington, D.C.: American Enterprise Institute, 1980), pp. 284-347.

3

The Constants of Presidential Leadership

Energy in the executive is a leading character in the definition of good government. . . . A feeble executive implies a feeble execution of the government. A
feeble execution is but another phrase for a bad execution; and a government ill
executed, whatever it may be in theory, must be, in practice, a bad government.

(Alexander Hamilton, Federalist No. 70.)

In order to lay a due foundation for that separate and distinct exercise of the different powers of government . . . essential to the preservation of liberty, it is evident
that each department should have a will of its own. . . . Ambition must be made to
counteract ambition. . . . This policy of supplying, by opposite and rival interests,
the defect of better motives, might be traced through the whole system of human
affairs. . . . These inventions of prudence cannot be less requisite in the distribution of the supreme powers of the State.

(James Madison, Federalist No. 51.)

Extreme centralization of government ultimately enervates society and thus, after
a length of time, weakens the government itself; but I do not deny that a centralized social power may be able to execute great undertakings with facility in a
given time and on a particular point.

(Alexis de Tocqueville, *Democracy in America.*)

Political systems, like organisms, confront key junctures in their development. Responses to these junctures help to determine adaptations to later development. Future responses, the historian Raymond Grew notes, are conditioned by
"the institutionalized patterns of behavior available," which reflect both responses
to previous crises as well as "the imprint of their initial formation."[1] Previously
successful patterns of response typically will be repeated again, although, of
course, not always successfully. Collective learning is always incomplete, and
prevailing patterns of response reveal characteristic blind spots. As with old dogs

and new tricks, the prevailing repertoires available from our collective experience are sometimes too narrow to adapt to stimuli not previously confronted.

In this chapter I outline some of the central elements of the American repertoire that bear on the prospects for generating central direction, and, to a lesser extent, their impact on the content of whatever direction is achieved. To what extent, in other words, are the prospects for presidential leadership affected by these central elements? As we shall see, the question is deceptively simple. Some elements have more direct impact than others, all depend upon both presidential goals and external conditions, and all interact with one another to produce an overall climate bearing on the predicament of presidential leadership. Five elements, obviously interacting with one another, are the special focus of my attention here. They are: (1) the architecture of the political institutions, (2) the political culture, (3) the character of American political parties, (4) the localistic, regional, and ethnocultural roots of American politics, and (5) the First Amendment freedoms that are constitutionally granted to the press. These are critical parameters, the heritage of an unusual historical development—distinct, for the most part, from other industrially advanced nations.

I refer to these elements as "constants," but this does not mean that they are constants in a mathematical sense. There are ebbs and flows among them, and they do not, as we shall see in Chapter 4, always have the same impact. In some instances too, modern trends have enlarged or accelerated their impact. Such trends are examined in Chapter 5. More properly, then, the constants, as I use this term, are the basic parameters of American governance.

Two matters need especially to be kept in mind. First, the relationships between the constant elements are strong and reinforcing, though the causal relationships among them are not always clear. Second, presidents themselves are variables. They are not solely the product of exogenous forces, although the success they enjoy (or fail to) and the agendas they face (or avoid) are not theirs alone to determine. To a somewhat greater degree, however, what remains within their grasp to determine are the values that infuse both their initial goals and their reactions to the events and issues imposed upon them. The constants do not affect all presidents alike but they are, in general, unkind to large-scale collective direction.

EARLY MODELS FOR THE POLITICAL SYSTEM— HAMILTON, JEFFERSON, AND MADISON

How are national goals to be determined? Ought they to be the product of a slowly emerging consensus shaped across diverse communities of interest reflected through different institutions? Or should they reflect the creative energies of a strong executive center? What model of the political process, in other words, underlies the operations of the American political system? The answers to these questions insofar as the intentions of the Founders are concerned inevitably contain ambiguities, for government obviously is different today from how it was two centuries ago. Our categories and frames of reference differ. Distance adds uncertainty to words, and time warps the context from which we derive meaning.

This, of course, hasn't stopped the flow of scholarly tracts devoted to interpretations of the Founders' ideas about, and behaviors affecting, the character of the emergent Republic. There has been more than ample room for interpreting the "constitutional tradition." Historical analyses of letters, papers, and documents have developed divergent and sometimes novel interpretations of the Founders' intentions and their intellectual frames of reference.[2] Since the Founders were both the political theorists and the political elites of the day, both thinkers and actors, and because behavior is rarely fully correspondent with theory, more controversy than conclusiveness often has resulted from discerning their intentions.[3]

Despite these hedges, I think that we can point to three broadly disparate conceptions of the political order referred to, at least in popular interpretation, as the Hamiltonian, Jeffersonian, and Madisonian models. In Table 3.1 I have extracted four key elements of each of these models of the political system. The first two elements contain assumptions about human nature and the desired relationship between citizens and authorities. They thus directly tap into the complex of beliefs and values that we commonly label "political culture." The third element consists of institutional structure, and the fourth, by interlocking culture with institutions, reflects an outline of the emergent regime implicit in each model. The summation represented in Table 3.1 is obviously judgmental. My concern here is not to elaborately document it (a fit subject for a volume itself), but to connect these summary judgments with how the political system has evolved, institutionally and culturally.

Of the three tendencies represented by Hamilton, Jefferson, and Madison, the conservative vision of Hamilton—a strong center of authority with limited citizen participation—has been mostly abandoned. Even so, the Hamiltonian vision of the political order in certain respects comports reasonably well with low visibility foreign and national security policy making. For example, Stephen Krasner, in a study of foreign policy making concerning raw materials investments, states that a state-centered interpretation focusing on the power of the president and the secretary of state best fits the data.[4] Krasner himself admits that strategic policy is probably a deviant case, that even "a state that is weak in relation to its own society can act effectively in the strategic arena. . . ."[5] He concludes, with some astonishment, that even in the more interest-infested area of materials investments an overriding and dominant cold-war ideology prevailed against interest group power in policy determination. Even so, he notes that the decline of American resources and power means that "the deficiencies of a weak political system may become more apparent."[6] For better or worse, according to Krasner's interpretation, the remnants of the Hamiltonian model of energetic central authority may be further eroded by externally imposed limits on American power and resources. Of course, the ominous

TABLE 3.1. Political Culture, Political Institutions, and Regime: Hamiltonian, Jeffersonian, and Madisonian Models of the Political Order

Models of the Political Order	Political Culture		Political Institutions	Regime
	Assumptions about Human Nature	Relationship To Authority		
Hamiltonian	Pessimistic	Deferential	Centralizing	Conservative modernizing (state-building)
Jeffersonian	Optimistic	Proximate	Decentralizing	Democratic and experimental (majority-building)
Madisonian	Guarded	Mediated	Noncentralizing	Republican and interest refracting (consensus-building)

if unlikely possibility exists that these new constraints on national power will lead to crises of effectiveness so severe that the executive authority and the powers of the state might end up being amplified well beyond even the Hamiltonian vision. For the most part, however, one must conclude that the Hamiltonian conception of the political order has not been kindly treated in the evolution of the American system, institutionally or culturally.[7]

That evolution has been, if in different respects, more kindly disposed to the Madisonian and Jeffersonian models. Madison emerges as the prime architect of our institutions, whereas much of the political culture is endowed with the Jeffersonian spirit. Madison evinces skepticism toward the wielding of power, while Jefferson is skeptical of the power wielders.[8] Though Madison was but one of a company of architects, the constitutional design owes deeply to his inspiration— most particularly that evidenced in Federalist 51 and 10. The institutions of the political system fragment political authority according to the Madisonian design, so that the system itself will be less susceptible to *ex parte* capture. The institutional blueprints have made it difficult to do that which their creation was meant to make it difficult to do: to concentrate power and enable government to be captured by a single faction. Such a system is naturally the bane of both party government theorists and social and technocratic planners who seek to engender, respectively, unity of will and rational purpose. It is at the same time their salvation when purposeful opponents have an upper (but rarely ever final) hand. Still, as Robert Dahl has persuasively argued, the fragmentation of power derived from Madison's famous Federalist 51 cannot by itself necessarily deter *ex parte* control even if it is likely to discourage it.[9]

Through institutional separation, the architecture discourages unity of the elite at the federal level. Through federalism it discourages the emergence of an elite unified across the many levels of government. The complicated political structure *in normal times* tends to diminish the capacity of ardent factions to impose their will upon the whole, thus discouraging sweeping and broad-scale change. But despite this cautious institutional framework, neither tyranny (for example, the suppression of black political and legal rights in the southern states) nor, on the other hand, sweeping political change could be fully deterred. Social conditions and political culture, Dahl and others rightly contend, are more fundamental to the deterrence of tyranny than is the arrangement of political institutions.[10] Still, as others have pointed out, the complexity of these arrangements does help make it abnormally difficult for authoritarianism to flourish at the national level.[11] The elaborate system of external or institutional checks alone would not suffice to prevent tyranny, but it would be biased against it. Similarly, while the Madisonian architecture would not preclude the possibility of efficient government, it also would be biased against it. At the same time, it might be easier for tyranny to flourish in isolated locales and cases, a concern expressed in Madison's Federalist 10.

The architect designed many doors, each seemingly with a different lock. In normal times there would be more locks than keys. Without the intervention of war (and, since Korea, even then), or the appearance of crisis, or the preponderance of likeminded majorities, the independence of institutions so greatly valued by Madison is conducive to the grinding, rather than the meshing, of gears. As Richard Neustadt points out, ours is a system not of separated powers, but of separate institutions sharing power.[12] Like separate siblings sharing candy, such a condition usually makes for rivalry, as it apparently was meant to. In Nelson Polsby's view, only a culture of moderate partisanship, of overlapping values, and of reasonableness could keep the president and the Congress from constant collision.[13]

Under certain conditions, namely when the White House and Capitol Hill are captured by the same party, stronger partisanship and more crystallized conflict could induce more institutional cooperation, yet potentially produce a more intensely divided society. The government that Madison divided could be united *or* even more deeply divided by the emergence of strong partisanship. But strong partisanship, Madison feared, would precipitate injurious social division.

What then of the spirit of American politics? If the institutions embody skepticism about the ravenous appetites of men, the culture is buoyed by a naive optimism and a populist rhetoric. One historian contends, in fact, that "It is within the constant tension between the revolutionary rhetoric and the conservative political structure of the fragmented American political system that one must perceive much of American history."[14] The insistent populist tradition, the pervasive localism, and the espousal of citizen rights have roots deep in the Jeffersonian tradition. If Madison was the most inspired of the architects, it was Jefferson's ideas about the relationship between citizens and authority that, by their intergenerational repetition, would illuminate the Madisonian design. This special contribution of a democratic, even radical, political culture was also discerned by Tocqueville. Regarding the unique relationship between authority and citizen in America, he wrote:

> [The society] may almost be said to govern itself, so feeble and so restricted is the share left to the administration, so little do the authorities forget their popular origin and the power from which they emanate. The people reign in the American political world as the Deity does in the universe. They are the cause and the aim of all things; everything comes from them, and everything is absorbed in them.[15]

And so:

> The lot of the Americans is singular: they have derived from the aristocracy of England the notion of private rights and the taste for local freedom; and they have been able to retain both because they have had no aristocracy to combat.[16]

The American system is an oddity. Republican institutions premised upon skepticism toward the *ex parte* exercise of power, in fact, are permeated by democratic ideals, by notions of proximity to authority, by a pervasive localism, and participant culture. Ironically, the combination of Madisonian skepticism (as reflected in the institutions) and Jeffersonian optimism (as reflected in the culture) has generated more a reinforcing of the diffusion of authority and a weakening of the authority of the state than a clash of opposite tendencies. Indeed, what the Madisonian system produced, our historical legacy and individualistic political culture have conspired to reinforce. A set of institutions designed to deter the unity of authority are reinforced by an individualistic political culture skeptical of authority. If the Madisonian system fragments political authority, the Jeffersonian aspects of the political culture effectively shorten the distance between political authority and the citizenry.

What emerges is not "a government," but many, often competitive and sometimes cooperative, governments; not a decisive point of decision making at the center, but a diffusion of decisional points; and not a state presumably representing a "common and durable interest," but a society whose abundant pluralism finds ready expression through the many conduits available in the polity. The constitutional system, then, has bequeathed us a government of disparate parts in which only rarely, and usually only momentarily, can a rough equivalent of "a government" be formed. Our pattern of development and our beliefs, in addition, bequeathed us a diverse and vibrant society, moved by populist impulses, and accepting of Lockean assumptions. Its contribution is a weak state—limited policy tools, a highly fragmented and negatively stereotyped bureaucracy, and a continuing suspicion of public officialdom. While there is an American state, there is no acceptable tradition of one, Hamilton notwithstanding. And that does amount to a distinction with a discernible difference. The difference is elaborated by Kenneth Dyson who claims that the impact of the state tradition

> is upon the autonomous exercise of public authority under law rather than participation or "citizen competence"; upon the unity of such authority, a monism that suggests the distinctive character of public affairs; upon technical criteria and the professionalism of bureaucratic mores rather than group conflict and adjustment; and upon an essentially moral, substantive concept of the public interest that is not viewed as simply emerging from a pluralist process in which groups openly compete. The state is seen as an agent or trustee whose authority is not merely derived from the "majority" or the "popular will."[17]

These are strange words. For in the tradition of the state lies a tradition alien to the American experience. In contemporary times, the architecture biases toward the prevalence of subgovernments, while the culture biases toward the dangers of no government. To be sure, any fully accurate account of how the American political system operates, and of how policy is made, will provide an inescapable array of evidence that fails to comport comfortably with these rather high-blown generalizations.[18] We have seen, for instance, that the Hamiltonian model is applicable in certain areas of policy making. Yet there is evidence to the contrary as well even in these policy areas. One scholar, for instance, studying changes in the character of international production and trade, and the impact of these changes upon both the American steel industry and international trade policy, observes that "accommodation to structural shifts in international steel production and trade is seen to be properly the job of the private sector—not of the government." In order to cope more effectively with such challenges, he further observes, there is a need "to develop greater institutional capacity and policy intsruments. . . ."[19] In their absence what results is an oscillation between market ideology (no government) and protectionist response (the prevalence of subgovernment). While weak government is prescribed by the culture, the representation of specifically aggrieved interests is facilitated by the institutional floor plan. On the whole, therefore, the continuing evolution of the American polity has been more beneficently disposed to the Madisonian and Jeffersonian visions than to Hamilton's.

Precisely where does this situate the presidency? The president is, after all, not the leader of "a government" but a leader who heads only a part of government—a chief of state in a society whose culture resists the idea (but *only* the idea) of the state. The American form of government handicaps ambition in the White House, and presidential success in accomplishing objectives hinges upon support generated across other institutions. The American culture, as well, inhibits ambitious government, and in some measure, therefore, ambitious governors. None of this is to say that presidents are powerless. A lot depends upon ther goals, their political agility, the times, and the strength of supporting partisan forces. These factors are too variable for blanket statements. The presidency would evolve into an energetic office, but so would others. The power to govern could never be assumed. It would always have to be struggled for in an environment of interdependence—the direct result of Madison's triumph, and the indirect result of Jefferson's conquest of the American political spirit.

While no one can say for sure what eighteenth-century politican-intellectuals would make of the twentieth-century United States, we might imagine their reactions. Madison, one suspects, would be impressed by the resiliency of the institutions in helping to preserve liberty—though he (more so than Hamilton) might be concerned about the growing judicial shadow. He might be concerned by the extent of partisanship within Congress and, thus, the unifying bonds it creates between Congress and the executive, however fragile these seem by contemporary standards of party government. Jefferson might be more disturbed: concerned about judicial assertiveness in the face of popular majorities, yet appreciative of the judicial defense of individual rights. He might be alarmed at the concentration of economic power within the society, and the erosion of state and local independence. Nonetheless, he probably would be enthused by the democratic and participant character of American politics, if less ecstatic about the social bias attached to political participation in the United States.[20] Hamilton, however, would have less reason to be enthused. The breakdown of deference, the continuing need for government to justify its being, the local orientations of "national elites," and the absence of directive guidance given by government to society are matters he likely would find disconcerting. In Samuel Huntington's view, "only a modernizing autocrat like Hamilton could advance in America the type of centralization favored by the democrats of Europe."[21] Huntington's observation clearly (and rightly) marks the Hamiltonian vision as anomalous, and, in turn, America as an anomaly.

GOVERNING WITHOUT "A GOVERNMENT"

Of course there is a government of the United States. On a daily basis, public officers authoritatively place the imprimatur of the United States Government on numerous pieces of official paper. Yet there is no unified government, no government of the day in the modern sense of that term. Instead, the design of the separation of powers system is predicated on the view expressed by Madison in Federalist 51 that such a system is essential for the maintenance of liberty. While in Federalist 51 Madison calls for the separation of governmental institutions at the federal level to deter the ability of a faction to capture the whole of government, his plea in Federalist 10 justifies a federal system on similar grounds. Here his contention is that enlarging the scope of a political unit likely would increase its diversity and thus decrease the dangers of a dominant, tyrannical faction.

> The influence of factious leaders may kindle a flame within their particular states but will be unable to spread a general conflagration throughout the other States. A religious sect may degenerate into a political faction in a part of the Confederacy; but the variety of sects dispersed over the entire face of it must secure the national councils against any danger from that source.[22]

While Hamilton speaks of "energy," Madison fears "oppression" and "tyranny." Though Madison did not win every battle, he won the war. The result is a government founded on defensiveness. Each of its parts can be assertive, but the assertiveness of the parts makes for an unassertiveness of the whole. The fissiparous nature of the government produced in Philadelphia would be biased against directive capacity, and faced often with the difficulty of arriving at, and deciding upon, national goals. In short the system of separated powers was (and largely remains) an institutional design meant to frustrate the exercise of power. This is so because American institutions do not so much divide *powers* as they divide *power*. In Samuel Huntington's well-turned sentence, "America perpetuated a fusion of functions and a division of power, while Europe developed a differentiation of functions and a centralization of power."[23] Clearly, whatever the virtues of these antique institutions, their strong suit is not the efficient direction of an active government.

The objective of countering ambition with ambition through the institutional framework was meant to preserve liberty, not generate action, at least beyond the most minimal collective goods functions. Regarding even these functions, however, Rogers Hollingsworth asserts that "the fragmentation of authority has made it increasingly difficult to govern in the interest of the entire society."[24] This difficulty was compounded by yet two further elements of the American constitutional system: first, the genuinely bicameral legislative body, and second, elections to each chamber (the House directly and the Senate indirectly) by a distinct territorial constituency. Bicameralism would provide a further dispersion of initiatory and veto points, while territorial constituencies would give unusual play to the representation of local or state and regional concerns.[25]

History is touched with ironies. One of these was that Madison had to live in the house he had done so much to design. Confronted with a remarkable diffusion of power and fragmentation of authority, Madison as president was unable to arrest the diffusive tendencies encouraged by the institutional design. In this regard, James Young persuasively argues that "Constitutional principles had triumphed, but at the cost of viable government."[26] And yet, as Young also observes, changes in the basic structure likely would be futile despite its grave inadequacies. Therefore, "the only . . . salvation for the nation lay in the development of a capacity for rulership within a constitutional framework deliberately designed to make rulership difficult."[27] A key would have to be found to enable presidential leadership to emerge. That key presumably would be the emergence of mass-based political organization—the inheritance of Jacksonian democracy. While there is evidence to suggest that party already had become a consistent predictor of voting alignments in Congress during the first decade of the Republic's existence, congressional party differences were usually greatly coincident with sectional differences.[28] Moreover, the mass base of parties had yet to emerge. Electoral politics could not as yet provide a mechanism for connecting presidential and congressional fates.

How strong parties could become as cohesive organizations able to provide coherent governing direction remains unanswered. Reponses to this question vary to some degree across different periods of American history. The dispersion of power, induced by the dispersion of governmental authority, makes strongly cohesive and highly disciplined parties improbable, if not always impossible. Together, federalism and winner-take-all elections would help produce parties that were largely localized and whose organizational structure was bottom-up rather than top-down. Thus, as Morton Grodzins once noted, there is apt to be a high degree of congruence between the form of the government and the form of the parties.[29] By European standards, certainly, American parties could only be pale imitations. They would be less cohesive and disciplined for certain than their European counterparts, not only because the structure of government in the United States impedes cohesion and discipline but also because the structure of conflict in the United States has lacked crystallization.

It is evident, however, that parties are critical instruments to the success of presidential programs. An historical study of the passage rate of presidential programs in Congress concludes, for instance, that "a key factor in Presidential legislative program success is the strength of his party, measured either by control of seats or internal cohesion."[30] American parties would be mostly loose organizations of the more or less likeminded. Likemindedness, even in the face of organizational deterioration, sometimes could provide a deceptively large degree of party responsibility. This would be low octane fuel, of course. Occasionally it would be enough to provide a basis for majority movement, but more frequently it would drive minority opposition. Still, the main bridge between the two ends of Pennsylvania Avenue would have to be constructed out of partisan material. The fragility of this bridge is well-known, especially in the present era.

The lack of disciplinary tools in the hands of the parties reflects their historically weak national organization, indeed, the lack of a clearly national politics. The American system, for the most part, remains highly localized. The terms of political discourse are often dissimilar between state or locale and nation. Variability in the content implied by a party label is broadened by these dissimilarities. Thus, as Nancy Zingale argues in the case of party identification among voters, "Only when the terms of political discourse are similar in both state and national arenas would we expect the tendency toward consistency."[31] Given this potential for divergence across arenas and the special sensitivity to local opinion, the moments of considerable cohesion would rest more on the consent of the likeminded than on the obligation of the officeholder.

The institutional design cuts in more than one way, however. The familiar side of it is that the enthusiasts of party responsibility must make do with a party system whose possibilities for rendering consistent support to presidents are partly determined by a system of government that defines accountability in terms of institutional checks rather than through electoral mandates. The less familiar consequence of the institutional design, however, is of some importance for presidents facing opposition majorities in Congress. Here the notorious lack of party discipline and the relative incohesiveness of the parties allows some maneuverability and bargaining room. Divided institutions in America, as in France, remain open to capture by different parties. It is not certain how the French party blocs would react to a situation they have not as yet had to face, but which has become commonplace in the United States: executive and legislative institutions controlled by different parties. From the standpoint of the executive operating under these circumstances, weak party discipline provides opportunities to penetrate the opposition, though at the same time one's flanks must be safeguarded. Rigid party discipline under conditions of divided government would mean certain stalemate, of course, unless a grand coalition could be concocted. Those who urge more party responsibility in a system of separable and thus potentially divided institutions, and of separated elections, need to acknowledge that what would be a gift to some presidents would inevitably be an albatross to others.

Regardless of the strength of the partisan bridge, however, Louis Fisher points out that presidents have inherent constitutional powers and from this he concludes that the Hamiltonian notion of an energetic and active presidency essentially was victorious.[32] How broadly or narrowly inherent powers are exercised depends to a large extent upon the varying assertiveness of different presidents, the political environment that conditions both their arrival in office and their behavior in it, and the relative vigor of other institutions. A presidency that is greatly dependent upon an exaggerated use of the inherent powers doctrine, however, likely would be either a wartime, war-making, or constitution-rending presidency. What powers do presidents have, in other words, when they are not otherwise preoccupied with any of the above activities? Most particularly, what capabilities do they have for moving an agenda? The answers lie less in what powers the president has than in what powers are also given to others. The relevant constitutional question in terms of how the design affects the operations of the political system is not whether the president is strong or weak in the abstract, but rather, is there a boss?[33] Was "the buck" meant to stop somewhere or to circulate everywhere? It is likely that the latter was intended, but it is undeniably true that it has been so constituted.

Governing by a seemingly endless circulatory process and through institutions that are often in competition with one another is governing that is normally incompatible with directive emphases. James S. Young describes the system as a dual one in which:

> We kept alive our constitutional system and the slow moving pluralist politics that go along with it, while building a contingency system around the Presidency, able to act alone and fast to provide disaster prevention and relief.[34]

In other words, we have the normal immobilization of power coexisting with the abnormal exercise of inherent powers. The institutional checks upon the assertive exercise of presidential power, in practice, are cast aside only in wartime, in clearly recognized crises, and by the sweep of an unusually wide electoral broom. One result, Stephen Krasner contends, is that "American central decision makers do not command the policy instruments that are important in countries like France and Japan [since] it is not clear in the United States where sovereignty rests, if indeed it rests anywhere at all."[35] At least in modern times, however, these limitations on the possibilities for presidential achievement are confronted by a secular rise in expectations about presidential performance.[36]

Operating within the framework of the day, even Hamilton's concerns for the unity of the executive, expressed in Federalist 70, were couched in terms of the division of powers. Yet, institutional fragmentation has helped to foment disunity in the executive, and to create, therefore, a nearly obsessive concern with its control.[37] From early on, the development of congressional specialization meant that executive heads of departments (and later other officials) would be subject to many pressures, and also, by virtue of that, be given many opportunities. The so-called "iron triangle" of today—the connection between executive agencies, congressional work groups, and affected interests—ironically could be seen in pale outline as early as the time of Madison's presidency. As James Young writes:

The committee system pushed the Presidency into the background and brought cabinet members to the forefront of executive dealings with Congress. With the establishment of congressional agencies for overseeing the work of the executive departments and passing upon substantive legislation affecting these departments, it was unavoidable that interaction should be intensified between the department heads and their superintending committees on the Hill. . . . Thus . . . a subsystem of political relationships between department heads and their supervising congressional committees came to supplant . . . the direct relationship between the President and his congressional party that Jefferson had enjoyed. The committee system caused the President to lose dominance over the communication channels to the community he needed to lead, and gave executive subordinates better access to the vital centers of legislative decision than the President himself had. *Men whose positions made them "the natural enemies of the President," as department heads have been called, became the principal spokesmen for the executive branch.* [38]

I have quoted Young here at some length in order to illustrate that concern about the impact of divided powers upon the unity of the executive is no recent issue. The phrase "men whose positions" made them into "natural enemies of a president" (the latter phrase, a quip from Charles Dawes) is especially revealing because it exemplifies what former presidential assistant John Erhlichmann sardonically called the "going native" syndrome—the reputed tendency of presidentially appointed officials to present their department's agenda to the president more enthusiastically than they present his to their departments.

It is true, of course, that the early specialization of Congress into committees was not mandated by the Constitution. Yet it was inevitable that an independent legislature would be a powerful legislature and that a powerful legislature would develop mechanisms by which to initiate policy, examine alternatives, and superintend the administration of the departments. In later years, as government became more complex, the executive-legislative channels would run along grooves dug deep into the various departments and agencies. Inescapably, then, given diverse outlets for pressing positions, the cabinet would be simply a collection of individuals rather than a collegial body of decision makers. Lacking a tradition of an independent, professional civil service with loyalties above the partisan fray, the bureaucracy also would become more obviously controversial as governmental functions grew. Mirroring the fragmentation of authority and of political power, the bureaucracy would be unified only in the epithets and suspicions of its many detractors. In fact, the compartmentalization of Congress would beget an equally compartmentalized bureaucracy—indeed, an executive divided within itself as Hamilton had feared. [39]

The uncertain constitutional proprietorship of the executive ultimately would beget strong White House efforts to gain central control over a bureaucracy subject to many influences. The belief that "the implementation of public policy could never be merely 'neutral,' and that the manner in which public services were delivered" counted, was implanted at least from the time of the Jackson administration."[40] In order to generate the elusive unity and energy of the executive for which Hamilton pleaded, in time, presidents would set out to construct cabinets composed of persons with little independent *political* status. This, however, would have to await both an environment conditioned to a more presidency-centered system, and a widened set of recruitment channels to the elite.[41] In time, presidents would seek to politicize the bureaucracy as well—to make "it" singularly responsive to their will—even if through forms different from those employed by Jackson. One commentator notes, in discussing the monitoring devices that replaced the traditional patronage mechanisms, that the movement of the Bureau of the Budget (BOB) to the Executive Office Building across from the West Wing of the White House was of great symbolic importance. In that site, the BOB would be expected to "serve presidential goals." Later, the assistant secretaries for administration in the departments would become political appointees. So too would the program associate directors at the Office of Management and Budget (the successor agency to the BOB). "The real motive," says Godfrey Hodgson, "for the politicization of the bureaucracy lay in the attempt, the perfectly understandable desire, of presidents to capture the bureaucracy, to shake it up and activate it as the instrument of an activist presidency."[42] Thus, the method for creating executive unity—to help presidents navigate through what in their eyes was indifference at best and hostility at worst—was to politicize the bureaucracy.

The unity of the executive, then, would remain in doubt. Its problems of unity would stem, however, more from the independence and complex organization of the legislature than, as Hamilton feared, from a failure to establish a single chief executive. As the functions of the executive multiplied, the more problematic adhesion would become. And the more problematic adhesion would be, the more presidents and their close associates would seek to have unity imposed from above—though the legally proper boundaries of this imposition often would remain obscure. A system, therefore, founded on the premise of checking the unity of government would contain an operational logic for checking the internal unity of its institutions as well.

As American government grew in its functions, it failed to grow commensurately in its unity.[43] With functional growth, questions inherent in the constitutional design would become more pressing while the answers to them remained enigmatic. To whom, for example, would the permanent legion of bureaucrats be accountable? The answer is to no single source of authority, and in that answer lies both a persistent quandary of American government and a persistent presidential response. The quandary is how to induce harmony in the executive branch and enable it to act with clear purpose; the response is to politicize the bureaucracy. Despite occasional victories, the myth of civil service neutrality, essential for the legitimation of the bureaucracy and the integration and professionalism of its officers, failed to take hold among the American political elite. Instead, the bureaucracy often would be perceived as "interested" and resistant to presidential goals. Moreover, in its fragmentation and disunity—one cause of its purported un-controllability—it would simply mirror its various would-be masters.

If all of these issues have been brought to the fore by the efforts of recent presidents to take full title to the executive, and by the quantum growth in governmental objectives, none is of entirely recent origin. The compact of trust needed to instill political leadership with an appreciation of bureaucrats' competence, and bureaucrats with a willingness to accept politicians' general directions, would prove to be elusive. For the American system of government is an edifice mounted on a foundation of distrust. Truly, even in the executive, ours would be not merely a government of strangers, to borrow Hugh Heclo's language,[44] but also from within itself a government estranged.

STATECRAFT WITHOUT "A STATE"

As divided sovereignty means that the United States lacks a single source of authoritative decision making (and thus, figuratively, lacks "a government"), so too the development of a distinctively American culture would deprive it of the idea of a permanent commonwealth both morally and authoritatively set off from the play of conflicting interests within society. Literally, of course, national sovereignty means that there is an American state. Figuratively, however, the interest-refracting notions implied by Madison are predicated upon the notion that the state is largely a medium for the play of interests rather than an autonomous presence providing continuous guidance. Madison's skeptical and defensive notions regarding the exercise of governmental power, however, would be permeated as well by both a strongly participatory ethos and a strongly privatizing one. The Jeffersonian legacy was political democracy and civic rights, while the Lockean legacy lay in the exalted status of property and contractual rights. As a result the practice of political democracy in America is more direct, less organized through instruments of political mobilization, more localistic, and more derisive of authority than elsewhere. So, too, the character of American development has shaped ideas about individual rights, about private entrepreneurship, and about the role of the state. Our political culture, then, tends to deny that which national sovereignty grants: the existence of a state. That denial, by default, also has denied a mobilized opposition to "the regime of the state," that is to say, a worker-based party founded in "Marxian" rhetoric.

Nevertheless, investigations of the role of the state in subsidizing activities within American society and in guaranteeing protection from risk, after all, confirm an expansive and undeniable presence.[45] Moreover, Americans hold attitudes that accept governmental involvement in specific social and economic activities, even though their generalized beliefs are usually less favorable to governmental involvement and, hence, more revealing of important cultural themes.[46] Even in the face of Reaganomics, an actively interventionist state, a large bureaucracy, and substantial welfare provision exist in the United States—though respectively less active, less well regarded, and arrived at later than in other Western democracies. Necessity requires an interventionist state and a bureaucracy to operate it. But state interventionism in America would be less inclusive, more reluctant, and always later to the mark. And, for public consumption at least, a bureaucracy without a longstanding tradition would become an easy target for derision.

The macrolevel evidence tells us that the United States government is busily engaged in social and economic activity, but these data fail to tell us much about the value orientation influencing its involvement or, for that matter, the structures through which involvement is channeled.[47] An almost religiously held belief in the market economy and in contractual rights, for instance, makes it especially difficult for government to intervene in the economy with anything but the bluntest macroeconomic policies. This reluctance makes it exceedingly hard to guide investment decisions or to develop wage and price policies. The dominance of the private sector has been ceded more than it has been imposed, but that dominance, as one student of the politics of comparative public finance points out, means that local governments in the United States are almost wholly dependent upon private markets for funding public investments. This dependence, in turn, forces investment decisions to be made on the basis of criteria acceptable to the private investment community.[48]

What we believe in, therefore, affects the tools that decision makers have to work with because it affects how actions must be justified. How actions must be justified also affects the ways in which policies and programs are administered. Indeed, it sets the tone of political debate.

Ideas matter, and policy patterns are related to ideas. But ideas do not spring *ex nihilo*. They are also the product of other factors. They follow from, are entangled with, and sometimes become indistinguishable from, the structure of interests and the structure of politics.[49] For example, while macrolevel expenditures indicate that the social security commitments of American government have risen rapidly in the past decade (although they still lag behind most European commitments), the punitive administration of some of these programs in the United States reflects the essential illegitimacy of their functions—the residue undoubtedly of the American ideology of "rugged individualism," but also of the absence of sustained mechanisms of political support. In contrasting, for example, the organization of social welfare policy in West Germany with that in the United States, Stephan Leibfried claims that

> The workhouse atmosphere is less prominent than in the United States where "work for relief" ("sing for your supper") programs are more systematically employed and where public job programs are specifically addressed to welfare clients and function as a more efficient device for testing within the framework of administrative control. . . .

> In the more socially diffuse context of American politics the emphasis of welfare programs is strongly negative. . . . Self-policing is intensive and "fraud campaigns" are widespread.[50]

If my emphasis here is on "political culture," I also recognize that this is something less than a very precise concept. It must almost always be inferred from evidence and, also, is typically indirect in its impact. Two researchers, for instance, caution us against its indiscriminate use as an explanation for political behavior. They contend, citing the case of Italy, that regional variations in political behavior are better explained by differences in the structure and organization of politics than by differences in the values held across the regions.[51] Of course, culture, interests, and institutions interact, but whether a mere symptom or a deep-rooted cause, culture helps "to account for limitations in the range of options, norms, and behaviors to be found in a population."[52] And yet because political culture cannot simply be reduced to individual attitudes and interpreted as the mere aggregation of these attitudes, it is difficult to point precisely at it.[53]

Thus, David Elkins and Richard Simeon observe that

> Individuals manifest or express their political culture without generally being aware of it. Political cultures consist largely of unconscious assumptions, so taken for granted that, except for a few rare and sensitive individuals, members of a culture seldom have occasion to question them.[54]

Though these assumptions affect the premises of our governance and at least indirectly the prospects for political leadership, they are not, if Elkins and Simeon are right, always susceptible to straightforward confirmation. Nor is it always self-evident how beliefs influence governance. Though these links are neither self-evident nor direct, there is ample reason to contend that the most prominent features of the American political culture first usually reinforce difficulties in imparting sustained political direction, and second often make social and economic intervention awkward.

We can, I think, distinguish between two very broad streams in our political culture. Each, in some measure, has to do with the state, but in somewhat different ways. The first refers to ideas and values regarding the relationship between citizen and political authority. These ideas give a special character to the democratic aspect of our political culture. The second refers to beliefs about the role of collective choice in society. Its roots are to be found in a society whose economic development was mostly privately generated, even if made easier by the government. The first stream requires the governing authorities to perpetually justify themselves, whereas the second stream seems to require the perpetual justification of government itself.

The case is stated boldly here. Realities are always more complex. The culture that we speak of is not uniform and homogeneous. Different views have been held on these rather large assumptions over the course of much of our history, and political forces have contended over them from the time of the Whigs and Demo-crats in the nineteenth century to that of the transformed Democrats and Republi-cans during most of the twentieth century. Moreover, what we claim to be culture merely may be a reflection of who has gained the upper hand politically, that is, whose values reign for the moment. In addition, elites and mass publics may not always be in concord or, if they are, it may be because leaders themselves set the tone for public consumption. These are obviously complex issues, and I raise them here without present hope of resolving them, simply because the value patterns that influence the range of acceptable action and permeate policy making and ad-ministrative implementation are not necessarily uniform across all sectors of the population.

There are, however, some very powerful and very special assumptions that Americans hold about the relationship of citizen to authority, and about the re-lationship of the state to society. These two broad but persistent themes in Amer-ican political culture have been briefly sketched. Now we will elaborate them and trace some of their implications for governance and presidential leadership.

The Democratic Ideal in America

The United States is the quintessential democracy buoyed by the ethos of egalitarianism. The language and symbols of American politics are saturated with notions about the sovereignty of "the people," who in political rhetoric at least are as unified as the governmental system is divided. Tocqueville, for instance, noticed that "Whenever the political laws of the United States are to be discussed, it is with the doctrine of the sovereignty of the people that we must begin."[55] The legacy of the successful American fight for independence, according to Rogers Hollingsworth, helped to explain the acclaim granted to popular sovereignty in our culture, and thus why the culture became so participant-oriented. "Not only did Americans believe that it was their right and duty to participate in government," he asserts, "but they very early believed that the government should be highly respon-sive to their demands."[56]

That participation occurred early in the United States—indeed, on a mass basis, well before any other country—meant that the body politic would suffer few enduring scars, although it also meant that few effective antibodies would be built up to resist the diffusion of power. With participation freely occurring among white males well before industrialization, the United States lacked the class rifts and grand social and political doctrines of later developing democracies. While there inevitably would be divisions, the sovereignty of "the people" would acquire a transcendent status. Where the European tradition would emphasize "the state" as the basis of legitimacy, continuity, and coherence, the robust American democ-racy would emphasize "the people" as the source of legitimacy (which they are) and the inspiration for guidance (which they cannot be). In contrast to Europe where "the people" were invoked by the left against conservative institutions, in the United States they are constantly invoked by all sides as the salvation against elitist ideas, policies, or organization—a political rhetoric of pantheistic populism. Being the object of such lavish rhetorical adulation, it would be easy to conclude that government should be always accessible and always responsive, and that failures of effectiveness would be better resolved by making government yet more accessible and responsive. If "the people" can do no wrong, then the source of perceived failures lies not in the immutabilities (or at least confounding perplexities) of social relationships or economic circumstances, but in the unresponsiveness and distance of government. "In sum," Samuel Huntington concludes, "the distinctive aspect of the American Creed is its antigovernment character."[57]

The democratic spirit is infectious in American society. It permeates political organizations and institutions. Although there have been relatively recent "surges" of democracy, promulgated by an expanded sector of people attentive to public affairs, by changes in organizational rules, and by the decline of stable intermediate organizations, the propensities for democratization always have been great. De Tocqueville noticed early on, for instance, the difference between European and American associations. Among their differences, Tocqueville claimed, were ones in the scale and scope of action that European and American associations each wanted to bring about:

> The means that associations in Europe employ are in accordance with the end which they propose to obtain. As the principal aim of these bodies is to act and not to debate, to fight rather than convince, they are naturally led to . . . centralize the direction of their forces as much as possible and entrust the power of the whole party to a small number of leaders.
>
> The Americans have also established a government in their associations, but it is invariably borrowed from the forms of the civil administration. The independence of each individual is recognized. . . .[58]

Perpetuated everywhere, democracy would reinforce fragmentation and decrease organizational coherence; it would lessen, therefore, the stability necessary to sustain agreement. Having little capacity to resolve conflict but having much to energize it, American institutions maximize politics.[59] What is true of American governing institutions is also true of its political party and interest group organizations as well. Skeptical of centralization, wary of discipline, and encouraging of independence, democracy in the United States would be peculiarly atomized and its politics unusually personalistic. A society imbued with the "civic culture" would also demand a large serving of microdemocracy. The distinctiveness of American democracy, in fact, would lie in the weakness of its organizational delivery systems. For Americans, and apparently now for the citizens of other industrialized democracies as well, the surface contradiction between a democratic political order and the lack of democracy in the organizations essential to its functioning is no longer easily reconciled.[60] Yet, a democracy characterized by the themes of individualism, "opposition to power, and suspicion of government,"[61] contributes to unusual perplexities in generating a democratically accountable scheme for decision making. Madison's system would work to confuse the issue of accountability. To achieve this less than democratic outcome, however, would require a remarkable assist from the pervasive spirit of democracy that flows through the American political culture. Together, institutions and culture would make collectively directed change arduous.

However poignant these characteristics are in our time, they are also etched in our past. The democratic impulse was elite-driven and skeptical of the authority of government. Individualism and skepticism of authority are at the core of the American democratic spirit. They work to atomize power, diffuse it, and localize it. The continunity of these themes is illustrated by James Young's excellent history of the early Washington political community. He observes that

> the antipower values of the governors would seem to explain, better than citizen demands upon them, the emergence of a constituency-oriented culture and social organization on Capitol Hill. Ambivalence about power among men in power would seem to explain better than their needs for political survival, why they preferred the behavior of constituency agents to the behavior of rulers. But the dogged commitment to internal democracy and the fragmentation into sociopolitical blocs . . . on Capitol Hill also raise—even more cogently for the congressional community—the same question that was raised by the antipower values and the fragmented structure of the larger governmental community. How could a system pregnant with such sources of conflict within itself perform the task of resolving conflict outside itself, in the nation at large?[62]

How does all of this impact upon the presidency? The answer is probably better addressed by a different question, namely, what is the effect on the capacity of government to formulate and carry through national goals? While no simple answer to this can be given, the American political style, being wide-open, entrepreneurial, constituency-oriented, and forever questioning of the legitimacy of authority, is better suited to opposing than to governing.

Ultimately, the populist tendencies of American democracy, spread indiscriminately, weaken the capacity to govern. Yet, with the advent of positive government and the mass media, a purposeful vision of governance would be commanded. In the modern era, presidents have become chiefly responsible for supplying the vision. They would suffer, accordingly, for being unable to govern. Invoking responsiveness to "the people" and deriding the legitimacy of government itself inevitably produces an asymmetry: large expectations and withered capacity. Heightened by contemporary trends, this would be the crux of the American governing predicament—a predicament, however, at least partly self-inflicted. Since, as Young notes, the elite "themselves regarded power as evil, power-seeking as corrupting, and politicians as unprincipled,"[63] it is not surprising that collectively this elite would become the object of scorn.[64]

The Antistatist Ideology

The hyperdemocratic American political culture tends to diffuse power still further among institutions designed to fragment it. Its impact is to make it even harder to get a handle on American government than the institutions alone could account for. The American propensity to avoid ceding effective political power to any source is also augmented by a general, but not always operational, belief that private action is to be preferred to public action. Only in the United States, for example, is private philanthropy highly valued. Elsewhere, it is expected that such undertakings are the proper responsibility of the state.[65] These first-order assumptions are especially relevant among the elite. "The most characteristic, distinctive and persistent belief of American corporate executives," David Vogel argues, "is an underlying suspicion and mistrust of government . . . [which] distinguishes [it] . . . from every other bourgeoisie. . . ."[66]

What Americans believe, and most especially what American political elites believe, Anthony King also contends, is that the state should play only a very limited role, and this belief, it is further argued, has much to do with the late development and the perceived quality of the public service.[67]

The role that the U.S. government plays is no longer so limited (even though it seems to be redirecting itself again toward that condition). There is, however, a less direct and nuanced state role in economic intervention than in virtually any other industrial society. Aside from public efforts in the area of education, American government was both later and less beneficent in arriving at a welfare role than other now comparable societies. Not all of this, obviously, constitutes a problem of governance. European governments that have to contend with strong pressures for expansive welfare benefits may have their flexibility limited in contrast to the United States where these pressures, and the interventionist assumptions behind them, are less powerful.[68] The cultural resistances in the United States to controlling the welfare state are apt to be less strong even though the system of government makes it easier to protect the status quo—whatever the status of the quo happens to be.

The populist and antistatist aspects of the political culture combine to generate backlash against both taxes and, at least in the abstract, government spending. These sentiments appear to be deeply rooted, almost reflexively so. "Americans," Susan Hansen remarks, "have complained about taxes at least as far back as the Boston Tea Party and the Whiskey Rebellion." Indeed, while Americans tend to complain most about taxes and "big government" (or at least find available channels for articulating their complaints), both taxes and social spending tend to be lower than in other industrial democracies (Table 3.2). Commenting upon the contemporary tax revolt, Hansen concludes that much of it is predicated upon "ignorance or anti-government sentiment rather than economic rationality."[69] A particularly impressive set of findings in this regard shows that support for Proposition 13 in California was substantial across the socioeconomic spectrum.[70]

TABLE 3.2. The Government Role in Comparative Perspective

(a)			(b)		
Percentage of private housing starts to all housing starts (1976) (*Source:* United Nations Compendium of Housing Statistics, 1980.)			Social security expenditures as percentage of Gross Domestic Product (GDP) (1974) (*Source:* United Nations, International Labor Organization Report on Social Security Expenditures, 1976. Housing & Education expenditures are excluded.)		
		% increase from 1970			
			Netherlands	—	24.8
United States	99%	+ 1	Sweden	—	24.4
Canada[a]	98%		France	—	21.6
West Germany	97%	+ 18	Italy	—	21.4
Norway	96%	+ 29	Denmark	—	21.0
Switzerland	94%	+ 11	Belgium	—	20.9
Austria	91%	+ 38	West Germany	—	20.3
Japan	91%	+ 4	Austria	—	18.2
Finland	87%	+ 4	Norway	—	17.8
Belgium	85%	+ 19	Finland	—	15.4
Sweden	78%	+ 36	United Kingdom	—	14.6
Denmark	76%	+ 5	Switzerland,		13.9
France[a]	65%		Canada	—	
Netherlands	63%	+ 11	United States	—	12.5
United Kingdom	48%	0	Japan	—	6.5

(c)			(d)		
Tax Revenues as percentage of Gross Domestic Product (GDP) (1975) (*Source:* OECD, Public Expenditure Trends, 1978.)			Government Spending as percentage of GDP (1975) (*Source:* OECD, Public Expenditure Trends, 1978.)		
Sweden	—	50.9	Netherlands	—	51.2
Netherlands	—	46.4	Sweden	—	49.4
Norway	—	46.2	United Kingdom	—	44.4
Denmark	—	44.7	Belgium	—	43.2
France	—	39.1	West Germany	—	42.1
United Kingdom	—	37.4	Italy	—	41.9
West Germany	—	36.0	Canada	—	40.9
Canada	—	35.4	France	—	40.3
Italy	—	32.3	Austria	—	40.2
United States	—	29.6	United States	—	34.0
Japan	—	21.3	Japan	—	23.4

[a]Canadian and French data are available only for 1970 (see 1974 Compendium). In contrast to 1970 data, private housing starts, as a percentage of all housing, have dramatically expanded across the board.

Naturally, such attitudes ebb and flow to some extent according to circumstances. High levels of economic growth make for a greater willingness at least to accept the particulars of welfare state spending (if not the idea), and a greater willingness to accept tax rates. Even deeply rooted sentiments can be conditioned by events. Such sentiments are also deeply influenced both by the issue agendas of elites, and by the nature and social biases of American political organization—most especially, the presence of a strong right-wing pro-market party, and the absence of a socialist alternative.[71]

While this antigovernment, antitaxing culture (one that is especially punitive toward "welfare" spending) most frequently is focused on the state and local level where pressure is more easily placed and where there are fewer interests to be dislodged, it is not without impact on national issue agendas or, from our point of view, presidential programs and programmatic success. For the most part, the antistate culture makes it exceedingly difficult, except under very unusual political circumstances, to openly generate sufficient support for new social service initiatives. Most of these initiatives have occurred during rare and short-lived bursts of reform. But perhaps it is precisely because the bursts are so short-lived (by European standards so retarded) and the resistances otherwise so great, that we must turn to cultural explanations. Surely, culture and political organization influence one another and whether the absence of a European-style social democratic party is the result or the precipitant of our ideas about the state, the fact remains that there is no strong political force compelling continuous attention to social welfare issues other than as matters either of administrative reform or of fiscal contraction.

The upshot is that presidents who want to promote great social change of this nature are (1) unlikely to get elected if this is the centerpiece of their agenda; (2) unlikely to successfully promote much of it unless they are endowed with massive majorities in Congress; and (3) likely normally to be sailing against prevailing winds. All of this is *ceteris paribus,* of course, and partly explainable by factors other than ideas, but that Americans hold unique beliefs about the welfare functions of the state there can be little doubt. The ideology of the middle class is nowhere effectively countered by a politically self-conscious working class.[72] Nor does there exist in recognizable form, in the land where the myth of rugged individualism prevails, a conservative ideology to provide legitimacy for the authority of the state. Institutionally, however, the same political design that discourages interventionist social reformers will also tend to be biased (once programs are secured) against large-scale change in the other direction.

Aside from the social welfare aspect of the antistatist culture, few tools are available (or are sought) for finely grained economic intervention. Writing in the 1960s during a period of dynamic growth in the Western economies, the late Andrew Shonfield asserted that "The United States is . . . one of the few places left in the world where 'capitalism' is generally thought to be an OK word. Elsewhere even a politician of the far Right, abusing socialism and the welfare state, will normally hesitate to base his appeal to popular sentiment on a call for the reassertion of good old capitalist principles."[73] In contrast to European governments, the American government exercises less discretionary adjusting and guiding of the economy—although, to be sure, it probably engages in more microregulatory activity than European governments. And as Table 3.3 indicates, there is a deep reluctance to allow government to own enterprises. Certainly, American government has more tools today than it had say a century ago, and capitalism is today more harnessed than it was then. Still, these instruments are weak in comparison with those available to most European governments. Most important, their availability and use is burdened by the belief that intervention is but a momentary expedient, a temporary act to adjust macroeconomic conditions, not a continuing basis for industrial guidance.

More tools obviously need not mean better economic management. Indeed, they can be only as useful as diagnostic accuracy and political possibilities permit. Ultimately, too, what is meant by better economic management must be referenced, in part, by political reaction. In short, the power to decide is not the power to control, nor would the power to control necessarily give greater weight to economic than political feasibility. In any event, the notion that the mature economies of the industrialized societies can be manipulated to resurrect the heady growth rates of the 1960s is no doubt vastly overblown.

Still, American presidents have less wherewithal typically to affect economic conditions than other chief executives. They have little at their disposal to help orchestrate economic change beyond what Congress and the Federal Reserve Board cede. Confronted with economic conditions they have little direct control over and affected by the view that government activity should only respond to specific problems rather than be a continuing and guiding presence, presidents are left to a fickle fate. As Shonfield comments

> Among the Americans there is a general commitment to the view, shared by both political parties, of the natural predominance of private enterprise in the economic sphere and of the subordinate role of public initiative in any situation other than a manifest national emergency. The West Europeans . . . have no such assumptions—for even the Right in Europe tends to believe in the abiding place of active paternalistic government.[74]

Granted this, there is still a simple point to be made: Whatever moves governments elsewhere can make on the economic chessboard, the U.S. government has fewer to make. Whether that is our good fortune or bad cannot be answered here, but that it is the president's bad fortune is likely. Under such circumstances, however, it seems, as Edward Tufte suggests, that the natural impulse of American presidents will be to zig and zag, to try to make blunt instruments do the work of fine tools, and to veer toward short-run policies that have visible benefits even if deferred and hidden costs.[75]

TABLE 3.3. Government Control of the Economy, 1975 (Approximate Percentages of State Ownership)

	Postal Service	Tele-communications	Electricity	Gas	Oil Output	Coal	Railroads	Airlines	Autos	Steel	Ship-building
Austria	100	100	100	100	0	0	100	75	100	0	NA
Belgium	100	100	25	25	NA	0	100	100	0	50	NA
United Kingdom	100	100	100	100	25	100	100	75	50	75	100
Canada	100	25	100	0	0	0	75	75	0	0	0
France	100	100	100	100	NA	100	100	75	25	75	0
Italy	100	100	75	100	NA	0	100	100	25	75	75
Japan	100	100	0	0	NA	0	75	25	0	0	0
Netherlands	100	100	75	75	NA	NA	100	75	50	25	0
Sweden	100	100	50	100	NA	NA	100	50	0	75	75
United States	100	0	25	0	0	0	25	0	0	0	0
West Germany	100	100	75	50	25	50	100	100	25	0	25

Note: There appears to be no consistent pattern as to whether reform or conservative governments were in power in the above countries when sectors of the economy became a part of the public sphere. Moreover, much government control of these industrial sectors is longstanding. In West Germany, for example, postal service, electricity, railways, telecommunications, coal production, and airlines were partially or wholly nationalized at the outset of their development. See, here, Anthony King, "Ideas, Institutions and the Policies of Governments: A Comparative Analysis —Parts I and II," *British Journal of Political Science* 3 (July 1973): 291-313.

Sources: The Economist and OECD, adapted from *The New York Times*, March 4, 1978, p. 93.

POLITICS WITHOUT PARTIES

An eminent American political journalist several years ago wrote a book decrying the ideological squishiness and indiscipline of the American parties. He entitled his book *The Party's Over.*[76] But perhaps it never much began. Recent years, we know, have been unkind to the ability of the American parties to monopolize the channels of access to politics, but the more important point is that the American parties never reached a stage of organizational maturation characteristic of parties in other industrialized democracies. In other words, if American parties in recent times have been weakened with regard to the performance of some of their functions, the point from which they have slid has not been exceedingly steep. If the American party system is the democratic world's oldest, it is also its most enfeebled.

Why are American parties so organizationally retarded? so incapable of acting as highly disciplined forces? and so internally ideologically diverse? Some answers are at hand: primary elections, campaign laws, mass communications, and single district winner-take-all elections. To be sure, these are all important, and some of them represent twentieth-century conditions. We may need, however, to stand back a bit further. After all, why does the United States alone have primary elections and campaign laws that frequently weaken party organization and activity? Why do mass communications seem to enervate the American parties so especially? Why should our form of representation, which mirrors that of Britain, produce substantially greater indiscipline within the American parties than within the British?

No single answer explains these conditions. A combination of reasons, however, may be derived from the design of the American political system and the character of American development. Together, political structure and social structure have inhibited the development of strong nationally organized parties because they largely also have inhibited a national politics. The complex structure of the American political system imposes significant impediments to organizational coherence, though at times these have been overcome. The persistent localism of the American system, structurally and culturally, meant also that if parties were to be effectively organized, they would have to be organized from the bottom up rather than from the top down. Their local character frequently would predominate especially in the presence of sectional divergences. At the national level, then, the parties primarily would be loose confederations of local organizations. (An irony of American political life, however, is that contemporary forces have helped nationalize the organizational character of the American parties while both weakening their local base and detaching public officeholders even further from the party base.) One important reason, of course, why the American parties failed to move past this retarded state and toward a truly national politics was that the United States never faced a crisis of participation (the struggle for black political rights aside) in the same degree as had the European countries. The early and universal participation of the white male American populace meant that political organization in America would be different from that in Europe. Having been granted the rights of citizenship with no discernible struggle and with a pervasive spirit of democratic egalitarianism afoot, there would be no fundamental challenge to the regime. There would be no significant prospect of a socialist party organized against the system, so there would be no obvious need for counterorganiztion from the right. In short, no organized challenge to the regime, thus no response.

We have talked about political parties in the American system as being relatively weak and underdeveloped. But in precisely what respects? It has been noted, for instance, that the concept of political party can be given different meanings. Frank Sorauf, for instance, suggests that it is useful to think of political parties in terms of a tripartite structure.[77] He first suggests that we need to think about the political party as an organization that serves both a mediating and a purposive function. In this sense, parties integrate and coalesce interests, recruit candidates for office, set forth goals for their own internal functioning, and propose manifestos (or platforms) for external policy-making purposes. Probably in all democratic polities parties have been somewhat deficient in these respects.[78] A second sense of party has to do with performance in office—the parliamentary party so to speak. By virtue of the separation of powers system in the United States, this aspect of party turns out to be a bit more complicated than in most other democracies. The third sense of party discussed by Sorauf is that which he calls the party-in-the-electorate, in other words, the relationship between the party and its rank and file followers—the extent to which the followers are psychologically identified with and loyal to the party. We may refer to these three aspects of party, respectively, as the *organizational party,* the *legislative party,* and the *psychological party.* An important consideration is whether there is a connection across these three levels. Without speculating as to causal sequence, it may be hypothesized that organizationally strong parties are connected to legislatively disciplined parties, and that these are also linked to a high degree of voter loyalty. In rough outline, such an argument has been advanced by one student of electoral cycles.[79]

The psychological definition of party presents some complications for historical analysis as well as for comparison across political systems. To the extent that its measurement is dependent upon the tools of survey research there are obvious limitations to historical comparison. We cannot, in short, be certain of how much waxing and waning there has been in the party loyalty of voters, though circumstantial evidence would suggest that political parties in the past have played a more powerful role in shaping voter behavior than at present. It is somewhat difficult as well to distinguish clearly between party attachment and voting behavior itself.[80] Moreover, the connection between party identity and voting loyalties in the United States is sometimes uncertain because of the concurrent existence of separated powers (meaning that elections are held across different sectors of government) and federalism (meaning that elections are held across different levels of government). Despite these caveats, there appear to be ups and downs in the salience of the psychological aspect of party within the electorate, and these may be related to the proximity to, or distance from, periods of fundamental political shifting or realigning.

Employing Sorauf's second aspect of party—the party in office—the American legislative parties at times have demonstrated considerable internal cohesion, conditions which are explored in more detail in the next chapter. However, by 20th century European standards, even these periods of robust cohesion have been dilute. One vital reason for this relative incohesiveness has to do with the unusual localism prevalent in the American system—a political system in which national identity remains incomplete. Hollingsworth argues, for instance, that

> Americans have had a less developed sense of national identity than the British, the people of the Scandinavian countries, or those of other European states with populations that are relatively homogenous ethnically. Throughout most of American history, there have been stronger ties to locality than to the national state, a condition resulting from the fact that the American political system is a federation of decentralized states.[81]

Even during a period of relatively strong party cohesion in Congress, a time in the 1840s and early 1850s dubbed "the shrine of party" by one historian, Hollingsworth concludes "the identity problem remained unresolved [because] . . . most Americans continued to identify with their region or with state governments to a greater extent than with their national government."[82]

The powerful impact of local forces in congressional elections vitiates what Donald Stokes has termed "the electoral logic of cohesion," i.e., the unity of parliamentary party induced by its members sharing a collective electoral fate.[83] By contrast with British elections, for example, Stokes finds that in the United States constituency forces are powerful buffers against national political tides. Put most simply, American members of Congress are apt to control their fates more readily than British members of Parliament. The logic of electoral cohesion in America is less compelling because for a member of the U.S. Congress such a logic might be downright irrational. Conflicts betwen party and district, therefore, are understandably likely to be resolved in favor of the district—evidence, in short, of a retarded national politics. While Stokes thought these district forces to be in decline and believed that American politics was in the process of becoming increasingly nationalized, more recent evidence indicates that local forces, at least insofar as the turnover of seats is concerned, have once again risen in the last twenty years.[84] Morris Fiorina here points to an electoral system that he and others argue has become (in my view has nearly always been) bifurcated. Motivations for presidential voting are separated from those of congressional voting. The result of this, he concludes, is that members of Congress can emphasize constituency-tending at the price of undermining support for a president of their own party.[85] That they can do so with relative impunity does not necessarily mean of course that they will, but

Fiorina's analysis indicates that they have little need to consider their fate and that of their president in common. These powerful local forces have always been with us, if not always with the same diffusive impact on congressional cohesion. As Stokes's data show, the distinctive contribution of constituency forces was most vast in the 1870-1910 period when party was king in Congress. Such a finding ought properly to open the question of what precisely party meant during this period to leaders and followers, and especially to national and local elites.

The puzzle of congressional party incohesion, however, cannot be explained alone by reference to these persistently powerful local forces. Other factors also have been important. In recent times, for instance, the great increases in information available to both mass publics and to elites probably has served to increase the independence of each. An analysis by Philip Converse is suggestive in thinking retrospectively about the impact of information supply on the retention of party loyalties. In earlier periods of information sparseness, he suggests, the stability of mass partisanship was likely to be very great because little information was available to disturb it. Thus, voting behavior presumably might more closely concide with underlying partisan loyalties.[86] The growth of information, increasingly relevant now in races for the House according to some analyses, means that constituencies are in a position to know more about their representatives than in earlier times when the supply of information was scarce.[87] The process also works in reverse. The availability of information helps members of Congress to maximize their electoral chances by placing district first; thus, when in doubt, constituency wins out. As Douglas Arnold has recently written, "Ordinarily, better information makes for better decisions. Here, vast improvements in the information available to congressmen have had the opposite effect. When computers inform everyone . . . of the incidence of local benefits under every imaginable formula, the stage is set for the complete domination of local politics."[88] While the forces of localism have always been strong, the ways in which the heavy dose of localism would come to interact with other factors, such as the supply of information, would shape members' incentives, and, thus to a considerable degree, the character of party cohesion in Congress.

The power of central leadership, at least within the House during the 1870-1910 period, undoubtedly also had much to do with enforcing cohesion, though it is not quite clear how the minority could enforce counter cohesion, nor is it clear how this could happen in the Senate which has managed to evade central forces of leadership with remarkable agility. The legislative party in the United States has rested on a unique bond between legislator and district (and senator and state)—a bond that ultimately would make it easy for members to resist party responsibility when it was in their interest to do so. When sectional forces also were at work, and when these were not fully congruent with partisan divisions, they would further weaken partisan forces.

Typically, then, Congress has been a bastion of localism. The tension built into our system between local pressures and national policies has never been much expunged by the appearance of national political parties, for the national political parties have been overshadowed at least in the past by local organization. The clashes between a potentially disintegrative localism and national coherence usually have been uneven. When such clashes have occurred, the two major American parties often have performed as though they were each a hundred parties, each principally interested in nurturing their constituent base rather than in generating national policy. As Theodore Lowi contends:

> The constituent orientation of the American parties, leaves us with a party system that splits regime off from policy. It leaves us with parties that virtually exist to keep leadership, succession, and the constitutional structure separate from the actual settlement of issues. Just as responsible programmatic parties like Europe's tend to centralize authority, so programmatic parties tend to democratize regimes by keeping legitimacy and policy in close association.[89]

With regard, therefore, to the third aspect of parties, Lowi's thesis is that organizationally American parties have been chiefly involved with distributing pork and patronage, and controlling the emoluments and perquisites of political office. Consistent with this view, corruption was rife at the local level of party organization and programmatic purpose was minimal even when political parties in America were at the peak of their congressional cohesiveness. The old local political organizations were hardly organized for indoctrinating, mobilizing, or programmatic purposes. At their peak they were heavily dependent upon the entrepreneurship of leading personalities and on the payoffs of a spoils system. What often has distinguished American political organization from its European form, in fact, is the issueless personalism of the former. Even the exercise of patronage—a vaunted tool for securing voter mobilization—appears to be disconnected from this fundamental purpose, as a study of the contemporary Democratic party organization in New Haven points out.[90] Lowi claims that this traditional divorce between organizational strength and policy commitments represents a retardation, a premodern element, in the development of the American political system—an argument of considerable persuasiveness inasmuch as the closest form of these old-line American political machines can be found in the least modern areas of Europe.[91]

Despite some counterflow of evidence, our parties rarely have progressed much past local and personal factions. Inevitably, the failure to fully consummate a national politics would inhibit the parties from attaining the status of being durable, effective, and cohesive forces at the national level. What the Constitution fragmented and what the culture reinforced, the party system for the most part has been unable to counter. Anemic as they typically have been at the national level, the American political parties have tended to adapt to and reflect their environment rather than overcome and redirect it. In so doing, they have reflected a politics that failed to join purpose with organization. The result at the national level has been a frequently disorganized and confusing politics—a politics with a significant social bias in the character of electoral participation, a strong emphasis on localistic concerns, and in recent times a special sensitivity to constituency-tending.

If the larger generalizations are that the American parties have reflected a traditional rather than modern definition of the political task (dealing far more in the currency of jobs, particularistic favors, the emoluments of office, and the furthering of personal ambition than in the generation of policy goals), these generalizations are not invariant over time or place. Some of these conditions, for instance, are changing and are discussed in Chapter 5. The American past too has shown variability in party functions across different periods in our history, in the mass attachment to parties, and in partisan cohesion. A politics of weak parties means quite obviously that presidents are denied disciplined support, and less obviously that presidents may have more leeway to set forth an heroic notion of the office and their role in it.[92] In the absence of supporting props, however, an heroic conception of the office may lead to much presidential tilting at windmills.

Although a strong case can be made for a strengthening of the political parties, vital political parties are neither an unrelieved blessing for presidents nor a panacea for effective governance. Politicians with executive responsibility for governing rather than merely articulating discover that not everything is reducible to abstract ideological propositions. They also discover that sometimes decisions with at least a short term adverse impact on their party's constituencies have to be made. Stronger parties with presidents beholden to them would likely, for better or worse, reduce this latitude. For parties have limited repertoires. They will tend to define issues in terms of familiar terrain—whether through accustomed ideological doctrine or their effects on key constituent groups, or both. In the whites of every partisan's eyes lies a passion to politicize everything—to turn issues of "fact" into issues of factiousness. Strong parties may help hold presidents to account but also can freeze them into inflexible postures. Moreover, given the fragile status of the American civil service and the potential vulnerability of the federal bureaucracy to deep partisan incisions, stronger parties also might mean an even more expansive spoils system. There is nothing in our past to indicate that a president's hand would be strengthened by such an arrangement.

The "energy" of the executive may be sapped by strong parties in yet other ways. Indeed, the Whig theory of government which emphasized strong parties also emphasized a powerfully directive Congress. The period of high partisanship in the 1840s and early 1850s, the period of the Whig ascendancy, was also a time of marked conflict between the White House and Congress—especially, but not exclusively, during the administration of President Tyler. During this period of what Joel Silbey has called the shrine of party, presidents were to worship, not to be worshipped.

Parties, finally, are limited by their relative insensitivity to technological or knowledge driven changes. Walter Dean Burnham, for instance, notes that "the extraordinarily complex and technical character of many key political issues" today provides fewer "partisan cues to the public . . . than in an age of fewer and broader political issues."[93] Political parties, by themselves, are apt to be blind to such issues, because they are exclusively political organizations attentive to spicy issues. If vital, they are better equipped to direct society according to their visions and priorities, but these are unlikely to be sensitive to technologically induced change. Properly, these are issues about which bureaucrats may have more to say, and to which parties can be expected to have little to contribute. Producing more partisan vitality, therefore, without an equal emphasis upon strengthening the institutions of governance—for example, a more integrated and autonomous civil service—is unlikely to provide much prospect for coping with the larger issues of governability. A condition of strong parties, in other words, without an equally strong bureaucracy (a balance of forces more nearly reached in Europe), induces a serious imbalance between politics and governance. Together, strengthened parties and a strengthened bureaucracy might actually simplify the maze of Washington policy networks, and reduce the need to layer in "loyal" personnel throughout the agencies. Thus, governance is aided by a more coherent politics, but it also requires more than that. A better organized politics, in other words, does not necessarily translate into more effective governance.

To all of these generalizations, I add a further qualification. I have been speaking of parties in the plural as though they were all of a single piece. They are not. Although the American party system is very weak by most European standards, it is also true that at any given time in any given party system some parties are better organized, more internally disciplined, and more capable of mobilizing relevant constituencies—better able, in short, to govern. In Europe, typically, greater discipline has come from the Left which in turn has induced it to a somewhat lesser extent on the Right.[94] In the United States, at least in the present era, the Republican party generally has been ridden with fewer factional splits than the Democrats, and certainly, as John Kingdon shows, it has been more salient to its members in the Congress than the Democratic party has been to its members.[95]

Still, with all of the qualifications and nuances we have added, the bottom line is that parties are essential to presidential programmatic support as Jeffrey Cohen's historical analysis has indicated.[96] Retarded as they are in their development, they still are the main bridges (flimsy though they often seem) connecting our political institutions. When the party bridge weakens, so too do the prospects for coherent direction.

CONTINUITIES IN THE STRUCTURE OF AMERICAN POLITICAL CLEAVAGES: SECTIONAL AND ETHNIC FRAGMENTS

Geographic Diversity

A nation as physically large as the United States was destined from its beginning to spawn regional cleavages. Diverse climates, resources, and patterns of development lead to distinct regional interests. Historically, American politics has been most sharply split along regional lines, though the precise structure of and issues behind these cleavages have been altered from time to time.

The American party system has mostly reflected this diversity. For example, a recent analysis of the ideological positioning of Democrats and Republicans in the U.S. House of Representatives reports that the overlap between individual members of the parties in Congress occupies a sufficiently large part of the ideological range that it is impossible to conceptualize exclusive Democratic and Republican spheres on that range (though, of course, the parties do occupy distinctive spheres). When these data are examined state by state, however, almost all of the overlap disappears. The political unit of the state itself, in other words, is responsible for the ideological space occupied by the parties. Invariably, the Democrats are on the left and the Republicans on the right of each state's spectrum, but the frontier between left and right varies markedly from state to state. Put slightly differently, it is only within each of the states and not in the nation as a whole that we may presume the Democrats to reside exclusively on the left and the Republicans exclusively on the right.[97] In this regard, we should take note that one of the highest tides of party cohesion and interparty dissimilarity within the House of Representatives (the decade and a half following the realigning election of 1896) was a period during which the parties were almost wholly coincident with sectional interests.[98]

The United States, of course, is not alone in possessing regional divisions. In Canada, the coincidence of party and region is now greater than it was even during the peak American sectional-party overlap produced by the realignment of 1896. West of Ontario, the Liberal party has fewer members of Parliament than Jimmy Carter had electoral votes west of the Mississippi. And despite its regional divisions, the United States has not been faced with the regional complications attendant to the geographic concentration of ethnic, religious, or linguistic groups as has, say, Belgium or Canada.

Rather, what is particularly interesting in the United States is the way in which regional divisions interact with the political structure. The Canadian system, for instance, squeezes regional divisiveness out of its parliamentary politics through a nationalized parliamentary party system (though the parties themselves strongly reflect regional interests). But while the Canadian system devolves greater authority to its provinces than is the equivalent case in the United States, it also enables the government in Ottawa to make decisions of national consequence—ones more difficult to make, for instance, in either Brussels or Washington.[99]

The cost of making national decisions in the face of serious regional splits is erosion of legitimacy, as the Canadian experience in dealing with bilingualism, oil royalties, and constitutional revision suggests. The cost of not making national decisions in the face of regional splits, however, is drift. Unlike the Canadian system which has a weak center (relative to the provinces) but a strong will, the American system has a potentially stronger center (relative to the states) but a weaker will. Whereas the parliamentary parties in Ottawa enforce direction, the American system mirrors its localistic and regional interests quite directly.

Among American public officials only the president can provide any prospect of articulating and generating support for "national interests" over and above regional and local ones. The president cannot, however, command the resolution of regional divisions—divisions that are typically articulated in Congress. Regional interests can be compromised, up to a point, as the connecting issues of national expansion, slavery, and political representation demonstrated until the 1850s, or as the more recent and less traumatizing issues of setting formulas for federal programs currently indicate. Truly difficult decisions, ones that clearly shift burdens and resources or disproportionately diminish largesse, are not easily compromised or resolved without the onset (or promotion) of crisis, as the slavery issue ultimately showed.

Presidents never have been immune from these divisions. The American political system places far greater value on legitimation and consent than upon decisive action or effectiveness. Implicitly, the assumption underlying our "localized" politics is that without legitimacy and consent there can be no effectiveness. Emphasis has been placed on patching, accommodating, or doing nothing when regional interests collide, at least until the costs of doing nothing either generate the consensus necessary for policy or lead to crisis and *ad hoc* responses. Neither our scheme of political representation nor our anemic tools for national politics enable presidents to easily surmount that which is mostly insurmountable.

While the regional differences have been with us from the outset—the gift of a large territory and later a diverse people—they have frequently changed form, alignments, and visceral intensities. They have directed our politics more than they have been redirected by our politics. While issues of distributive equity are raised in all representative political systems, in few places have these issues evaded national decision making so successfully. And that undoubtedly is because in few places "is the ability of the political actors to function as a national public" so weak.[100]

Ethno-Cultural Diversity

American diversity was reflected by sectional forces very early on. Not until later was diversity also reflected through ethno-cultural forces. These did not, however, threaten the territorial integrity of the nation; they would not, in other words, spawn a nationality or separatism problem. Nevertheless, ethnic and religious subcultures would be politically relevant. The coincidence of these subcultures and partisan divisions has been even greater (though also frequently correlated with region) than those between region and party.[101] As Paul Kleppner has written:

> Nineteenth-century American partisanship was not rooted in economic distinctions. Neither gradations in wealth nor perceived differences in status nor shared orientations toward the work experience were at the core of partisan commit-

ments. Partisan identifications mirrored irreconcilably conflicting values emanating from divergent ethnic and religious subcultures. And nineteenth-century political parties were not aggregations of individuals professing the same political doctrines but coalitions of social groups sharing similar ethno-cultural values.[102]

Ethno-cultural diversity, among other things, would act to inhibit a politics based strongly on vertical economic distinctions. Friedrich Engels, for instance, claimed that "American conditions involve very great and peculiar difficulties for a steady development of a workers' party. . . . To form a single party [in the face of great ethno-cultural diversity] requires," he concluded, "unusually powerful incentives."[103]

As with regional factors, however, the interaction between political structure and ethno-cultural diversity helped to produce a peculiar outcome, one that avoided either ethno-cultural segmentation or separatist potential, and instead promoted a high degree of ethno-cultural permeability throughout the political system. Ira Katznelson asserts in this regard that the separation of workplace and community in American social structure means that "it is at the level of community that ethnicity has defined the basic social and political units of the social structure, and thus has defined the phenomenal terms of group conflict."[104] While inhibiting the development of a working class based political movement, ethnic factors in public life would be facilitated greatly by a noncentralized system in which the parties were more sensitive to ethno-cultural than to social stratification distinctions, and by a culture that stressed ethnic incorporation without forcing cultural assimilation. Ethno-cultural considerations, therefore, have been expressed as part of the constituent focus of the political parties. Recently, they have even more saliently appeared in the form of interest group activity. In a political system that reveres pluralism, ethnic group political activity has long been considered a normal basis of interest expression in the system. Ethno-cultural diversity, of course, preceded an expansive tolerance for its expression, but a highly penetrable political system would make that expression inevitable.

The ethno-cultural features of American politics are an enduring part of the landscape, though their bases and the forms of their expression have been alterable. What previously had been largely expressed through the parties is now more directly articulated by interest groups. In recent times, the permeability of the political system to salient ethno-cultural interests would produce new constraints on presidential policy making, especially in the area of foreign affairs which presidents usually have identified as their special preserve. The interaction of political structure and ethnic interest formations is notable in this regard for, as Theodore Lowi observes, Congress has a tendency to convert foreign policy issues into constituency problems.[105] By doing so, it provides a natural outlet for ethnic group influence. Although ultimately presidents are usually able to set their course even in the midst of significant ethnic group pressures, no executive leader must be so sensitive to these constraints as the American president. This is perhaps as it should be in a society so diverse. Legitimacy often has been enhanced by this sensitivity and that is no modest achievement. But it also has required subjecting foreign policy to many of the same currents that are at work in domestic policy processes. Presidents with large-scale diplomatic master plans had best be prepared for equally large-scale modifications.

FISHBOWL GOVERNMENT: THE FIRST AMENDMENT AND THE MEDIA

In all democratic polities, there is a potential conflict between "state interests" and a free and open press. Viewed from a comparative perspective, however, this conflict is weighted substantially toward the media in the United States, though the tugging and pulling between the two forces alters the magnitude of the relative advantage from time to time. Much of the media's advantage, and certainly much of their impact both on the conduct of politics and of government, would come later—the product of technological and social trends. The media's legal advantage, however, would be defined at the outset of the Republic's existence via the First Amendment to the Constitution. The potential impact has come to fruition with the advent of the electronics media (which is among the few national institutions in American society).

Relative to other constitutional polities, the press in the United States has had a long tradition of unfettered freedom to probe and inquire. The longstanding legal tradition of an unrestricted press also coincides here with the populist elements of the democratic culture. As Edward Shils has noted, "The United States has been committed to the principle of publicity since its origin . . . [since] Repugnance for governmental secretiveness was an offspring of the distrust of aristocracy."[106] The American tradition of openness contrasts vividly, for instance, with British or French obsessions with secrecy. In all of the industrialized countries, politics has become saturated with media coverage as a result of modern technological and social trends, but only in the United States are the exercise of media coverage and, above all, the absence of restrictions against publication exalted as an absolute constitutional right. More than the media elsewhere, the American media have extraordinarily broad legal scope to inquire and publish. This means that the American media are well-positioned to counter the deceptions in which all presidential administrations engage, but it also means that the size of the deception, the importance of the gaffe, and the relevance of the foible are all magnified by the enlarged capacity to uncover them.

The press in Europe frequently is restricted by law from inquiring into everything that its own government considers privileged information, and the electronics media are usually at least partly nationalized. In contrast, the press in the United States is an active, if inadvertent, participant in the governing process itself. It is a ready and available source for leaks, trial balloons, back stabbings by policy losers, and knife twistings by policy winners.[107] As contrasted with other flourishing constitutional systems, the American press has a unique capacity to hang out all the governmental wash, and a strong tendency to emphasize personalities (and conflict between them) and politics at the expense of examining policies.[108]

The media, of course, interact with political structure, and they are influenced by elements of our culture. A politics of personalism, after all, begets attention to personalities. A politics that thrives on suspicion of government also begets skepticism about government and the motivations of officeholders. A government of diffused powers and responsibilities invites an involved press.

Everywhere in a free society, the media (at least the elements that are not governmentally controlled) thrive on controversy. In the United States where virtually no element of the media is governmentally controlled and where constitutional legal guarantees are very significant, the latitude for attending to controversy remains larger, and the availability for participating directly, if unintentionally, in policy making is unprecedented. Much of this is relatively recent, but the potential for it has been given by the Constitution itself. The implications of this now realized potential are more fully explored in Chapter 5.

CONCLUSION

Throughout this chapter presidents have been treated as though they were only acted upon rather than acting; their situation determined wholly by exogenous factors rather than influenced by their own behavior in office. Naturally, this is much too simple a picture, for the individual president is obviously a variable in the governance equation. How the "constants" discussed in this chapter affect presidents will also depend upon the presidents themselves—their ambitions and goals, the scope of directive change they seek, and the particular focus of their policy objectives. Those with large ambitions for generating nationally directed change, however, typically will face singularly large obstacles.

The first of these impediments to the execution of presidential will lies at the foundation of the political system: A system designed to rein in the opportunities for temporary majorities to achieve their goals, in practice, tends to prevent presidents from achieving theirs. Big changes in the American political system typically require great consensus. The virtues of the design lie in its ability to promote representation, its openness to popular currents, and, by virtue of its multiplicity of policy sources, its capacity to inspire (but not consummate) innovation. The limitations of the design, on the other hand, are bound up with its capacity to resist coherently directed change, and certainly to resist it on any kind of sustained basis. Resistance does not mean that such change is impossible however. Rare electoral sweeps provide moments of opportunity, but the sweet tonic of victory, it turns out, must be gulped quickly rather than savored.

A second major obstacle to generating coherently directed change reflects our culture—the unique beliefs that Americans hold about government. The governors, themselves bereft of the idea that government should be granted autonomy, would also fail to develop an ideology of governance. Beliefs, of course, have been outpaced by necessities. Government is involved in society, but in ways that reflect skepticism about its legitimacy. Thus, presidents are frequently denied policy tools possessed by heads of other democratic governments. What they, like their counterparts elsewhere, are not denied are enlarged expectations about what they may be able to pull off.

A fragmented government and a weak state, for the most part, have produced weak parties. Modern parties promote that which both the institutional framework and the spirit of our politics have prejudiced against: a capacity to put forth, pass, and sustain an agenda. American parties provide only a moderate and often unpredictable degree of adhesion. In this, they more or less reflect our system of government and our beliefs about government. In regard to the latter, Richard McCormick argues that "the whole history of American parties suggests that the American people have never wanted strong political parties for the same reasons, essentially, that they have not wanted strong government."[109]

However important parties are for bridging the constitutional separation between the president and Congress, the American parties have generally mirrored the localism imbedded in the political system. Organization typically was strongest at the local level (and often pathologically venal), and the parties themselves could mean different things in different locales. Lacking potent disciplinary forces (a testament to the importance of locality over party) in a system of representation that exposes the personal visibility of officeholders and candidates, members of Congress often behave essentially as local emissaries to Washington.

Interlocking with a political structure that diffuses power and emphasizes constituency politics, the diversities of American society readily find expression in the political arena. The lack of a central authority coupled with a mode of representation that emphasizes local interests often makes it difficult to find national solutions to issues that entail regional divisions. Such an arrangement in the face of regional cleavages means a fine line has to be found between legitimacy and impasse, and between the distribution of benefits that may need to be locally or regionally concentrated and their irrational diffusion across a myriad of congressional districts.[110]

In a system that celebrates diversity, ethno-cultural forces, too, have been a staple of American politics. Ethnic groups easily become interest groups because the institutions of the system are highly penetrable. This phenomenon by itself is hardly astonishing. Multiethnic societies are more nearly the norm than not, and dispensations to various ethnic groups are a common enough procedure for minimizing the potential for unrest.[111] Yet, the weakness of the American state, the lack of a fully integrated national identity, and the ease with which ethnic interests can be facilitated makes it especially complicated to arrive at policies considered opprobrious by organized ethnic groups, most recently in the heretofore special presidential preserve of foreign policy.

Finally, by virtue of the First Amendment, the American media cut a wider swath than that in other countries with consequences that are obviously good for politics, and less obviously so for governance. The technological potential for putting government in a fishbowl has been quite recent, but the legal possibilities to do so have been longstanding. Moreover, the cultural tradition for it has been substantial.

In this chapter, then, I have focused attention on the broad environment of American politics. I have done so because it is only within that context that we can fully appreciate the special difficulties attendant to the exercise of political leadership and of governance in the United States. This environment structures the conditions under which directive leadership can take place. I have called attention here to a set of factors, though sometimes variable in form, that structure those conditions. They make presidential governance unusually difficult, by which I mean to imply neither that this was unintended by the framers, nor that giving direction to government is only a quaintly American problem. Nor have I meant to imply that providing direction in the American system is hopeless. It isn't. But it also is quite difficult, and requires circumstances that occur only very rarely. If all of this seems entirely obvious, it is. But it also at times has escaped the attention of those amongst us who are the most politically attentive. For our attentiveness to, and excitement about, politics sometimes leads us to ask more from it than can be had, more from those who practice it than they can produce. Sometimes it leads to a dimmed perspective. From that standpoint, it is perhaps advisable to conclude here with an historian's words:

> We read a good deal in the press that novel and untoward developments—especially the breakdown of party discipline in Congress, the power of lobbies, the rise of single-issue political movements—are transforming U.S. politics in a startling and unprecedented way, crippling the presidency, and rendering the republic ungovernable. . . . From the historical perspective, columnists and other commentators would seem inordinately excited about what are, in fact, the standard conditions of American politics.[112]

NOTES

1. Raymond Grew, "The Crises and Their Sequences," in *Crises of Political Development in Europe and the United States,* ed. Raymond Grew (Princeton, N.J.: Princeton University Press, 1978), p. 30.

2. For instance, see Garry Wills, *Explaining America: The Federalist* (New York: Doubleday, 1981), and his *Inventing America: Jefferson's Declaration of Independence* (New York: Vintage Books, 1979).

3. For an analysis that attempts to discern Jefferson's true intentions regarding party politics and majority-building by laying stress on his deeds rather than his words, see James MacGregor Burns,

The Deadlock of Democracy: Four Party Politics in America (Englewood Cliffs, N.J.: Prentice-Hall, 1963), pp. 24-46.

4. Stephen D. Krasner, *Defending the National Interest: Raw Materials Investments and U.S. Foreign Policy* (Princeton, N.J.: Princeton University Press, 1978).

5. *Ibid.,* p. 70.

6. *Ibid.,* p. 352.

7. What remained of the deferential culture, Ronald P. Formisano argues, was effectively terminated by 1840. In Formisano's interesting thesis, the collapse of Whig culture preceded the political collapse of the Whigs as a party. See his "Deferential-Participant Politics: The Early Republic's Political Culture, 1789-1840," *American Political Science Review* 68 (June 1974): 473-487.

As for institutions, it is difficult to know precisely how strong Hamilton wanted the Congress to be relative to the president—there being more than the usual room for interpretation on this. It is clear, however, that Hamilton's concerns lay in the efficient exercise of state power. In Hamilton's words: "When you have strongly connected the virtue of your rulers with their interest; when, in short, you have rendered your system as perfect as human forms can be; you must give power." As quoted in Louis Fisher, *President and Congress: Power and Policy* (New York: The Free Press, 1972), p. 259.

For a heterodox interpretation of the thinking of the framers, one which sees more similarity in their assumptions and their thinking than difference, see Wills, *Explaining America*. And, for an interpretation linking the Declaration of Independence and the Constitution to the same web of thought, see also his *Inventing America*.

8. There is one sense, however, in which the Jeffersonian tradition is more optimistic even about the power wielders than was Madison. Whereas Jefferson's concern lay with the emergence of "a political class"—a separation between the governors and the governed—he was less skeptical about the democratic exercise of power. While Jefferson was skeptical of the elite, he was hopeful about the citizenry. In this regard, Madison's skepticism encompasses both the rulers as well as the ruled.

9. Robert A. Dahl, *A Preface to Democratic Theory* (Chicago: Phoenix Books, 1963).

10. *Ibid.* Rabushka and Shepsle also argue that "the resolution of intense but conflicting preferences [is not] manageable in a democratic framework," and that where they are made manageable the cause may be found in traditions and "integrating" exigencies rather than in institutions. Alvin Rabushka and Kenneth A. Shepsle, *Politics in Plural Societies* (Columbus, Ohio: Merrill, 1972) as cited in J. Roland Pennock, *Democratic Political Theory* (Princeton,N.J.: Princeton University Press, 1979), p. 251.

11. Thus, in contrasting the American penchant for politics with the European stress on the unity of the state, Richard Rose notes that while the latter may make for a more efficient government it also has produced, in the past at least, the suppression of politics. See Richard Rose, "Government Against Sub-Governments: A European Perspective on Washington," in *Presidents and Prime Ministers,* eds. Richard Rose and Ezra Suleiman (Washington, D.C.: American Enterprise Institute, 1980), p. 288.

And, in logic supportive of that expressed in Madison's Federalist 10 and 51, Seymour Martin Lipset has argued that "Intolerant movements, while often powerful, have never been able to endanger seriously the normal processes of American democracy." This is so, Lipset claims, because of "the involved structure of the constitutional system, the division of powers, the juridical protections, the complex and diverse sources of opinion and interest differences. . . ." In other words, he concludes, "it is relatively easy to build a new extremist movement in this country; it is difficult if not impossible to build a party." See Seymour Martin Lipset, "Three Decades of the Radical Right: Coughlinites, McCarthyites, and Birchers—1962," in *The Radical Right,* ed. Daniel Bell (Garden City, N.Y.: Doubleday, 1963), p. 369.

12. Richard E. Neustadt, *Presidential Power: The Politics of Leadership from FDR to Carter* (New York: John Wiley, 1980), pp. 26-27.

13. Nelson W. Polsby, *Congress and the Presidency,* 2nd ed. (Englewood Cliffs, N.J.: Prentice-Hall, 1971), p. 147.

14. J. Rogers Hollingsworth, "The United States," in *Crises of Political Development,* p. 177.

15. Alexis de Tocqueville, *Democracy in America,* vol. 1 (New York: Vintage Books, 1945), p. 60.

16. Tocqueville, vol. 2, p. 316.

17. Kenneth Dyson, *The State Tradition in Western Europe* (New York: Oxford University Press, 1980), p. 270.

18. Joseph LaPalombara properly provokes my anxieties over this. He argues vigorously that while political scientists are least likely to draw large-scale generalizations about the American political system (probably because of the richness of our information about it), they are readily drawn to such generalizations concerning other societies for which (or precisely because) there is a paucity of information. I hope at least to have reversed the nature of the problem that LaPalombara refers to by demonstrating more caution in my remarks about other systems than in those I offer about the U.S.! See Joseph LaPalombara, "Macrotheories and Microapplications in Comparative Politics," *Comparative Politics* 1 (October 1968): 52-78.

Lending credence to LaPalombara's cautions, the editor of a volume examining the making of public policy in Japan concludes that the studies undertaken "reveal some of the many complexities of Japanese policymaking and defy oversimplified judgments about the totality of that country's politics and society." See T. J. Pempel, "Conclusion," in *Policymaking in Contemporary Japan,* ed. T. J. Pempel (Ithaca, N.Y.: Cornell University Press, 1977), p. 323.

19. Robert S. Walters, "Industry and Government Approaches to the Crisis in Steel: Protectionism, Structural Shifts and International Economic Peacekeeping." Paper presented at the Eleventh World Congress of the International Political Science Association, 1979, Moscow.

20. For evidence of this, see especially Sidney Verba and Norman H. Nie, *Participation in America: Political Democracy and Social Equality* (New York: Harper & Row, 1972), pp. 334-343.

21. Samuel P. Huntington, *Political Order in Changing Societies* (New Haven: Yale University Press, 1968), p. 129.

22. Clinton Rossiter, ed., *The Federalist Papers* (New York: New American Library, 1961), p. 84.

23. Huntington, *Political Order,* p. 110.

24. Hollingsworth, "The United States," p. 187.

25. A comparison of national legislative elites in seven countries, for example, reveals that American members of Congress not only emphasize the facilitating function more than any other function, they also emphasize it far more than parliamentarians in the other countries do. That some of the variance here is accounted for by the nature of the scheme of representation is indirectly indicated by evidence from another country in which some legislators are elected by district and some by proportional representation. Members of the German Bundestag who are elected by district are substantially more likely to emphasize facilitative functions than their colleagues elected through proportional representation. See Joel D. Aberbach, Robert D. Putnam, and Bert A. Rockman, *Bureaucrats and Politicians in Western Democracies* (Cambridge, Massachusetts: Harvard University Press, 1981), pp. 94-102.

26. James S. Young, *The Washington Community 1800-1828* (New York: Columbia University Press, 1966), p. 252.

27. *Ibid.*

28. See John F. Hoadley, "The Emergence of Political Parties in Congress, 1789-1803," *American Political Science Review,* 74 (September 1980): 757-779. Although Hoadley's stress is on the emergence (temporarily) of congressional parties, he also notes that "both new parties retained a distinctively sectional character." Thus, "Given the great cultural and economic differences between the regions, it should not be surprising that the parties were so distinctively regional." (p. 772.)

29. Morton Grodzins, "American Political Parties and the American System," *Western Political Quarterly* 13 (December 1960): 979-998, esp. p. 994.

30. Jeffrey E. Cohen, *Passing the President's Program: Presidential Congressional Relations, 1789-1974* (Ph.D. thesis, The University of Michigan, 1979), p. 161.

31. Nancy H. Zingale, "Third Party Alignments in a Two Party System: The Case of Minnesota," in *The History of American Electoral Behavior,* ed. Joel H. Silbey, Allan G. Bogue, and William H. Flanigan (Princeton, N.J.: Princeton University Press, 1978), p. 132.

32. Fisher, *President and Congress,* pp. 32-33.

33. In Norton Long's memorable phrase, this was the unanswered question of the American political order and remains, therefore, the constant plague of administration. See his, "Power and Administration," in *Bureaucratic Power in National Politics,* 3rd ed., ed. Francis E. Rourke (Boston: Little, Brown, 1978), p. 16.

34. James S. Young, "The Troubled Presidency: II," *New York Times,* December 7, 1978, p. 23 as quoted in Charles O. Jones, "Congress and the Presidency," in *The New Congress,* ed. Thomas E. Mann and Norman J. Ornstein (Washington, D.C.: American Enterprise Institute, 1981), p. 246.

35. Krasner, *Defending the National Interest,* p. 62.

36. See, for instance, Richard Rose, *Managing Presidential Objectives* (New York: The Free Press, 1976), p. 158.

37. See, here, Long, "Power and Administration"; Joel D. Aberbach and Bert A. Rockman, "Clashing Beliefs Within the Executive Branch: The Nixon Administration Bureaucracy," *American Political Science Review* 70 (June 1976): 456-468. For evidence suggesting the prospects of control (but also the great effort required to achieve it), see Richard L. Cole and David A. Caputo, "Presidential Control of the Senior Civil Service: Assessing the Strategies of the Nixon Years," *American Political Science Review* 73 (June 1979): 399-413, and Ronald Randall, "Presidential Power versus Bureaucratic Intransigence: The Influence of the Nixon Administration on Welfare Policy," *American Political Science Review* 73 (September 1979): 795-810.

38. Young, *The Washington Community,* pp. 204-205. Emphases are mine.

39. As James Q. Wilson has written: "If our bureaucracy often serves special interests and is subject to no central direction, it is because our legislature often serves special interests and is subject to no central direction." James Q. Wilson, "The Rise of the Bureaucratic State," in *The American Commonwealth—1976,* ed. Nathan Glazer and Irving Kristol (New York: Basic Books, 1976), p. 103.

40. Matthew A. Crenson, *The Federal Machine: Beginnings of Bureaucracy in Jacksonian America* (Baltimore: The Johns Hopkins University Press, 1975), p. 174.

41. See, here, the analysis by Nelson Polsby in his "Presidential Cabinet Making," *Political Science Quarterly* 93 (Spring 1978): 15-34; also see his "Interest Groups and the Presidency: Trends in Political Intermediation in America," in *American Politics and Public Policy,* ed. Walter Dean Burnham and Martha Wagner Weinberg (Cambridge, Massachusetts: MIT Press, 1980), pp. 41-52.

42. Godfrey Hodgson, *All Things to All Men: The False Promise of the Modern American Presidency* (New York: Simon and Schuster, 1980), pp. 98-99.

43. A point, however, that Richard Rose insists is endemic to the growth of government generally. That is, the more the functions of government expand the more contradictory become its objectives. See Richard Rose, "What if Anything Is Wrong with Big Government?," *Journal of Public Policy* 1 (February 1981): 5-36.

44. Hugh Heclo, *A Government of Strangers* (Washington, D.C.: The Brookings Institution, 1977).

45. For a veritable mountain of evidence thereof, see Thomas J. Anton, Jerry P. Cawley, and Kevin L. Kramer, *Moving Money: An Empirical Analysis of Federal Expenditure Patterns* (Cambridge, Massachusetts: Oelgeschlager, Gunn & Hain, 1980).

46. See, for instance, Lloyd A. Free and Hadley Cantril, *The Political Beliefs of Americans: A Study of Public Opinion* (New Brunswick, N.J.: Rutgers University Press, 1967). Along this line a *New York Times*/CBS News survey indicates that while only 32% of Americans approve of "most Government sponsored welfare programs" specific programs all gained more approval, and roughly four-fifths of the public approved of food stamps, aid to families with dependent children, and health care for the poor. A national health care program was approved by an almost two to one margin. See Robert Reinhold, "Public Found Hostile to Welfare as Idea but Backs What It Does," *New York Times,* August 3, 1977, pp. 1, 49.

47. In contrasting social security policy in Britain and France, for example, Douglas Ashford suggests three main features of any policy comparison: (1) the value-orientation underlying the policy; (2) the relationship between policy and political authority; and (3) the organizational links between pol-

icy and government. See Douglas E. Ashford, "The British and French Social Security Systems: Welfare States by Intent and by Default." Paper presented at the 1981 Annual Meeting of the American Political Science Association, New York.

48. Alberta Sbragia, "Borrowing to Build: Private Money and Public Welfare," *International Journal of Health Services* 9 (May 1979): 207-226.

49. I do not intend here to get into the debate, raised by John Manley, regarding the direct explanatory role of culture and class (or other) interests. Suffice it to say, culture and structural factors are related to one another, but the case that culture flows solely from the class basis of socioeconomic relations simply has not been convincingly made. I do not claim knowledge of the precise relationship, and I am skeptical of its capacity to be empirically known. See John F. Manley,"Neo-Pluralism: A Class Analysis of Pluralism I and Pluralism II," *American Political Science Review* 77 (June 1983): 368-383.

50. Stephan Leibfried, "Public Assistance in the United States and the Federal Republic of Germany: Does Social Democracy Make a Difference?" *Comparative Politics* 11 (October 1978), p. 61.

51. Samuel H. Barnes and Giacomo Sani, "Mediterranean Political Culture and Italian Politics," *British Journal of Political Science* 4 (July 1974): 289-303.

52. David J. Elkins and Richard E. B. Simeon, "A Cause in Search of Its Effect, or What Does Political Culture Explain?," *Comparative Politics* 11 (January 1979), p. 137. For a Marxian emphasis on the structural (class-based) roots of this culture, see Manley, "Neo-Pluralism."

53. On this point, see Edward W. Lehman, "On the Concept of Political Culture: A Theoretical Reassessment," *Social Forces* 50 (March 1972): 361-370, and Elkins and Simeon, "A Cause in Search of Its Effect," pp. 127-146.

54. Elkins and Simeon, "A Cause in Search of Its Effect," p. 137.

55. Tocqueville, *Democracy in America,* p. 57.

56. Hollingsworth, "The United States," p. 177.

57. Samuel P. Huntington, *American Politics: The Promise of Disharmony* (Cambridge, Mass.: The Belknap Press, 1981), p. 33.

58. Tocqueville, *Democracy in America,* p. 205.

59. Rose, "Government Against Sub-Governments," p. 288.

60. For example, one democratic theorist contends that, "For a democratic polity to exist it is necessary for a participatory society to exist, i.e., a society where all political systems have been democratized and socialisation through participation can take place in all areas." See Carole Pateman, *Participation and Democratic Theory* (London: Cambridge University Press, 1970), p. 43.

61. Huntington, *American Politics,* p. 33.

62. Young, *The Washington Community,* p. 108.

63. *Ibid.*

64. Richard Fenno notes, for instance, that in working their constituencies members of the House of Representatives try to differentiate themselves from others in Congress, attack Congress as an institution, and portray themselves as combatants against institutional deficiencies. In other words, he concludes,

members tend their own constituency relations and even attack Congress from time to time to reinforce their customized political support at home. Whether or not such behavior contributes to the decline of confidence in Congress, it surely does nothing to balance the scales. . . . Representative government . . . also requires the governing of constituents. . . . Most members of Congress have enough leeway at home, if they have the will, to educate their constituents in the strengths . . . of their institution. They have more leeway than they allow others—even themselves—to think.

Yet, they seem afraid to acknowledge that strength in order to help govern the country. See Richard Fenno, *Home Style: House Members in Their Districts* (Boston: Little, Brown, 1978). Statements are taken from pp. 167 and 246-247.

65. See, for instance, Jeffrey Obler, "Private Giving in the Welfare State," *British Journal of Political Science* 11 (January 1981): 17-48; also see Jonathan Kandell, "Private Charity Going Out of Style in West Europe's Welfare States," *New York Times,* July 2, 1978, pp. 1, 4.

66. David Vogel, "Why Businessmen Distrust Their State: The Political Consciousness of American Corporate Executives," *British Journal of Political Science* 8 (January 1978), p. 45.

67. See Anthony King, "Ideas, Institutions and the Policies of Governments: A Comparative Analysis—Part III," *British Journal of Political Science* 3 (October 1973), p. 421. With regard to the public service and the unflattering stereotypes surrounding it, see, for instance, Daniel Katz, Barbara A. Gutek, Robert L. Kahn, and Eugenia Barton, *Bureaucratic Encounters: A Pilot Study in the Evaluation of Government Services* (Ann Arbor, Michigan: Institute for Social Research, 1975). See also Charles T. Goodsell, "Looking Once Again at Human Service Bureaucracy," *Journal of Politics* 43 (August 1981): 763-778. For somewhat contrary views emphasizing an activist but chaotically organized state role, see Theodore J. Lowi, *The End of Liberalism: The Second Republic of the United States,* 2nd ed. (New York: W. W. Norton, 1979), and Stephen Skowronek, *Building a New American State: The Expansion of National Administrative Capacities, 1877-1920* (Cambridge, England: Cambridge University Press, 1982). For a different, but also contrary, view emphasizing the instrumental nature of such beliefs for the maintenance of a capitalist and class-based social order, see Manley, "Neo-Pluralism."

68. See, here, Richard Rose and Guy Peters, *Can Government Go Bankrupt?* (New York: Basic Books, 1978), and Samuel Brittan, "The Economic Contradictions of Democracy," *British Journal of Political Science* 5 (April 1975): 153-175.

69. Susan B. Hansen, "The Tax Revolt and the Politics of Redistribution." Paper presented at the 1981 Annual Meeting of the American Political Science Association, New York, p. 3.

70. *Ibid.,* see Table 2.

71. The absence of a socialist party, according to L. J. Sharpe, means that

> the Federal government has to conduct periodic bursts of activity, "carried out on a stretcher," in order to maintain some sort of parity of welfare with comparable countries in relation to the poor. . . . Instead of being the product of a continuous doctrinal battle within the political system about the speed and direction of the secular trend to greater equality within society (which is very roughly what seems to happen in other Western democracies), social amelioration has often to come from on high, from the Executive branch in large doses dressed up as emergency measures to combat a temporary national crisis.

See L. J. Sharpe, "The Social Scientist and Policy Making in Britain and America: A Comparison," in *Social Policy Research,* ed. Martin Bulmer (London: MacMillan, 1978), p. 310. For an argument, on the other hand, that suggests that the critical political variable in social provision is not the power of the Left, but rather the strength of a right-wing party in opposition to the social welfare state, see Francis G. Castles and R. D. McKinley, "Public Welfare Provision, Scandinavia and the Sheer Futility of the Sociological Approach to Politics," *British Journal of Political Science* 9 (April 1979): 157-171. And, finally, for an analysis that suggests the irrelevance of political ideology to social policy expenditures, see Harold Wilensky, *The Welfare State and Equality: Structural and Ideological Roots of Public Expenditures* (Berkeley: University of California Press, 1975).

72. Sidney Verba and Kay Lehman Schlozman argue, on the basis of survey data from the 1930s, that few of the unemployed developed much sense of class consciousness, and they conclude further that "there is nothing . . . to indicate that members of the contemporary working class have either abandoned their individualistic assessments of their own situations or acquired a sense of class consciousness." See their, "Unemployment, Class Consciousness, and Radical Politics: What Didn't Happen in the Thirties," *Journal of Politics* 39 (May 1977): 292-323. (The quote is on p. 323.) For a fuller treatment of this theme, see Kay Lehman Schlozman and Sidney Verba, *Injury to Insult: Unemployment, Class, and Political Response* (Cambridge, Mass.: Harvard University Press, 1979).

73. Andrew Shonfield, *Modern Capitalism: The Changing Balance of Public and Private Power* (London: Oxford University Press, 1965), p. 298. Obviously, this was written in the pre-Thatcher era.

74. Shonfield, *Modern Capitalism*, pp. 298-299.

75. Edward R. Tufte, *Political Control of the Economy* (Princeton, N.J.: Princeton University Press, 1978), p. 143. See also Henry W. Chappell, Jr. and William R. Keech, "Welfare Consequences of the Six-Year Presidential Term Evaluated in the Context of a Model of the U.S. Economy," *American Political Science Review* 77 (March 1983), 75-91.

76. David S. Broder, *The Party's Over: The Failure of Politics in America* (New York: Harper Colophon Books, 1972).

77. See Frank J. Sorauf, "Political Parties and Political Analysis," in *The American Party Systems: Stages of Political Development,* ed. William Nisbet Chambers and Walter Dean Burnham (New York: Oxford University Press, 1967), pp. 37-38.

78. Anthony King, "Political Parties in Western Democracies: Some Sceptical Reflections," *Polity* 2 (Winter 1968): 111-141.

79. Paul Allen Beck, "The Electoral Cycle and Patterns of American Politics," *British Journal of Political Science* 9 (April 1979): 129-156.

80. See here, for example, Everett Carll Ladd, Jr. and Charles D. Hadley, "Party Definition and Differentiation," *Public Opinion Quarterly* 37 (Spring 1973): 21-34.

81. Hollingsworth, "The United States," p. 166.

82. See Joel H. Silbey, *The Shrine of Party: Congressional Voting Behavior, 1841-1852* (Pittsburgh: University of Pittsburgh Press, 1967). Also, for the quote, see Hollingsworth, pp. 192-195.

83. Donald E. Stokes, "Parties and the Nationalization of Electoral Forces," in Chambers and Burnham, *The American Party Systems*, p. 202.

84. *Ibid.* But for evidence of renewed localism, see, *inter alia*, Thomas E. Mann, *Unsafe at Any Margin: Interpreting Congressional Elections* (Washington, D.C.: American Enterprise Institute, 1978), and Fenno, *Home Style*.

85. Morris P. Fiorina, *Retrospective Voting in American National Elections* (New Haven: Yale University Press, 1981), pp. 208-211.

86. Philip E. Converse, "Information Flow and the Stability of Partisan Attitudes," in Angus Campbell, Philip E. Converse, Warren E. Miller, and Donald E. Stokes, *Elections and the Political Order* (New York: John Wiley, 1966), especially pp. 150-157.

87. For data on name recognition, see Mann, *Unsafe at Any Margin*, pp. 26-33.

88. R. Douglas Arnold, "The Local Roots of Domestic Policy," in *The New Congress*, p. 285.

89. Theodore J. Lowi, "Party, Policy, and Constitution in America," in Chambers and Burnham, *The American Party Systems*, p. 256.

90. Michael Johnston, "Patrons and Clients, Jobs and Machines: A Case Study of the Uses of Patronage," *American Political Science Review* 73 (June 1979): 385-398.

91. For an example of such, see Judith Chubb, "The Social Bases of an Urban Political Machine: The Case of Palermo," *Political Science Quarterly* 96 (Spring 1981): 107-125.

92. James MacGregor Burns associates this, in part, with Hamiltonian conceptions of leadership. In his interpretation of the Hamiltonian model, Burns asserts that the president is likely to have "far more leverage in manipulating personal and presidential power than if he were the responsible leader of a unified and disciplined party." James MacGregor Burns, "Three Approaches to Presidential Leadership," in *Classics of the American Presidency*, ed. Harry A. Bailey, Jr. (Oak Park, Illinois: Moore, 1980); pp. 64-70. The quoted material appears on pp. 68-69.

93. Walter Dean Burnham, "Party Systems and the Political Process," in Chambers and Burnham, *The American Party Systems*, p. 305.

94. For evidence of the traditionally greater political discipline of the Left in Europe at least insofar as legislative cohesion is concerned, see Duncan MacRae, Jr., "Intraparty Divisions and Cabinet Coalitions in the Fourth French Republic," *Comparative Studies in Society and History* 5 (January 1963): 164-211, and Giuseppe DiPalma, *Surviving Without Governing: The Italian Parties in Parliament* (Berkeley: University of California Press, 1977), esp. pp. 132-184.

95. John W. Kingdon, *Congressmen's Voting Decisions,* 2nd ed. (New York: Harper & Row, 1981), pp. 110-123; see also Douglas Rivers and Nancy L. Rose, "Passing the President's Program: Public Opinion and Presidential Influence in Congress." Paper presented at the 1981 Annual Meeting of the Midwest Political Science Association, Cincinnati. Rivers and Rose conclude "that a Democratic president with the usual Democratic congressional support (about 60% party strength) can expect only slightly greater congressional approval rates than a minority Republican president (about 40% party strength)." (p. 22.)

96. Cohen, *Passing the President's Program.*

97. See K. G. Armstrong, "Party, State and Ideology in the U.S. House of Representatives, 1967-76." Paper presented at the 1981 Annual Meeting of the American Political Science Association, New York.

98. See Jerome M. Clubb and Santa A. Traugott, "Partisan Cleavage and Cohesion in the House of Representatives, 1861-1974," *Journal of Interdisciplinary History* 7 (Winter 1977): 375-401, esp. pp. 382-383.

99. In Canada the key appears to lie in party government in Ottawa, however coincident the parties are with sectional forces. See Robert W. Jackman, "Political Parties, Voting, and National Integration: The Canadian Case," *Comparative Politics* 4 (July 1972): 511-536, and Norman C. Thomas, "An Inquiry into Presidential and Parliamentary Government." Paper prepared for the 1979 Conference on Legislative Studies in Canada, Vancouver.

100. Samuel H. Beer, "In Search of a New Public Philosophy," in *The New American Political System,* ed. Anthony King (Washington, D.C.: American Enterprise Institute, 1978), p. 22. Beer notes, however, that this is not exclusively a result of localistic and sectional pressures, powerful as they are, but also a product of the connecting functional interests of bureaucrats, legislative personnel, and policy specialists.

101. Aside from party identification itself, the most powerfully consistent predictor of voting behavior (as well as attitudes toward policy issues) is race.

102. Paul Kleppner, *The Third Electoral System, 1853-1892* (Chapel Hill: University of North Carolina Press, 1979), p. 144.

103. Letter from Friedrich Engels to Friedrich A. Sorge, December 4, 1893, as quoted in Kleppner, p. 238.

104. Ira Katznelson, "Considerations on Social Democracy in the United States," *Comparative Politics* 11 (October 1978), p. 96.

105. Lowi, *The End of Liberalism,* 2nd ed., p. 161.

106. Edward Shils, *The Torment of Secrecy,* as quoted in Huntington, *American Politics,* p. 46.

107. For a discussion of this, see Bert A. Rockman, "America's *Departments* of State: Irregular and Regular Syndromes of Policy Making," *American Political Science Review* 75 (December 1981), esp. pp. 916-918.

108. According to one student of the press, "newsmen tend to analyze their society in terms of personalities, rather than institutions comprising a social and cultural system." Another contrasts American political reporters with the intellectuals who write for the prestige European press, and contends that when Washington reporters talk about public affairs, "they primarily exchange speculations on the prospects of getting a bill through Congress, a candidate's chances of getting elected, the personality of a cabinet officer, or who has the real power in a department." See Stephen Hess, *The Washington Reporters* (Washington, D.C.: The Brookings Institution, 1981), p. 124. The second reference is to Hess himself. The first, as quoted in Hess, is from Warren Breed, "Social Control in the Newsroom: A Functional Analysis," *Social Forces* 33 (May 1955), p. 331.

109. Richard P. McCormick, "Discussion," in *The American Constitutional System Under Strong and Weak Parties,* ed. Patricia Bonomi, James MacGregor Burns, and Austin Ranney (New York: Praeger, 1981), p. 69.

110. See, for instance, Arnold, "The Local Roots of Domestic Policy," and Alice Rivlin, *Systematic Thinking for Social Action* (Washington, D.C.: The Brookings Institution, 1971).

111. See, for example, regarding ethno-partisan criteria in recruitment to the Belgian bureaucracy, Léo Moulin, "The Politicization of the Administration in Belgium," in *The Mandarins of Western Europe: The Political Role of Top Civil Servants,* ed. Mattei Dogan (New York: Halsted Press, 1975), esp. pp. 168-177.

112. Arthur M. Schlesinger, Jr., "Can the Party System Be Saved?" in Bonomi et al., *The American Constitutional System,* pp. 115, 117.

4

The Cycles of Presidential Leadership

As American history has shown time and again, there are concrete reasons why successive electorates feel they have "had enough." Both conservatives and liberals take over the government in a spirit of zeal and dedication, convinced that truth crushed to earth has risen again. But neither group can stand more than a certain amount of success; thereafter the quality of their performance tends to deteriorate. The desire to continue in power encourages timidity and compromise; holding office as a means tapers into holding office as an end.

(Arthur M. Schlesinger, *Paths to the Present*, pp. 90-91.)

The third political resource of a President is the type of electoral victory that brings him into power. In this century there have been three complete cycles. . . . Each cycle contains three types of Presidencies according to a different phase of the cycle. Each type of Presidency reflects different political conditions in the country, and therefore Presidential goals, styles, and strategy are likely to differ accordingly.

(Erwin C. Hargrove, *The Power of the Modern Presidency*, p. 186.)

An epoch of Hardings and Coolidges produces, by the scale of the problems to which it gives rise, its own regeneration. The weak president . . . comes from the fact that a strong predecessor has set the feet of the nation on level ground. He is chosen because, after a diet of strong occasions, a nation, like an individual, turns naturally to the chance of a quiet time.

(Harold Laski, *The American Presidency: An Interpretation*, pp. 52-53.)

Both the timing and size of the President's program respond to the ebb and flow of time, information, expertise, energy and, most importantly, capital. The dual cycles of declining influence and increasing effectiveness affect the pressures on the President to move the agenda. . . . Ultimately, the cycles produce countervailing pressures.

(Paul C. Light, "The President's Agenda: Notes on the Timing of Domestic Choice," *Presidential Studies Quarterly* 11 [Winter 1981]: 81.)

The culture of American politics and the structure of American government each predispose against the prospects for achieving and then sustaining coherent direction. To be sure, the obstacles to achieving direction are not at all times equally severe. Opportunities for directive leadership ebb and flow, the product of cycles of longer and shorter duration. Within these cycles are phases during which some of the normal constraints on leadership are relaxed, and, of course, times during which these constraints become more inhibiting. In the modern era, we tend to think of these opportunities and restraints as granted to, or visited on, the president. We now naturally equate the potential for leadership in the system with the presidency.[1]

In this chapter, I distinguish between three types of cyclical patterns: (1) long term and epochal; (2) metacyclical—those of more modest duration but independent of the presidential term; and (3) termcycles—short-term cycles dictated by the logic of the presidential term. The notion of a cycle implies a uniformly regular and recurring pattern. It is often very difficult, however, to distinguish clearly the tides that move to and from the shore from the erosion of the shoreline itself. It is not always clear, especially with regard to the longer-term patterns, whether one is talking about recurring phenomena or about evolutionary trend lines. Whatever the case, the epochal and metacyclical patterns move to a less regular rhythm than do the termcycles.

As difficult as it sometimes is to chart the contours of the epochal patterns with definitive precision, we still can discern a pattern of presidential-congressional relations over the long term that reflects the relative weight of these institutional forces in the matrix of American government. With somewhat more regularity and precision, we can also point to cycles of electoral politics that link political change to policy change. At their realigning peak, the electoral cycles can help presidents exert a more powerful directive force, though this has not always been so in the past. Within these broader historical patterns are the metacycles—oscillating moods and expectations—that help to define for a time the presidential role and the receptivities of the public. Finally, we can point to the term patterns—the logic of action and reaction dictated by the character of incumbency and the fixed term.

Insofar as the presidential-congressional relationship is concerned, periods of congressional assertiveness need not be at the expense of policy coherence, or even necessarily result in the clipping of presidential wings. Despite the natural tendencies for each of these outcomes to occur, much depends upon how Congress asserts itself and through what channels it does so. A lot, in fact, will depend upon whether Congress can be effectively referred to with the singular pronoun "it" or whether Congress is better characterized simply as a structure housing an atomistic collection of individual members and loosely organized interest clusters. A great deal rests, in short, on the power of Congress as a decision-making institution as distinct from the power wielded by its individual members. Both the powers of central leadership in each chamber and the extent of members' institutional consciousness are linked to whichever model of Congress is appropriate—collectivity or mere collection.[2] Whatever the case, it is Congress with which presidents must deal on a regular basis if they hope to achieve programmatic success. Across both institutions lies the shared burden of producing direction. Thus, it is the presidential relationship with Congress and the patterns governing that relationship that are the main focus of our attention.

The relationship between president and Congress also can be affected by the cycle of electoral realignment. The process of realignment crystallizes issues and sharpens the structure of conflict. Consequently, opportunities for broad-scale policy change tend to occur as a result of realigning electoral change. As the vitality of partisan forces decays, however, coalitions become more difficult to organize because the issues that helped organize them recede in prominence. The deterioration of issues and coalitions linked to past realigning periods frequently reduces substantial party majorities in Congress to apparitions; the presence even of large numbers often cannot compensate for the reduction in partisan cohesion.

Swings of mood and priority that can affect both presidential behavior and the perception thereof are characteristic of metacycles.[3] Like the annual showing of Parisian *haute couture,* newness is defined by the prevailing fashion of the immediate past. Presidential style and organization are often similarly influenced. In the immediate aftermath of the Watergate scandals, for instance, the institutional esteem of Congress momentarily soared in opinion surveys while the contentiousness of the Nixon presidency and the broad-scale assertion of prerogatives it advanced were in disrepute. The importance of reestablishing trust and the restoration of a constitutionally restrained presidency was accorded a more pressing priority than the direction and development of large policy agendas or a forceful leadership style. Despite the electoral rebuff to Gerald Ford such an atmosphere seemed still prevalent in the forces moving Jimmy Carter from obscurity to the presidency. By the time the gas lines of 1979 appeared, however, the old mood was eclipsed by the newer urgencies. Carter's perceived difficulties in effectively meeting those urgencies assured him a return to obscurity.

In contrast to the epochal patterns and metacycles outlined above, termcycles operate in a more regular, though very compressed time frame. The rhythms of presidential activity and popularity seem to be more common than different across the relatively few presidential administrations for which acceptable data can be marshalled. In this compressed time frame the rhythm of activity is heavily influenced by the compelling logic of a fixed electoral clock, by the array of institutional contenders and events against which presidential agendas rub, and by the entropic features of leadership change itself.

How do these various patterns affect presidents and their agendas? The *epochal patterns,* like enabling statutes, require a lot of filling in of detail by those on the scene. They provide both broad constraints and opportunities. The epochs of presidential-congressional relationship are likely to affect similarly presidents of the same era. The *metacycles,* which are especially relevant to modern times, can affect presidents within the same era differently, but also may overlap administrations. Among presidents of the modern era, the *termcycles* should lead to a somewhat different pattern—one revealing an apparently similar rhythm of presidential behavior across different administrations. In the preceding chapter, we discussed the more or less fixed features of the system in which presidents work. In this chapter, we examine the opportunities that exist when some of the normal constraints are loosened, as well as the inhibitors that come into play to harden the grip of these constraints.

The following analysis of these cyclical patterns and their possible effects on prospects for political direction, for presidential success, and for presidential behavior is more suggestive than conclusive—aimed merely at providing a useful context in which to think of leadership opportunities. "Suggestive" and "useful context," unfortunately, are specimens of gloriously unspecific phraseology. Almost everything can be suggestive and thus lead to the "everything is related to everything else" conundrum. The problem, I am afraid, is more recognizable than its solution.

While an analogue does not resolve the problem of empirical-theoretical specification, I suggest one useful to the overall design of my analysis—the sport of baseball. It is governed by a basic structure that has remained relatively unchanged (like the constants of Chapter 3). Yet, it also moves in cycles that influence opportunities; the pitcher (at least in the National League) must regularly come to bat—a splendid opportunity for the defense and a constraint on the offense, but still only a probabilistic determinant of the outcome. Indeed, like the cycles of presidential opportunities and constraints, the sport of baseball has similar irregular longer-term cycles that advantage (and also disadvantage) some of the players (the liveliness of the ball, the shape of the stadiums, and the texture of the playing surface). These also help to define the style of the game (emphasis on offense or defense, power or speed). The short-term cycles occurring within the game itself are very regular (the batting order, for example), and tend, like termcycles, to dictate available strategies.

The analogy of baseball to the subject at hand may be taken yet a step further: The managers of baseball teams, like presidents, increasingly are subject to intense scrutiny, continuous measurement of how they are faring, and are dependent upon critical resources held by others (general managers and team owners). Their opportunities are tactical ones—making do resourcefully with what they have at their disposal. One other thing they have in common, especially recently: short tenure.

EPOCHAL CYCLES

Presidential-Congressional Relations

Although Congress is constitutionally granted a crucial role in the governing process, it is an institution ill-suited to initiate and achieve broad policy direction.

To begin with, it is really two institutions composed of members whose perceived mandates are derived from overlapping constituencies. Congress itself, like the government of which it is a part, is not of a single piece but is instead reflective of the Madisonian logic of "divide so that none shall conquer." Yet for large parts of American history, especially throughout the nineteenth century, Congress has been the dominant political institution eclipsing the presidency for all but rare interludes.

For much of this period, and for many reasons, the Federal government was remote and weak—out of sight and, for the most part, out of mind. The governmental policy load was light, and Congress carried most of it. Although ups and downs will be found in the balance between Congress and the executive in all eras, it is during the twentieth century, in an era of vastly increased federal activity, expanded international involvement, and rapid development of mass communication, that the presidency has been mostly on the upswing, and certainly at the center of attention. That the presidency has grown in expected power does not by itself mean that Congress has been on the downswing, nor that acrimonious confrontation has been constantly prevalent. Government has grown in importance relative to a century ago, and both institutions have generally grown in their activity levels,[4] as indicated in Figures 4.1 and 4.2.

Despite the growth in absolute levels of activity, tension between the two institutions inevitably is promoted by the constitutional design. The tension can be eased by a number of factors, chief of which is a similarity in the partisan identity of the president and the congressional majority. Still, as James Sundquist has observed, "The Constitution, in effect, put two combatants in the ring and sounded the bell that put them into endless battle. . . . On essential matters that would define the boundary . . . and the relations between them, the Constitution was silent or ambiguous."[5]

While Sundquist sees the existence of alternating tendencies between strong presidencies and placid congresses, and weak presidencies and assertive congresses, he believes these to be more expressly a function of the style and aims of the president than of the Congress. For the last half century, he notes, the "decline" of Congress is best accounted for by the assertiveness of presidents—in other words, by the decline of the Whig theory of the presidency in the attitudes of the White House occupants.[6] This hypothesis is hard to test precisely. Whatever the case, however, it is certainly likely that presidents who assert themselves on behalf of causes popular in Congress and acceptable to it are apt to be granted a wider berth than those who do their asserting on matters unacceptable to congressional majorities. Procedural issues of institutional power are likely to recede in the face of substantive agreement across institutions. In the absence of such agreement, however, and from whichever source (White House or Capitol Hill) the push to power asserts itself, there is tension in the relationship between the executive and the Congress. Persistent challenges to institutional prerogative emanating from the White House will surely bring forth congressional reaction; yet, the appearance of congressional disarray also invites presidential assertiveness.

FIGURE 4.1.   Presidential Messages Sent to Congress, 1789-1976 (averaged by eras)

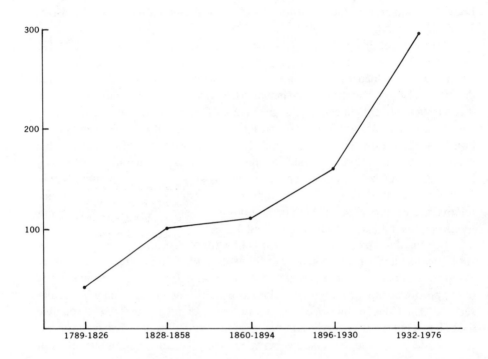

Source: Adapted from Jeffrey E. Cohen, "Passing the President's Program, Presidential-Congressional Relations 1789-1974." Paper presented at the 1979 Annual Meeting of the Midwest Political Science Association, Chicago, Illinois.

FIGURE 4.2.   Amount of Legislative Activity Requiring Presidential Action, 1789-1976 (bills acted on, averaged by eras)

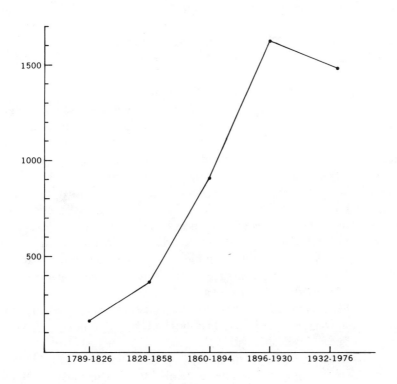

Source: Adapted from Cohen, "Passing the President's Program," 1979.

Another student of the historic relationship between the executive and the Congress, Lawrence Dodd, identifies four epochs in this relationship—an era of confrontation (1789-1860), an era of expansion (1876-1910), an era of consolidation (1920-1965), and an age of protest (1960s and 1970s).[7] The first stage of this historic cycle, characterizing the American Republic from birth to the onset of the Civil War, is labeled the "Era of Confrontation," a period during which Congress served as a forum of debate. This was a time during which the federal government cast a miniature shadow, an era during which president and Congress were relatively inert, and in which politics was dominated by a few notables. Professionalization of politics had not yet developed. Although there would be from time to time presidencies of notable assertiveness—Jefferson, Jackson, and Polk—they mostly would be followed by presidents less able or willing to assert similar authority—Madison, Van Buren, and Taylor/Fillmore. Sporadically, however, partisan forces would be especially strong within the American context, even in the absence of a professionalized politics. Jefferson and Jackson both adopted the style of party leader and, as Joel Silbey shows, partisanship was in full stride throughout the 1840s, apparently a result of the galvanizing issues of the immediately preceding Jacksonian era.[8] If partisanship was strong (until the decade of severe regional conflict in the 1850s), so too was the Whig theory of institutional powers. As yet, neither institution clearly predominated but within the period of contest, assertive presidents inevitably invited congressional counter-reactions when their assertiveness proved unpopular or threatening.

In the post-bellum era through the end of the nineteenth century and into the first decade of the twentieth, professional politics had come to fruition and, along with it, powerful party leadership within Congress.[9] The emergence of powerful central party leadership on Capitol Hill was not a presidential tool, *per se*. For the Whig theory emerged triumphant despite the demise of the Whig party. Congressional prerogatives were expansive and presidents disinclined to challenge them. Nevertheless, even within this era of congressional predominance, not all presidents were equally meek. Both Cleveland and the first Roosevelt moved to assert a presidential agenda, although certainly with fewer expectations than today about congressional compliance. This second period in the historic cycle of executive-legislative relations is labeled by Dodd as the "Era of Expansion," a period during which the national government became more active and relatively more powerful.[10]

With the revolt against Speaker Cannon in 1910, a new phase of the cycle, an era consolidating the role of the national government, emerges characterized by the development of a more or less autonomous committee system. The flow of power devolved from the Speaker to the committees, each of which now became a pocket of authority. The "iron law of seniority" enhanced the powers of committee chairs and vitiated those of the Speaker. In the process of power dispersion, the loser was the party leadership and the winner a new set of committee barons. Thus, reversing the process of state-building, it might be said that the nobility triumphed at the expense of the crown. Power was both diffused and segmented, and integrative capacities were obviously eroded. What occurred in the House, with different particulars, was mirrored in the Senate. In this more individualistic chamber the position of the majority leader also was weakened. Never strong formally, the loss of central leadership was principally one of deference to entrepreneurial leaders, induced to some considerable extent by the Seventeenth Amendment (ratified in 1913) providing for the popular election of senators.

These changes meant more autonomy for members of Congress and a strengthening of congressional substructures at the expense of its integrative abilities. In one respect, the more important the members became (as evidenced at least by their willingness to continue standing for the job), and the more autonomous the committee structure became, the more power gravitated to the members (at this point, however, still a select few) at the expense of the institution. The iron rule of seniority, however, assured that the diffusion of power would be limited principally to the committee barons, who were rarely held to account in exercising it.

No simple summary of this third era suffices. Within it there were periods of congressional dominance and relatively inert presidents. But there also were periods of active presidents and congresses responsive to presidential initiation, as occurred during the early period of the New Deal, during wartime crisis, and in the early moments of the Johnson administration. Indeed, from the period of the war years to the Vietnam War, congressional deference to presidential foreign policy initiatives was considerable. At the same time the weak position of the party leadership vis-à-vis the committees meant that presidential initiatives on domestic issues generally met rougher sledding, at least until the middle to late 1960s (Figure 4.3).

Throughout the late 1960s and much of the 1970s, the age of protest, Congress moved in two directions; one that would vastly increase its knowledge base and coordinative capabilities, the other that would proliferate further the resources of political power and initiative and promote accountability while frequently diminishing responsibility. During this fourth period, the Democratic majority in the House spread subcommittee chairs to over two-fifths of the majority caucus membership. (So widespread was the diffusion of authority that one former official in the Carter administration waggishly observed that it was always prudent to greet an unfamiliar Democratic member of the House as "Mr. Chairman" since chances were good that this appellation would be appropriate!)

Heightened by the prevalence of divided government during this period, conflict between the president and Congress was at least as great as it had been since the Truman presidency. The Watergate crisis epitomized this tension and during both its protracted unfolding and its aftermath, Congress enacted laws and created mechanisms to strengthen its oversight of the executive, to arrest the disintegration of institutional policy discipline, and to invigorate its technical support capabilities. The Budget, Impoundment, and Control Act of 1974 is one of the

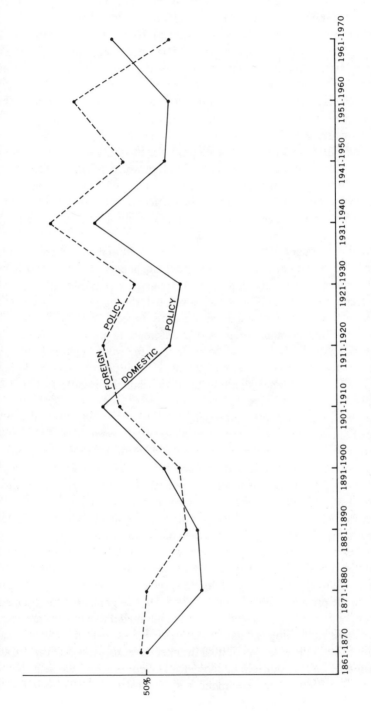

FIGURE 4.3. Presidential Legislative Success in Foreign and Domestic Policy, 1861-1970 (averaged within decades)

*Figures are based on percentage of enactments of presidentially submitted legislative proposals.

Source: Adapted from Jeffrey E. Cohen, "A Historical Reassessment of Wildavsky's Two Presidencies Thesis," *Social Science Quarterly* 63 (September 1982), p. 552.

leading examples of these efforts. But while they were taking place, fragmentation was also keeping pace with if not, in fact, outdistancing the potentially integrative tendencies. In addition, the "new blood" that filtered into Congress during the 1970s became a torrent, especially after the 1974 elections. An institution noted at the beginning of the 1970s for the stability and durability of its membership, and for the benefits that would accrue to those who were patient, would be radically changed in all of these respects before half the decade was gone. As with the congresses of over sixty years ago, democratization and responsiveness to the members was a theme behind which to devolve power. Now, however, the dispersion was far more massive than it had ever been.

Perhaps as relevant as the diffusion of internal authority was the renewed emphasis on external accountability, occasioned during a period of congressional reform and pursued by emergent "public interest" pressure groups. Thus, in the House, another congressional response was to enhance the visibility and, therefore, the vulnerability of its members. As the Progressives of an earlier era had helped to weaken party control and discipline, so the inheritors of the middle class reform tradition, by their emphasis on accountability and open government, would help to make the members more vulnerable to intense constituency and pressure group opinion. The Legislative Reorganization Act of 1970, itself the product of intense lobbying efforts by "public interest" groups, increased the ease with which recorded votes could be taken in the House. By helping to make members more visible, it increased the members' accountability to highly attentive interests in their constituencies and further reduced their responsibility to the institution. The dramatic increase in the number of recorded votes in the House (Figure 4.4) owes much to the Legislative Reorganization Act, but since a lesser increase is also spotted in the Senate, it may be indicative as well of a general increase in floor activity and a weakening of the containment structures formerly dominant in the House (notably the power of committee chairs and the norms for junior members of quiescence and acquiescence). The upsurge in recorded votes owes to no single factor, but it is a reflection of increased congressional activism. The more recent decline noted in Figure 4.4 (though curving up in 1982) indicates both the briefly successful application in 1981 of the integrative budgetary reconciliation procedure prescribed by the 1974 Act, and a more general decline in legislative initiatives while budgetary concerns remain paramount.

As the objects of "reform" in any period are frequently the products of a previous generation's definition of reform, so too do the results of the 1970s democratization surge in Congress contain the seeds of a new (fifth) congressional cycle, especially in the House. Whether these will bear fruit will depend greatly on climatic conditions. But many of the tools for integrative change are already in place. For example, while congressional reformers in the 1970s weakened the prevailing authority structures (the committee chairs) mostly diffusing power further, they also strengthened the Speaker's powers to structure major omnibus legislation. The potential of the party caucus also was revived, if not the inclination to im-

FIGURE 4.4. Total Recorded Votes in the U.S. Congress Overall and the House and Senate, 1967-82

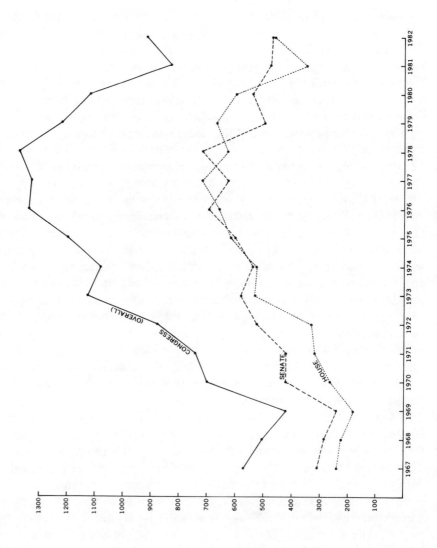

Source: Compiled by the author, from *Congressional Quarterly Almanacs 1967-82.*

pose "party government." Similarly, an instrument for arresting the piecemeal decision-making process in Congress—the budget reconciliation process—provides a vehicle by which to promote institutional responsibility. Under the right conditions such tools could be used to compel the legislative branch to do that which it does only with great reluctance—arrive at binding limit-setting decisions. There are traces, in other words, of a new congressional order, but for the time being only traces. They do not necessarily foretell change, particularly in view of the more compelling forces operating outside of Congress that structure the behavior of its members.

As always, it is easier to point to where we have been rather than where we are going. Even in looking backward, however, our summaries of the past inevitably are simplified in some important ways; they do not capture all of the details or nuances. Exceptions within each era abound, but they remain exceptions. In spite of these cautions, the four cycles of Congress that Dodd describes may be characterized according to three factors: The nature of the congressional-executive balance, the structure of internal authority in the Congress, and the evaluative tools available to Congress for achieving policy integration. In Table 4.1, I set forth these three variables in order to summarize each of the four phases of the congressional cycle. The characteristic subject to the greatest degree of apparent cyclical variation is the balance of congressional-presidential relations. The structure of internal congressional authority mostly has been diffused, with the exception of the brief period of powerful central leadership. Finally, the capabilities for integrated policy making (of the sort needed to deal with a more expansive set of governmental activities) is mainly a phenomenon of the post-World War II era—indeed, largely a phenomenon of the post-Watergate era.

What is especially striking in Table 4.1 is the historical relationship between internal authority structure and tools for policy development. As Congress has gained more of the evaluative tools for policy development and integration and as it has acquired the technical expertise to make informed decisions, it has lost much of its capacity to assert an institutional will. Put somewhat differently, as the power of the members has grown, the power of the institution to assert itself as a corporate entity has seemingly declined. When its unity was the expression of political centralization, its policy capacities were weak, though in accord with the prevailing functions and conceptions of government in the last quarter of the nineteenth and first decade of the twentieth centuries. Now, its policy capacities have grown, but so too has the expression of diversity within the institution. Where once Congress had will (if nothing more than the power formally and informally granted to its leadership), it had by contemporary standards little proficiency or expertise. Now it has proficiency, but by past standards relatively little will to act in a coherent manner. "Party battalions" having once given way to "committee suzerainty,"[11] the contemporary House of Representatives has devolved still further. There is nothing, perhaps, so symptomatic of its contemporary internal morselization than the proliferation of three dozen regional, ascriptive, and func-

TABLE 4.1.   Characteristic Phases of the Historic Congressional Cycle

Congressional Cycle	Congressional-Presidential Relationship	Internal Structure of Authority	Tools for Policy Development and Integration
Phase I (1789-1860)	Frequently adversarial; mostly congressional dominant	Variable: diffused early, but oligarchic for most of period	Weak
Phase II (1876-1910)	Congressional dominant	Centralized	Weak
Phase III (1920-1965)	Variable: cooperation and adversarial relations; mostly presidential dominant	Oligarchic—"committee barons"	Moderate to weak (growth in post-World War II era)
Phase IV (Mid 1960s, 1970s)	Adversarial; both assertive	Decentralized—triumph of the subcommittees	Moderately strong (particular growth in post-Watergate era)

Source: Compiled by the author. Four phases based on Lawrence C. Dodd, "Congress, the President, and the Cycles of Power," in *The Post-Imperial Presidency,* ed. Vincent Davis (New Brunswick, N.J.: Transaction, 1980).

tional caucuses.[12] By comparison with the 1950s and 1960s, congressional capacities to secure information and analysis grew markedly, while Congress's ability to arrive at decisions became even more feeble. Then, as Norman Ornstein contends, "'obstruction' as often as not meant a committee chairman killing a piece of legislation, while today, obstruction means any of 535 legislators . . . altering a bill, delaying action, or tying the institution in knots for an indeterminate period of time . . . thus obstructing a score of bills awaiting debate and/or action."[13]

Over the course of American history the Madisonian conception that no institution should emerge as a definitive source of authority seems to be well sustained. The relationship between president and Congress normally has been something less than blissful, calmed largely by the limited expectations of the president as a sponsor of legislative programs throughout most of our history and, during much of the Phase III period, by the onset of foreign crisis following economic crisis. What presidents want, Congress mostly has. That being the case, it is normally presidents who must sue for peace. But what Congress has, it may choose not to exercise. So, while it is true that the strength of congressional reaction often is a function of the severity of the presidential prod, the powers that presidents take mostly are those given (and thus taken away) by Congress. When Congress has given way before assertive presidents, the decision has been, in the final analysis, of its choosing.

Table 4.2 summarizes the expected relationship between the institutions across each of the four phases of this cycle. I have chosen purposefully not to use the word "power" here. For the formal congressional power, as distinct from the profile it projects, is remarkably stable. The more ambiguous prerogatives of the presidency have been altered in part by expectation, governed in part by tides of congressional assertion and acceptance, and influenced in part by the activities of particular holders of the office. What varies, of course, is not constitutional power, but assertiveness. Assertiveness, however, is deeply influenced by expectation. And it is, of course, expectation that varies.

Thus, in two of these broad phases there was a tendency for one or the other institution to be a dominant force. The era of congressional dominance in Phase II, however, was far more decisive, albeit within an environment of restricted government, than was the subsequent era of presidential assertiveness. In recent times, the relationship between the president and the Congress can be characterized as aggressively adversarial. Some of this relationship is accounted for by the frequency of divided government, but there is more to the story than this. Indeed, outside of the early part of the Johnson administration and at least the first year of the Reagan administration, the period that is roughly coincident with Phase IV has been almost unrelievedly adversarial.[14]

The early Reagan successes with Congress in 1981 may have reflected special political skills. But to ensure longer-term prospects for success, the impetus needs to be political rather than personal. Although these successes were not repeated in

TABLE 4.2. Modal Congressional and Presidential Profiles Across Historical Epochs

	Congressional Profile	
	Higher	Lower
Higher	Phase IV	Phase III
Presidential Profile	(Mid 1960s, 1970s)	(1920-1965)
Lower	Phase II	Phase I
	1876-1910)	(1789-1860)

Source: Compiled by the author. Four phases based on Lawrence C. Dodd, "Congress, the President, and the Cycles of Power," in The Post-Imperial Presidency, ed. Vincent Davis (New Brunswick, N.J.: Transaction, 1980).

1982, it is still too early to tell whether they are the product of political change stimulating enhanced partisan cohesion. We now turn to such political forces and the electoral cycles that apparently spark them.

The Electoral Cycle

The electoral cycle of realignment and dealignment links mass political change to elite change and, ultimately, to policy change. I focus on this cycle, and map it in Figure 4.5, because it appears to relate intimately to the prospects for policy direction. Simply stated, the process of realignment means the emergence of new policy (elite) majorities resulting from the build-up of new political majorities in the electorate. According to this line of argument, the new political majority will be more strongly partisan, and the strength of this partisanship will be reflected (perhaps even caused) by the new policy majority in the leadership stratum. The process of decay in the tensile strength of this bonding, according to some, has tended to be fairly predictable, at least until recent times during which partisan decomposition seemingly has continued unabated.[15] My mapping of this process in Figure 4.5 does not settle the matter of assigning causal inference to determine whether mass partisan revitalization is essential for stronger elite partisanship, or vice versa. Evidence linking the two, however, is abundant.[16]

FIGURE 4.5. The Realignment-Dealignment Cycle

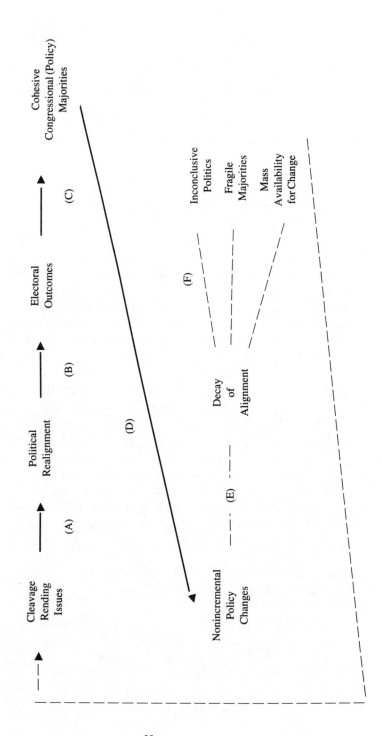

Critical elections certainly are related to, indeed, are apparently preceded by, the onset of critical issues that produce new lines of cleavage. In an analysis of party conflict between 1844 and 1968, Benjamin Ginsberg shows that the salience and structure of interpartisan conflict can be classified into three principal systems. Two of these conflict systems, he claims, were initiated immediately prior to the onset of electoral realignment, while one was concluded during such a period.[17] During the 1852-1860, 1892-1896, and 1928-1936 periods two distinctive systems of high interpartisan issue conflict were found by Ginsberg. The first (1852-60) had to do largely with issues that were the byproduct of the Civil War; the second (1892-96, 1928-36) reflected the same issue cluster (essentially, industrialism) but advantaged different sides in each of the two different electoral eras. According to Ginsberg's analysis, however, the 1944-68 period has lacked the same salience of interpartisan conflict that characterized the earlier periods. The message of Ginsberg's analysis is clear: Issue salience reflected in partisan positions is associated with significant (realigning) electoral change.

If critical conflict, as Ginsberg calls it, is associated with realigning electoral circumstances, then two additional links need to be established as suggested by Figure 4.5. The first lies in the strengthening of partisanship among the elite, and the second lies in the relationship between a strengthening of partisan unity and the promotion of substantive policy change. Longitudinal studies of partisan voting in both the House and the Senate reveal a fairly clear picture of the relationship between partisan cohesiveness within the Congress and the impact of salient (often realignment induced) partisanship among the electorate.[18] While other factors also influence partisan cohesion on floor votes in Congress, the realignment process is powerfully associated with sharpened interparty divisiveness and heightened partisan unity among the political leadership stratum. This is so, Clubb and Traugott hypothesize, because the circumstances of national crisis associated with realignment tend to narrow issue concerns and polarize around them the electorate, the political elite, and the political parties. Accordingly, realigning periods should produce higher levels of partisanship in Congress and declining levels in the years following.[19] Despite the apparent presence of a long-term decrease in party voting on Capitol Hill, the realignment cycle also seems to account for significant fluctuations in partisanship. From their analysis, Clubb and Traugott conclude that "Party cohesion in the House . . . has been characterized by a long-term declining trend and by shorter-term cyclical decline which has apparently been associated with the realignment process."[20]

While evidence of increased partisanship is expressed among the political elite in accordance with realigning periods, to what extent is enhanced partisan unity related to policy change? The answer, argues David Brady, is that "critical elections have the effect of creating conditions which facilitate the building of partisan majorities in the legislature capable of enacting clusters of policy change."[21] By comparing the results of realigning eras with those immediately beforehand, Brady notes that there is a dramatic rise in the partisan structuring and competitiveness of salient issues in the immediate aftermath of a realigning electoral result. This consequence of realignment coincides with a heavy turnover of committee membership (the result of electoral defeats) and with unusually strong partisan allegiances among these members newly elected from districts previously held by the other party.[22] In sum, on the relatively rare occasions when partisan temperatures run high, when candidates identify (or are identified) with polar positions, and when a new congressional majority and a president of the same party are elected, the conditions for party government exist. When these conditions are met it is likely that substantial nonincremental policy change will occur. Indeed, recently this argument has been extended to include not only the pivotal role of Congress, but also the Supreme Court and the bureaucracy.[23]

Two important points emerge from this analysis. First, it is obvious that the conditions for substantial policy change come infrequently and apparently do so as a result of accumulated tensions developing in the society but, heretofore, not directly and clearly resolved through the political system. Second, and perhaps less obvious, the price of large policy change may well be strident partisanship—a game that may have big winners and big losers. Put bluntly, the more disconcerting side of party government and of majority rule is to be found by focusing on the discontents of the losers.

The cyclical tides of the realignment process, nonetheless, produce conditions during which political capacity can be marshalled on behalf of expansive agendas. Yet, from the standpoint of presidential leadership, *per se,* there are some limiting considerations. One of these is that the realignment processes of the nineteenth century appear to have been more complete at the mass level than the New Deal realignment has been. Walter Dean Burnham claims that "When one compares the realignment patterns of the 1850s and 1890s with the critical elections associated with the 1929 Depression and the New Deal, the latter suggest a far muddier pattern of electoral readjustment than the former."[24] At the same time, congressional party cohesion also has been considerably weaker during the latter period. Table 4.3 illustrates the relative inability of the New Deal realignment to stir up partisan cohesion in Congress in contrast with that associated with the realignments of the middle and end of the nineteenth century.

For whatever reason, then, the earlier realignments not only were more complete at the level of mass electoral shifts, but they also resulted in a stronger expression of partisanship within Congress. To a considerable degree, the greater partisanship of earlier eras within the Congress was spurred by the greater powers held by congressional party leaders. It is interesting to observe from Table 4.3 that even the later phases of the 1850s realignment (the low tide of the cycle) evidence higher levels of party consciousness in the House than does the earlier phase of the New Deal realignment (the high tide). Similarly, even while the low tide of the 1890s realignment reflects the dramatic upward shift in the powers of the committees in the House and the commensurate decline of those of the party leadership, the indicators of partisanship in the House for this low-tide period are only barely below the averages for the high tide of the New Deal realignment (Table 4.3).

TABLE 4.3. Partisanship in the House of Representatives during Three Realignment Phases[a]
(entries are averages for each period)

	Average Party Unlikeness[b]	Percentage of Party Votes	Mean Association (Lambda) of Vote with Party
1850s Realignment			
—High Tide, (1861-1877) 37th-44th Congresses	56.2	73.3	.43
—Low Tide (1877-1896) 45th-54th Congresses	52.1	64.6	.40
1890s Realignment			
—High Tide (1897-1913) 55th-62nd Congresses	63.7	72.8	.56
—Low Tide (1913-1932) 63rd-72nd Congresses	42.4	54.6	.31
New Deal Realignment[c]			
—High Tide (1933-1949) 73rd-80th Congresses	46.3	56.6	.33
—Low Tide (1949-68) 81st-90th Congresses	35.2	48.7	.24

Source: Adapted from Jerome M. Clubb and Santa A. Traugott, "Partisan Cleavage and Cohesion in the House of Representatives, 1861-1974," *Journal of Interdisciplinary History* 7 (Winter 1977): 382-383.

[a]The cutoff of sixteen years at the high tide and twenty at the low tide of each realignment cycle is somewhat arbitrary. In all three cases, however, a downward trend can be clearly spotted at this point although the trend lines for the latter two realignment-dealignment cycles contain fewer perturbations than the downward line of the 1850s cycle.

[b]Party unlikeness is a measure of partisan cohesion on votes containing a high degree of partisan conflict. The index of party unlikeness is produced by calculating the percentage of each party's members voting in favor of a measure and subtracting the smaller percentage from the larger one. The indexes produced for each roll call were then averaged across for each session. The actual cell entry is the average of these averages for the periods specified in the table.

[c]To maintain comparability with the other two realignment-dealignment cycles, the low tide of the New Deal realignment was cut off after a twenty-year period. The data for subsequent congresses are markedly lower in the partisanship indicators than even the low tide averages.

The principal impact of the electoral cycle seems to have come at a time in the nineteenth century when party leadership in the Congress was very strong, when Congress itself played a larger initiating role (over a much smaller government of course), and when presidents, for the most part, kept a much lower profile than they have grown accustomed to in recent times. In other words, until the less robust New Deal realignment, presidents were not always the principal political directors behind these surges of political movement.

What then of the present era of activist presidents? After all, the New Deal realignment produced significant programmatic change. And the Johnson administration, although energized for a shorter time, also briefly produced significant programmatic change. Quite possibly, too, as David Brady notes, had the Republican presidents of the 1920s been more disposed to legislative activism, they would have been in an advantageous position to stimulate significant change.[25]

Naturally, we cannot assume that if realigning forces were to emerge partisanship would be restored to the level of past realignments, even that of the relatively limp New Deal realignment.[26] At the elite end of the realignment equation, however, Brady shows from roll-call votes in the U.S. House that the key to sharpened partisan cohesion in a realigning period is to be found in the flood of new members who have won election from districts previously held by the party now threatened by the realigning of political forces.[27] It is this group that will be pivotal to the intensification of partisanship. Table 4.4 updates Brady's findings to recent congresses in which a substantial number of members were elected from districts whose prior incumbent was of a different party. Since 1974 (mostly because of retirements), subsequent congressional elections have produced a larger than usual infusion of new members from switched-seat districts. The advantage went to the Democrats in 1974 and 1976 and to the Republicans in 1978 and 1980. As the data in Table 4.4 show, the massive dose of Democratic representatives from switched-seat districts registered only a moderate upturn in party voting in the Ninety-fourth Congress and vitually none in the Ninety-fifth. On the other hand, the differences among the Republicans in the Ninety-sixth Congress are about the same as those appearing among the Democrats in the first New Deal Congress, and those in the Ninety-seventh Congress *are even larger*. At the elite level, then, one—but only one—of the symptoms of realignment appears.

Interesting as they are, these data are only a part of the more puzzling diagnosis of realignment. To take them any further is merely speculative. Still, it is worth pondering whether the classic symptoms of realignment—the sociological shifting of political allegiances—will result in the equivalent of a political earthquake (the displacement of partisan majorities) as did the New Deal realignment.[28] The midterm election results of 1982 do not encourage such an interpretation, however. Neither does the fact that party support in the second term of the Ninety-seventh Congress fell off markedly among the new switched-seat Republican members of the House—74 percent above the party mean in the second term compared with 92 percent in the first. As to the prospects for sustaining partisanship, I

TABLE 4.4. Party Support among Members of the U.S. House of Representatives by Switched- and Non-Switched-Seat Districts for the 55th, 73rd, 94th, 95th, 96th, and 97th Congresses

Party Support Scores	1896 (55th)		1932 (73rd)		1974 (94th)	
	Switched-Seat Republicans	Non-Switched-Seat Republicans	Switched-Seat Democrats	Non-Switched-Seat Democrats	Switched-Seat Democrats	Non-Switched-Seat Democrats
Percent above party mean	76	47	65	48	70	59
Percent below party mean	24	53	35	52	30	41

Party Support Scores	1976 (95th)		1978 (96th)		1980 (97th)	
	Switched-Seat Democrats	Non-Switched-Seat Democrats	Switched-Seat Republicans	Non-Switched-Seat Republicans	Switched-Seat Republicans	Non-Switched-Seat Republicans
Percent above party mean	64	62	74	56	83	56
Percent below party mean	36	38	26	44	17	44

Table is partially adapted from David W. Brady, "Critical Elections, Congressional Parties and Clusters of Policy Changes," *British Journal of Political Science* 8 (January 1978): 97.

Sources: Congressional Quarterly Almanacs, 1975-81.

offer here an anecdote regarding two first-term House members who in 1981 voted for the president's budget and tax proposals. Saddled with high unemployment in their districts, they voted in 1982 "for *both* the liberal *and* conservative alternatives to the Reagan budget."[29] The moral, if any, to this story is that members believe their fates are theirs to mold. That belief decreases their incentives to plant themselves firmly,[30] and, in turn, helps deter the consummation of political change implied by realignment.

In fact, one interesting analysis asserts that the key elements of realignment have taken place: New and distinctive party positions on salient issues, an accurate perception of such by the electorate, secular shifting within the parties, and a tendency for party identifiers to reflect the new party issue cleavage. In the view of these analysts, there is a clear and discernible shifting of the seismic plates (a realignment, in their view) without as yet (or possibly ever) producing the equivalent of a political earthquake such as that of 1932. Realignment, they argue, is a continuous and evolutionary process rather than a discrete event and, consequently, may not result in a relatively straightforward outcome as suggested by the New Deal model.[31]

In its classic form, the long-term electoral cycle at high tide generates spurts of political energy. The electoral cycle now, however, seems to be encapsulated within an era of long-term partisan decomposition at the mass level and indiscipline at the congressional level. These long-term forces inevitably dam the tides. The high tides of the electoral cycle have brought forth moments of party government, but the times themselves are now less likely to sustain these periods. Paradoxically, too, when the spurts of directed political energy were stronger and better sustained, presidents were noticeably weaker.

METACYCLES

Metacycles, though of narrower range than epochal cycles, may overlap several presidencies leaving each with similar constraints or opportunities. Unlike the epochal cycles, the metacycles may swing back and forth within the confines of a single term. To be sure, the timing of metacycles is not clearly bounded. Moreover, how the metacycles impinge on presidents is affected by modernity and the instruments of communication which it bestows. Four cycles are noted here: (1) the business cycle, (2) the international threat cycle, (3) the issue-attention cycle, and (4) the leadership style and organization cycle.

The Business Cycle

The cycle of prosperity and bad times, familiar to the capitalist economy, is irregular. The swings of the cycle vary and so does the duration of any particular cyclical phase. Modern forms of communication and the availability of an impressive array of government generated indicators help make the effects of the business cycle more publicly prominent than in earlier eras. Indeed, so important is the modern element of communications that two researchers have coined a term, "sociotropic politics," to describe both voter awareness of aggregate economic conditions and its influence on their voting behavior.[32] Perhaps the single most important aspect of this analysis is that it highlights the relevance for political behavior of social information over personal experience. In their words:

> People "morselize" their private experience: the events and details of daily life are typically not interpreted as instances of broader themes, political or otherwise. . . . At the same time, information about national economic conditions is available in a quite different form. From the mass media, such information comes predigested, comparatively coherent, and abstract. . . . And of course, information about national conditions is typically conveyed at a level of abstraction appropriate to nationally-oriented political judgments.[33]

Yet another analysis points to the power of public judgments about presidential economic policy performance and the astonishing weakness of personal economic circumstances as a predictor of presidential public approval.[34]

The point seems clear enough. In modern times news travels fast. Its impact is to diminish the political acceptability of the down side of the business cycle. The American economy has become increasingly interdependent with global economic forces and, thus, subject to their influence. A period of simultaneous high inflation and low growth, popularly called "stagflation," has spanned several presidencies, although these conditions presently seem to be abating. The phenomenon has afflicted leaders in nearly all of the advanced industrial societies (all of which did relatively worse in the 1970s than in the 1960s). The consequences for presidents (and other leaders) in such an era are severe. Having been made more politically vulnerable, they become more willing to resort to rash fiscal adjustments. The pressures to fine tune the economy and to be held accountable for its performance have been growing as the efficacy of the former and the relevance of the latter are increasingly in doubt.[35]

Not all presidents will react the same way to similar phases of the cycle. Eisenhower, Carter, and Reagan (in 1982 at least) did not do what several postwar presidents have done: engage in economic stimulus efforts to coincide with short-term political needs. Despite Eisenhower's prestige, he also suffered, as did Carter and Reagan, losses in popularity and at the polls, although, of course, Carter's losses were steeper and more personal. While it is not clear that presidents can extricate themselves from the nadir of the business cycle, it seems entirely reasonable for them to try in ways that will both increase their political prospects and induce other economic maladies.[36]

The International Threat Cycle

A widespread recognition of international threat normally produces a more consensual atmosphere and lessened political conflict. The perception of external threat, after all, clearly concentrates the national mind. It produces, therefore, a setting that is conducive to presidential direction at least insofar as the conduct of foreign affairs is concerned. A widespread belief in international peril, therefore, is generally beneficial to the exercise of presidential initiative primarily because it leads to self-restraint among other contending power centers. Perilous times, however, mean that the presidential agenda is apt to be reactive and loaded toward national security measures.

Not all perceived international perils result in wars, nor are all wars necessarily either consensus producing or even perceived as responses to threats. Indeed, modern protracted warfare appears to be positively dissensus producing. Perceptions of peril are really what is crucial. However, since data on these perceptions are very limited, especially historically, the international events themselves will have to suffice as our guideposts.

To the aphorism that "states are war-makers and wars are state-makers,"[37] we may add that wars tend also to be president makers. There are limits, however, to the addendum. First, war constricts presidential agendas. Second, war is kinder to the success of presidential initiatives than is its aftermath. For, as the author of one study assessing the relationship between presidential direction and foreign policy crisis notes, "In crisis periods, power tends to gravitate toward the Presidency, but eventually Congress has always moved to reassert its position."[38] Third, there appears to be something (or some things) in the contemporary political environment and in relatively recent military conflicts that makes war a less powerful predictor to presidential programmatic success than it used to be.[39]

Notably, as previously seen in Figure 4.3, the general pattern of "ups" and "downs" regarding congressional support for presidential foreign policy initiatives is verified. The specific relation between war periods and foreign policy initiatives is somewhat more open to question because the data are not disaggregated either into particular years or by war-related and other types of requests. However, nothing in the pattern leads us to discount the relationship between war periods and legislative success in foreign policy. The presidential relationship with Congress on foreign policy matters, then, seems to be marked by the following features:

1. the modern presidency, spanning World War II, Korea, the cold war, and Vietnam, show this to be a period of considerable presidential discretion in foreign policy;[40]
2. from 1973 on, presidential discretion in foreign policy has been weakened considerably;[41]
3. from 1861-1932 war was an independently more powerful predictor of presidential legislative success than it has been subsequently.[42]

Regarding the first point, this period coincides with a phase of fairly continuous threat. The threat appears to be responsible for the lowered congressional profile in foreign policy. Consequently, greater presidential discretion in foreign policy is engendered.

However, the second point is indicative of a reaction to this period of both protracted and frequent military engagement. Most direct and immediate, of course, was the impact of the protracted and unsuccessful intervention in Vietnam—an engagement that in its later stages sharply divided opinion makers and political elites. The reaction, aided also by other factors, produced a steep decline in support within Congress for presidential foreign policy initiatives, and a restriction of presidential discretion in foreign policy generally. It represents, in other words, a periodic reassertion of congressional prerogative during which presidential venturesomeness has been relatively inhibited. From acceptance of presidential initiatives to obstacles to presidential assertion in foreign policy, the swing of the pendulum has been accompanied by a dissolution of the consensus that earlier existed regarding the cold war. The consensus that once centered around a world view of polar antagonism has dissolved, but no other has taken its place. The result is greater congressional constraint in foreign policy, *whatever the policy.*[43] In the absence of a shaping consensus, skepticism reigns, and skepticism is the foe of presidential initiative.

The third point indicates simply that, *as an independent factor,* war had a more powerful effect on presidential legislative success in the premodern presidency than in the modern era. This does not mean, however, that the evidence upon which points one and two rest is illusory. It means only that in the modern era, when adjusted for other variables, war is a less important predictor of legislative success. Important to such success at all times, according to an analysis by Jeffrey Cohen, are the seats in Congress held by the president's party and, above all, the cohesiveness of his legislative party. In the modern era, however, the president's activism and his election and electoral victory margin become significant variables.[44] These data are coincident with modern presidential claims of plebiscitory mandates, claims that some believe have been responsible for extravagant assertions of presidential authority.[45]

Threat increases presidential prerogative, for the most part, because it decreases the willingness of other institutions to assert their prerogatives. For a threat to exist, not only must there be a consensus about what it is, but also a rough consensus on a course of action. (What defines a crisis, after all, is the widespread agreement that there is a threat and a need for a dramatic response.) Even those presidents, however, whose prerogatives have been acceded to as a result of threatening international events are granted latitude that is both limited in duration and concentrated in scope.

The Issue-Attention Cycle

The two metacycles examined thus far have appeared with historic regularity, though each is especially sensitive to the modern environment. However, a third type of metacycle, having to do with the birth, life, and death of public issues and moods, is probably relevant only in the modern era since it is so dependent upon a high level of media saturation. This phenomenon is called by Anthony Downs the "issue-attention cycle."[46]

To what extent, and for how long, can public attention be focused to provide opportunities for the mobilization of political support? Downs suggests that for certain classes of issues the issue-attention cycle will be relevant to their prospects for being institutionalized as public policies. As Downs puts it: "Any issue gains longevity if its sources of political support and the programs relating to it can be institutionalized in large bureaucracies."[47] This means, according to Downs, that a problem first has to be recognized and then dramatized to provoke and maintain public interest, the *sine qua non* for generating political support on behalf of a solution. The problem must, in other words, be exciting and dramatic.[48] When it loses these qualities, attention fades and with it the opportunities to create political support.

As Downs is careful to point out, not all issues are likely to be affected by the issue-attention cycle. Issues that deal with longstanding and powerfully held elements of political belief are unlikely to be so affected, as are subgovernmental issues involving a limited set of actors and focused around very definable interests. The example Downs employs in his discussion has to do with environmental policy making, but an equally plausible example is the issue of energy conservation and development. After the Arab oil embargo of 1973-74 and the lengthy gasoline lines it helped produce, the energy issue evaporated. Old habits were resumed as though a recurrence was impossible. The price increases for petroleum products stabilized (in fact, real prices declined) after sharp increases during the 1973-74 period. For all practical purposes, energy as an issue had reached what Downs calls the "post-problem stage."

Upon his election in 1976, President Carter moved shortly thereafter to make energy concerns a leading priority of his administration, delivering four addresses on the subject within a short span in the early months of his term. These were followed dutifully by a set of legislative proposals. After being subjected to radical alteration by Congress over a period of nearly two years, these proposals were finally passed in 1978. They passed the Congress in a form virtually unrecognizable from when they had been initially submitted. Nonetheless, the energy bill was duly proclaimed a legislative victory by an administration desperate for one. Less than a year later gasoline lines emerged again. Prices at the pumps and throughout a petroleum dependent economy soared, and discontent simmered. Another energy program was produced by the administration following on the heels of its self-proclaimed legislative victory. These proposals made their way through Congress far more quickly and overall in far better shape than had the prior package. Why? No single explanation suffices, of course, but in the absence of a significant recognition of energy as an issue, and thus without support behind a particular definition of the problem and set of accompanying policies, little could be accomplished. In the presence of a widespread recognition of a problem in 1979, a program closely resembling that urged by the president was passed. Obviously, many other factors were at work, among them the skills or ineptitude of the president and of members of the presidential staff. But whether or not presidents can exhibit issue leadership depends greatly upon what issues they select and what opportunities avail themselves.

Whereas President Nixon's environmental proposals offered in 1970 were designed to capitalize on an issue that had already been created, Carter's energy proposals in 1977 seemed more nearly to create, or at least to resurrect, an issue. By 1979, events had revived energy as an issue and, thus, also revived the legislative prospects for an energy program. At the same time, these events helped diminish Carter's electoral prospects.

An unfortunately sobering conclusion within reach here is that political opportunities for presidential assertion normally are spasmodic or crisis induced. High levels of public attentiveness, however, can help produce policy overkill, especially on technically complex matters. Drama helps produce attentiveness but also, as a consequence, policy escalation—the specification of large-scale ends without a specified set of means or an evaluation of tradeoffs.[49] The product frequently is a deductive mode of policy making from which means must be discovered to produce the stated ends; thus in implementation the ends must be continually evaluated and adjusted, and frequently resolved through the courts. Oddly, this is precisely the opposite syndrome of that discussed and celebrated by David Braybrooke and Charles Lindblom—"disjointed incrementalism."[50] The strategy of disjointed incrementalism is an experiential and inductive strategy through which ends are discovered rather than specified. Disjointed incrementalism requires bargaining tactics, but such tactics seem inappropriate for issues that depend upon the infusion of high drama and policy entrepreneurship.

Dramaturgy and incremental bargaining are simply two poles in a continuum of strategies, and they may be employed during different stages in the development of the same policy. Both occur in nearly all political settings. Yet the nature of the mix is important. In a system in which presidents believe, and are encouraged to believe, in the desirability of going to "the people," drama inevitably will be a tool used to excite public attention. (Even Carter, despite his pedantic style, was attentive to symbols and dramaturgy, just inept in their use.) Perhaps no harm comes of this—just a peculiarly American way of trying to govern. One can't be sure. But if drama produces enlarged expectations and unrealistic promises, then a policy process so dependent upon the use of this instrument for gaining political support will produce large costs in unmet expectations, unstable elite relations, and the use of the judicial process to settle that which might otherwise be bargained over.[51]

Presidential Style and Management Cycles

Another set of cycles within the broad rubric of metacycles, and one that is again heavily influenced by a media saturated environment, has to do with presidential leadership ambition and temperament, and styles of managing the presidency. Table 4.5 distinguishes two polar styles of leadership drive and temperament, their likely relationship to different patterns of management, and the probable stereotypes produced by such patterns of management. Ambition and temperament, on the one hand, and presidential management, on the other, need not be related but are likely to be.[52] I apply the label "drivers" to the style of presidents with expansive agendas and expansive tastes for personal intervention. They are likely to make the White House the center of executive activity and the oval office the nucleus within that. They are likely, in other words, to seek to maximize their control of the levers of power. On the other hand, the tag "coasters" is given to those who are apt to address matters only after they first have been ingested by other officials and staff or administrative units. The premise here is that important and unresolved issues will necessarily arrive in the president's in box in due time. Inevitably, as Richard Rose rightly claims, "the way in which a President exercises his chieftainship in Washington must reflect his own vision of the kind of President that he wishes to be."[53]

Certainly this is true, but not fully sufficient. For what presidents wish to be is, in some measure, a reflection of what they are wished to be. The epigrams which began this chapter, particularly those of Laski and Hargrove, remind us of the cyclical character of demands on leadership. They suggest, in other words, a cycle of expectations about the presidency itself. Such expectations primarily derive from the thinking of opinion leaders, particularly the tendency of political journalists to divine public moods and, thus, inevitably to help create them. What critical elites think is the reality tends to become reality, in part, through self-fulfilling behavior.[54]

In government, as in the physical world, it takes more energy to generate direction than to sustain inertia. The energies often produce a future desire for more tranquil occasions, and, conversely, too many troubles and too little motion whet the appetite for more energetic leadership. Times during which energetic presidential leadership is most in demand are those usually associated with a preference for a "driving" leadership style and a tendency toward a White House-centric perspective. This preference usually follows upon a "coaster" style of presidency (or succession of them) which induces a sense of drift. Larger-than-life presidents, on the other hand, tend to encourage a desire for less urgency and a more delegated and consensual style of governing.

Probably no president fits very neatly or consistently into these categories (set forth in Table 4.5). Policy ambition and style need not be related, for example.

TABLE 4.5.   Styles of Presidential Leadership and Management

	Driver Style	*Coaster Style*
Presidential Policy Ambitions	Expansive	Incremental or maintaining
Leadership Temperament	Entrepreneurial, chief operating officer	Ratifying, chief executive officer
Management Characteristics	Centrist, interventionist, use of informal channels and uncertain jurisdictions	Decentralized but hierarchical, delegative, use of formal channels and certain jurisdictions
Negatively Stereotyped As	Ruthless, intolerant, isolated	Contradictory, inefficient, incompetent
Presidents Most Likely to Fit Type	Johnson, Nixon, (Kennedy, Roosevelt)	Eisenhower, Ford

Each column is rather more like a set of as yet unmeasured indicators of a type, that is, a set of variables en route to a summary index. If no president is apt to gain a perfect score on either index, the two "indexes" still are likely to be inversely correlated. In all presidents mixed characteristics abound, but more so in some than in others. Carter, for instance, while a highly activist president in terms of the breadth of his agenda, was not clearly a White House centrist—at least until the famed seance at Camp David in the summer of 1979. Nor was there a clear organizational scheme within the Carter White House itself, perhaps at any time. The early, and unusual, combination of Carter's activist agenda and noncentralized administration made the negative stereotypes associated with the "coaster" style of presidency especially poignant. Activism taxes coordination. When the former is present and the latter absent, presidents are made to look foolish. The style of presidential organization that resulted has been facetiously referred to as "multiple adhocracy".[55]

It was, of course, Jimmy Carter's fate to become president at a time when a low-profile politics occasioned by a disillusionment with political leadership was prominent and when the rhetoric of the day was still punctuated by cries of an "imperial" and "isolated" presidency. Indeed, campaigning on the promise of openness, a low-profile politics emphasizing the style of a life-size presidency was Carter's meal ticket to the White House itself. Subsequent frustrations with Congress and the country's frustrations with both gasoline lines and economic troubles, plus the appearance of American impotence in the world, changed the mood from one of reasonable satisfaction with honesty to one demanding inspiration and results. In any event, the combination of openness, featured especially in the early days of the Carter White House, and an activist agenda inevitably served to dramatize the multiplicity of direction inherent in a complex government.

In certain respects, what has been said of the Carter administration is equally true of the Reagan administration despite the dramatic personality and work habit differences of the two presidents. Carter's compulsion was to gain control more of policy detail than of the reins of government, that is to try to comprehend the solution at the expense of understanding the political mechanics. In contrast, Reagan seems literally more strongly compelled to control the reins of his horse than those of either policy detail or the mechanics of government. In both the details and mechanics of policy he has been willing to delegate considerable authority subject to his final approval. Like Carter, Reagan has an active agenda, and though loaded with fewer discrete requests, each one contains more megatonnage. Unlike the Carter administration, however, the Reagan presidency appears united on first principles regardless of the disagreements that flow from second and third principles. The ideological binding has been sufficiently robust to quell the unseemliness of internal disagreement and of contradictory direction that marked its predecessor. On those occasions, however, when either such cues have been lacking or when first principles have simply failed to travel very far, the Reagan presidency too has been subject to tendencies for bureaucratic politics to surface visibly. In the Carter administration, this situation often presented the White House with problems of consistency of agenda and contradictions in high policy. In the Reagan administration, the conflicts that have surfaced have involved fitting high policy to operative decisions.

Penchant for leadership tends to follow fashion, and so too do styles of presidential management. The latter produces an oscillation between tighter and slacker central control in the White House and in the government. Within all administrations there is probably a tendency over time to tighten the reins, or as aptly coined by Colin Campbell, there is a transition from "spokes in a wheel to wagons in a circle."[56] While the chief executive style of President Eisenhower gave way to the more urgent and interventionist operations of Presidents Kennedy, Johnson, and Nixon (a chief operating officer style), the traumas of Vietnam and Watergate led to fears of an "imperial" and "sealed-off" presidency. After Nixon's departure, Ford helped to lower the temperature. He was welcomed not for being extraordinary, but for being ordinary; not for being seized with purpose and vision, but for his mental stability. He promised, and mostly delivered, to delegate authority and to have an "open" and decentralized administration.[57] But openness invites the appearance of chaos, of weak hands on the tiller and loose cannons on deck.

Carter's campaign was the first election held after presidential power had become once again unfashionable. (Its fashionability was reasserted however during, and because of, the Carter incumbency.) As a result, Carter became the apostle of openness, a posture that made the inevitable tightenings later appear especially clumsy and embarrassing. Unlike Ford, however, Carter had a busy agenda and a nominal congressional majority to help him enact it. Yet, following and even exaggerating the early characteristics of the Ford White House, the Carter system lacked central coordinating mechanisms. The consequence, whatever its real accomplishments, was that it appeared uncertain, confused, and unable to filter its internal diversity. Therefore, Bruce Miroff contends:

> After a brief flirtation, in the days of Watergate, with the language of virtue and modesty, American political commentators . . . renewed their propensity for declaiming about leadership. A pervasive sense of drift amid mounting domestic crises . . . produced pleas from spokesmen of diverse political positions for a recrudescence of dynamic political leadership.[58]

The resurgent phase of strong leadership in the face of economic drift and other problems helped propel Reagan to the White House and to a highly successful first year in securing legislative passage of his programs. It helped also that there was a belief, promulgated by a *New York Times* reporter, that "Politicians in both parties say people are tired of seeing Presidents fail and want to see this one succeed."[59] Whether this is the reason or not, it does appear that Reagan has achieved the image of a strong leader without a highly energetic or interventionist presidency.[60] For the most part, there has been a good bit of operational delegation to both leading White House staff officials and department heads. In this case, the adhesive is a remarkably consensual vision. This consensus has been forged to a considerable degree by the effective implantation of loyalists into key positions in the departments. It will be tested by issues that do not lay claim in direct fashion to those loyalties or the ideologies on which they are based. Nonetheless, an orderly system of delegation and reliance on officials in both the White House and the departments may well be dependent upon a clear projection of public purpose, whatever its content. If the chief executive style of delegation appears to conflict with the appearance of competence, however (which it is always at risk of doing), and if a siege-like atmosphere develops, it will not be surprising to see a reemergence of White House centrism.

TERMCYCLES

The epochal cycles and metacycles help to determine the prospects of particular presidents whose fate it is to fall at one point or another in these cycles. They also help shape presidential behaviors, strategies, tactics, and modes of organization. But within the presidential term itself there are frequent recurring patterns of both constraint and opportunity. Three that I focus on here are the cycles of succession, declining support, and growing effectiveness. They are together relevant to the setting of the presidential agenda, and to its achievement.

Succession Cycles

"Let us continue," intoned Lyndon Johnson to a joint session of Congress shortly after the assassination of John F. Kennedy. But, in truth, few leaders fresh to their jobs want to continue the tasks of others. Some, like Johnson, come to office under circumstances in which deference initially must be paid to continuity. Generally, however, new leaders have an interest in distinguishing themselves from their predecessors. After all, leadership successions are often the result of changed political environments that typically cast the deposed or retired leaders in a less favorable light. Except for unusual circumstances such as when the deposed leaders leave office either as heroes or in heroic form (the latter meaning when the deposed are also departed), they are typically less well thought of and less influential than when they began. The choosing of new leaders is occasion for renewal, and for the victors to interpret generously their accession as an opportunity to proceed with promised change.[61] Valerie Bunce, who has studied leadership succession and policy change in both capitalist and socialist countries, discovered, with considerable regularity, that innovations occur when leaders (even within the same party) turn over.[62] These results, in fact, seemed so pervasive that they defy explanation based on the idiosyncrasies of any particular country, however much national conditions mold both the patterns of succession and the opportunities of successors. Stated most boldly, then, the claim is that "New leaders mean new policies and old leaders mean the continuation of old priorities."[63]

Why does succession have this effect? Several factors may be at work in helping to trigger these policy spurts. The struggle for leadership in any system is a process that encourages one or more of the following: (1) sharpened rhetoric; (2) increased partisanship; (3) the making of promises to groups important to the outcome.[64] The process of being chosen also is occasion to converge one's aims with their apparent justification and approval by the (s)electors. Making it to the top anywhere is a heady experience; the more democratic the process of selection, the more intoxicating the experience. What one wishes to do thus quickly becomes what one has been mandated to do. Additionally, the process of changing leaders also alters an older coalition and means that a new set of expectations and pressures are to be satisfied. Diverse motives or needs, in other words, seem to beat a path to much the same outcome: Change of leaders occasions change in policy.

As a general matter, opportunities never seem so ripe as they do at the beginning of an executive's tenure. At this point the glow of political victory is undamped, and the promise of new policy proposals untested. Neither awareness of, or at least acceptance of, the intractabilities of problems has as yet set in, nor has the sobering of early enthusiasms by the antidote of experience. Enthusiasms tend to be entropic: They are generated by talking (the politician's forte) and countered by doing (the task that befalls the executive leader).

There appears, then, to be a natural cycle of policy development according to Valerie Bunce. Because of the forces behind it, leadership succession is a powerful stimulant to policy change. As change settles into routine, however, it is tempered over time and a more normal pattern of incremental policy making comes to dominate.[65] Indeed, Bunce's empirical analysis implies a piece of advice to new executive leaders: Strike early and seek to be different. The evidence is that they do. In this respect at least, American presidents seem little different from their peers elsewhere; in the broadest sense they are moved by similar forces. In less than the broadest sense, however, the forms through which these forces operate do differ, and the special complications attached to building majorities in an independent legislature lacking in party discipline create a heightened sense of executive urgency.

Declining Support

Nearly all newly chosen leaders are offered a period of relatively little criticism—in the popular parlance, a honeymoon. This honeymoon period varies in length, but ultimately in the case of American presidents, their standing plummets largely as a curvilinear function of time. Presidential popularity declines steadily and then curls upward modestly at term's end.[66] The effects of time (in essence, the decomposition of a winning coalition) are both buffered and reinforced by particular events and circumstances, though these are too weak to disturb the main tendency. Even with the benefit of this uplift at the end of the presidential term, the recovery leaves incumbents considerably beneath where they began. Why this happens deserves a fuller accounting and some of the forces behind it are discussed in the succeeding chapter. For now, however, I want only to focus on its occurrence and its consequences.

The consequence of a drop in public approval is anything but a settled matter. We have to ask how is public (dis)approval interpreted and by whom? Perhaps the most celebrated answer to this question was formulated by Richard Neustadt in his book, *Presidential Power*. Public approval, Neustadt claimed, is a measure of a president's public prestige, and public prestige is in turn a factor in his influence.[67] Yet, public prestige is neither measurable by a single instrument, nor interpreted in a simple way by those whose judgments affect the president's fortunes in Washington.

The Gallup (and other) surveys, however, do provide a common denominator for both politicians and political scientists to assess the president's standing with the public. Gallup's reading of the president's public standing is a simple, very general measure from a national sample which corresponds to no senator's or representative's constituency. Polticians, being more resourceful than political scientists, rely on other readings as well. But by virtue of being reported in numerous newspapers across the country, the survey data inevitably influence elite reaction. If public standing is an element in presidential influence, it still remains to be specified *what type* of influence it can be translated into as well as *how it is interpreted.*

Although presidents attempt to influence the actions and alter the expectations of numerous actors within and outside their official administrations, the link between public prestige and political influence is supposedly most relevant to presidential efforts to influence Congress. One reason for this lies in the role of Congress as a representative political institution and, therefore, its presumed responsiveness to currents of opinion. If presidential standing is thought to be especially relevant to presidential success on Capitol Hill, how is approval translated?

Between Gallup and the legislative gauntlet there are filters and intermediate steps to consider. Insofar as presidential fortunes with Congress are concerned, presidential approval is a factor that operates in a complex way. Certainly, there is a relationship. From the Eisenhower presidency through the second year of the Reagan presidency, the raw (Pearson r) correlation coefficient between the averaged annual presidential approval score and the president's legislative success score is .43. This association is graphically illustrated in Figure 4.6, and while it is strong it is very far from perfect. Also, as we can see from Figure 4.6, the coincidence of the trend lines varies somewhat across different presidencies.

We are left with some tantalizing questions for which answers are not immediately on tap. First, is a coefficient of .43 high or low? Is the glass half-full or half-empty? What, in other words, are our expectations? Second, can we be certain that public standing is more of an element in a president's success with Congress than his legislative success is in his public standing? This latter question is not presently solvable for technical reasons, but it is certainly not unreasonable to assume that the appearance of success or failure begets more of the same. After all, that also is the premise behind the notion that public standing influences persuasibility. Whether the raw correlation between approval and legislative success is high or low, therefore, cannot be answered straight away since that depends upon analytic premises. These premises, in turn, help to determine how direct or indirect will be our model of how approval is interpreted and, thus, of influence on legislative success.

A more exacting analysis of the relationship between public approval and presidential success with Congress, in fact, reveals that the strength of a president's electoral performance in a member's district or state, and the party affiliation of the member, are the most direct predictors of a member's support for presidentially endorsed legislative proposals.[68] In deciphering the relationship between public prestige and legislative support for presidential proposals, this

FIGURE 4.6. Relationship between Presidential Popularity and Legislative Success from Eisenhower to Reagan

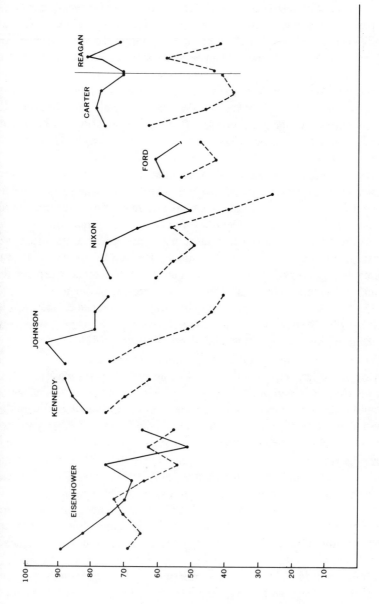

- - - - Averaged annual approval scores (Gallup).

———— Legislative success rate on issues where president has taken a position (*Congressional Quarterly*).

118

analysis concludes that "members of Congress seem to respond not to presidential prestige among the public or their district as a whole but *to presidential prestige among their own electoral supporters.*"[69] Declining presidential approval, therefore, is likely to impact most on members of the president's party who, then, will be less inclined to take risks on behalf of a president of diminished prestige, especially as that is defined by partisans within the member's district. This finding is especially relevant to Democratic members and, thus, to Democratic presidents.[70]

Approval is a measure of public prestige, and prestige a factor in presidential relations with Congress. Slippage of approval, therefore, is an indirect source of a weakened president on Capitol Hill. Other things being equal, Democratic presidents have a more fragile partisan base of support than Republican presidents, and are more affected within their party by alterations in public approval. Independent of other factors, therefore, Democratic presidents are legislatively more vulnerable to declining public approval. This is a part of the spiral of declining influence marked also, as the succession cycle suggests, by declining presidential energies and initiatives, and by a growth in the number of matters to be reacted to rather than acted upon.[71] One additional reason why the downward spiral of public approval negatively influences the level of presidential success with Congress is that the midpoint slump in presidential approval also contributes to a loss of congressional seats. That loss reduces presidential prospects for legislative success.[72] Lowered public standing, consequently, reduces both a president's leverage in Congress and the size of his partisan base in it, with the latter being the more directly critical of the two.

Growing Effectiveness

Whereas the passage of time erodes presidential influence with forces outside the administration, Richard Neustadt contends that the key years for making the presidential record are the third, fifth, and sixth.[73] By this, Neustadt obviously means much more than a crude measure of legislative victories can convey. The problem here is how to measure presidential effectiveness beyond the crude indicators of legislative success available to us. These indicators are simple outcomes not necessarily traceable to a president's exertions. Neustadt is obviously trying to make us look at more subtle issues, an effort that is as sensible as it is nonspecific. Clearly, what he is trying to make us see is not easy to operationalize or to subject to quantitative analysis.

Neustadt seems to be driving at the incumbent's understanding of his office, his sensitivity to his opportunities, and an ability to link these to his goals. Can the incumbent become, in other words, increasingly effective in relating objectives to opportunities and in sharpening tactics on the whetstone of power? If presidents learn successfully, they presumably become more effective in understanding the levers of the office they hold, in displaying sensitivity to the institutions and publics relevant to their success, and in perceiving the power stakes behind the decisions they make.

The problem is that all of this may be true without our being able to measure a discernible consequence. Although not all presidents (perhaps not many) are apt to be discerning students of power, the longer they hold office the more astute they are likely to become whatever the base of knowledge with which they began. The more discerning among them will profit especially by their experience in office. But how can we know what, if any, difference their growing effectiveness will make?

In recent times, one difficulty has been a notable shortage of presidents who have seen, in any normal sense, a fifth or sixth year. Neustadt could speak of Roosevelt, Truman, and Eisenhower with some assurance that these presidents were typical in the time they would have to serve. But the only subsequent president to have a sixth year, and only a portion at that, was Richard Nixon, who fled office under duress.

A more important dilemma, however, is that a president's growing effectiveness may come to naught. The tendency for presidential approval to decline principally as a function of time means a very uncertain relationship between a growing command of presidential tools and successful legislative outcomes, since the latter is mediated by the declining public prestige of the president. The irony, as Paul Light has noted, is that the cycle of decreasing influence intersects the cycle of increasing effectiveness.[74] As presidents get to know better their office and resources, and acquire the skills and experience to manipulate them, their best opportunities will have passed them by. Over time, presidents may learn better how to play the "insider" game of Washington politics, but they will have lost the enthusiasms of novel undertakings, of shared if still distant visions, and of a fresh expression of public support. All leaders, as Valerie Bunce's analysis suggests to us, appreciate this. A system in which legislative support is so dependent upon these enthusiasms, however, sharpens this ironic gap between learning in office and declining resources to achieve.

CONCLUSION

In this chapter three general types of cycles that bear on the presidency are identified: long-term historical or epochal patterns, metacyclical patterns whose occurrence is independent of the presidential term, and cycles that pulsate to the rhythms of the presidential term (termcycles). The effects of the shorter cycles are nested within the longer ones, and I have not here attempted to precisely integrate them into a single structure of explanation. Instead, my more modest purpose has been to identify these cyclical phenomena and point separately to their consequences for presidential leadership, influence, and success.

Two epochal patterns are especially pertinent to a discussion focusing on presidential leadership potential. One is the pattern of relationship between president and Congress; the other, the long-run cycles of electoral politics and of partisan invigoration and decay.

The presidential-congressional relationship is the *sine qua non* of effective programmatic leadership. To achieve programmatic success, Congress has what presidents want—the authority to enact. Congress reacts, however, to what presidents claim, and the stronger the presidential claim the more energetic the congressional counter. Periods of adversarial relations have alternated throughout American history with periods during which one institution (mostly Congress) was generally dominant, and with rarer periods of close cooperation (mostly, and quite selectively, in recent history when the policy agenda has been dominated by international threat). Over time Congress has exhibited two contrary tendencies—on the one hand, a greater diffusion and fragmentation of internal authority and, on the other, a greater capacity for policy integration. While ways have been developed for Congress to act as an informed and unified bargaining partner with the president, the will necessary to achieve this has been slower to develop. Thus, a remarkable growth in the capacity of Congress to act in an integrated and unified manner has foundered in the face of politically disintegrative tendencies. Over time, also, the activity levels of both president and Congress have increased, and the assertiveness of each is now the understood norm.

Decline in the rate of governmental growth now suggests a downturn in the level of congressional activity.[75] The more Congress focuses its attention on budgets, probably the less legislative activity there will be. From a president's point of view, however, this does not necessarily mean that Congress will be any less a hurdle. Representation, rather than decision making, continues to be the hallmark of the institution. Of course, the abilities of presidents to work with Congress and the demands they make of Congress will vary according to their partisan resources and their own resourcefulness.[76] But the phase of the congressional tide will define the parameters of the relationship.

The capacity to pass a presidential program through Congress requires (a) the existence of a presidential legislative program, and (b) the presence of disciplined and fervent supporters in the Congress. The first factor, we have seen, is a relatively recent feature of the presidential role.[77] The second factor is connected to great electoral shifts that bring rising partisan temperatures and new coalitions to the surface. Such shifts bring about more political discipline and greater party cohesion within Congress. The bolstered partisanship in Congress resulting from realigning periods, however, withers over time. So, to the extent that a president is reliant upon his partisan base of support within Congress, the closer or further his accession to office from the surge of partisanship produced by realignment, the better or worse his legislative prospects are likely to be.

Ironically, however, the most powerful and durable effects of realignment on partisan virility occurred when presidents had lower profiles and Congress was clearly the more assertive and prominent institution. Indeed, only the most recent generally recognized realignment (that associated with the New Deal) coincides with the onset of the modern programmatic presidency, and its effects on partisan cohesion have been weaker and more vulnerable to rapid erosion than those of earlier realigning periods. Hints of renewed partisan fever in Congress and equally tentative evidence of realigning tendencies in the electorate have now reappeared, although neither mirrors the symptoms identified in the classic model of realignment. Whether these fragments of evidence signify the long-awaited development of a new era of partisan redefinition and cohesion or merely a momentary deviation from a longer-term pattern of partisan decay cannot as yet be conclusively answered, however important the answer is for the prospects of presidential success with Congress. But these developments look less likely now than during the Reagan administration's first year when it was basking in the glow of electoral victory and legislative success.

Cycles independent of the presidential term but occurring within the larger historical patterns are labeled metacycles, and four of these are discussed. For the most part, the effects of metacyclical phenomena on presidents are exaggerated by their interaction with the time-compressing and attention-exposing character of the modern media. The cycle of economic fortune, for instance, shapes presidential maneuverability and electoral chances, and induces potentially hazardous efforts to prime the cycle. The cycle of international threat, however, tends to enhance presidential authority, but this is because threatening crises generally supercede other, more divisive elements of the presidential agenda. The deference granted to presidents in a time of international crisis appears to be in the form of a nonfungible currency. Apparently, the consensual belief that an international crisis exists is the key stimulant to deference toward presidential authority. All-out unconditional warfare (a rather unlikely condition in the nuclear age) or a pervasive sense of threat such as evidenced in the first decade of the cold war will promote deference to presidential leadership insofar, *but only insofar,* as responses to the specific situation are at issue. Indeed, the so-called "two presidencies" thesis (deference to the president by Congress in foreign, but not domestic, policy) is itself derived from measuring presidential success with Congress in foreign policy during a period of perceived intense threat. Easing of the latter weakened foreign policy consensus thereby reducing, for better or worse, presidential latitude. In recent times, it has been more difficult to arrive at an agreed upon definition of international peril. Not surprisingly, presidents of late have not fared well in regard to their foreign policy initiatives.

A third metacycle is that of issue attentiveness. The cycle of public attentiveness on issues about which belief is relatively unintense and not deeply anchored makes the enactment of policy proposals dependent upon spasms of momentary political pressure. Under such circumstances, the imperative, Do! supersedes the question, What are we doing? Moreover, policy proposals designed for long-range problems are especially subject to the vicissitudes of public attentiveness. As the leading agenda setter, of course, a president might concentrate in a very single-minded way so as to keep alive an issue (and a set of proposed policies) whose fundamental importance is likely to outlast the normal phase of public attentiveness. This process is often called "setting priorities." A single-minded focus, however, means just that; it means that other issues on an agenda will either be thrown overboard or at least stowed below deck. A presidential willingness to sacrifice all for the achievement of a particular set of policy objectives will no doubt bolster the prospects of those objectives, but the price of unwavering purposiveness can be high.

Among the metacycles, there is, finally, the cycle of leadership style and presidential management. In an odd way, presidents tend to beget their opposites. The more forceful among them challenge a system that yields authority reluctantly to a single power holder. Such presidents also create strong resistances and eventually induce a desire for what a former president inelegantly called "normalcy." On the other hand, a lowered presidential profile often is thought to leave problems unengaged and unresolved and, therefore, begging for a more forceful hand. Leadership style, of course, is in large part imagery, but it is also, to some degree, reflective of the scope and intensity of presidential policy and management ambitions. Styles of leadership are also naturally influenced by events, and it is the quickened pace of events that is behind the rapid displacement in contemporary times of preferred leadership styles. In its lower-profile past, the presidential leadership norm was to minimize the stirring up of tempests. Occasionally, the norm was interrupted by presidents more willing to engage the office in constitution stretching ways. Now, the reverse is closer to the mark. The generated demand for inspired leadership is now interrupted only by reactions to unusually extravagant presidential claims and deeds.

Termcycles, those whose patterning occurs within the term of incumbency, are the last set of cycles discussed in this chapter. One such pervasive cycle is the pattern of energy and entropy characterizing terms of leadership. For the mere fact of leadership change also begets policy change which then tapers off to incremental adjustments in the course of incumbency. The virtually universal character of this pattern is impressive and necessarily gives rise to a hunt for generalized explanations. Specific elements of such explanations, however, are apt to vary across national political contexts. One set of specifics relevant to the American presidency in this regard notes the intersection of declining support for the president at the same time he and his administration are gaining in experience and effectiveness. As with the aforementioned issue-attention cycle, this paradox of declining support and increasing effectiveness promotes a tendency toward bold plans and unclear thoughts, a failure to engage in what Richard Neustadt calls "backward mapping."[78]

Such a tendency appears to be at work in *all political systems,* if the evidence of policy energy early in office is indicative. It is likely to be most acute in the United States, however, for several reasons including the lack of continuity in the executive office of the president (EOP), the frequent estrangement of the presidential administration from the permanent administration, and the frequent absence of prior experience on the national scene of newly elected presidents and their close associates. Probably the most important factor, however, is the tenuous situation that presidents face during the most crucial stage of the policy process, that of gaining legislative majorities. Of course, heads of government in multiparty coalitions face similar constraints, but the process of putting such coalitions together usually inhibits high-risk strategies. Alone at the top, however, presidents in the United States find themselves in the uniquely high-risk situation of having to cash in their chips early since they will be, at best, only sporadically stronger than they are at the present moment.

To sum up, in this chapter I have discussed recurring patterns influencing the prospects for direction, and particularly presidential leadership. Yet, the character of recurring patterns is affected, influenced, and altered by trends coursing through society. In the following chapter, therefore, I focus on these trends and examine their impact on capacities for leadership, especially presidential leadership.

NOTES

1. Thomas Cronin's argument in 1970 that "An inspection of introductory American government and related political texts indicates a strong endorsement of the activist-purposeful-progressive and powerful presidency" has been modified somewhat throughout the decade of the 1970s. More recently Cronin has pressed the argument that innovative leadership is likely to be found outside of governmental institutions rather than inside them (1980). A recent review of textbook portrayals of the presidency by Douglas Hoekstra, however, uncovers a view consistent with a newly diminished presidency:

> The recent Carter presidency and popular reactions to it—in the seeming dominance of the "moral" dimension, the "depomping" of the office, the administration's feel for presidential constraints . . . bore a striking resemblance to the strictures emphasized by the new textbook presidency.

The irony is that this latter-day model of presidential behavior, at least as embodied in the Carter presidency, apparently will serve to reendorse the model of activism and purpose that Cronin originally had critiqued. See Thomas E. Cronin, "The Textbook Presidency" (unpublished paper, 1970). For a similar account, and also for his view that innovative leadership will come from sources beyond the presidency, see Cronin's *The State of the Presidency,* 2nd ed. (Boston: Little, Brown, 1980), chap. 2 and 11. For evidence of the revised "textbook presidency," from which the quoted material is taken, see Douglas J. Hoekstra, "The 'Textbook Presidency' Revisited: 1974-1980." Paper presented at the 1981 Annual Meeting of the Midwest Political Science Association, Cincinnati, Ohio.

2. See, for an analysis of the individual-institutional relationship, Glenn R. Parker and Roger H. Davidson, "Why Do Americans Love Their Congressmen So Much More Than Their Congress?," *Legislative Studies Quarterly* 4 (February 1979): 53-61.

3. The term originates with Colin Campbell. See his, "The President's Advisory System Under Carter: From Spokes in a Wheel to Wagons in a Circle." Paper presented at the 1980 Annual Meeting of the American Political Science Association, Washington, D.C.

4. See, for instance, Robert A. Dahl, *Democracy in the United States: Promise and Performance,* 3rd ed. (Chicago: Rand McNally, 1976), pp. 208-209.

5. James L. Sundquist, *The Decline and Resurgence of Congress* (Washington: The Brookings Institution, 1981), p. 16. This constitutional ambiguity is not always accepted by the judiciary, however, as the Supreme Court decision concerning the legislative veto indicates. (Chadha vs. U.S.)

6. Sundquist, *Decline and Resurgence,* p. 20.

7. Lawrence C. Dodd, "Congress, the President, and the Cycles of Power," in *The Post-Imperial Presidency,* ed. Vincent Davis (New Brunswick, N.J.: Transaction, 1980), pp. 71-100; also see Lawrence C. Dodd, "Congress, the Constitution, and the Crisis of Legitimation," in *Congress Reconsidered,* 2nd ed., ed. Lawrence C. Dodd and Bruce I. Oppenheimer (Washington: Congressional Quarterly Press, 1981), pp. 390-420.

8. Joel Silbey, *The Shrine of Party: Congressional Voting Behavior, 1841-1852* (Pittsburgh: University of Pittsburgh Press, 1967).

9. The professionalization hypothesis based on analysis of the Senate from 1869 to 1901 is advanced in David J. Rothman, *Politics and Power: The United States Senate, 1869-1901* (Cambridge, Mass.: Harvard University Press, 1966). Alternative hypotheses based on the virility of shared beliefs and interests accounting for the stunningly high degree of partisanship during this period are offered in William G. Shade, Stanley D. Hopper, David Jacobson, and Stephen E. Moiles, "Partisanship in the United States Senate: 1869-1901," *Journal of Interdisciplinary History* 4 (Autumn 1973): 185-205.

10. See Dodd, "Congress, the Constitution, and the Crisis of Legitimation," pp. 394-395.

11. The polarity of these forces is suggested by Charles O. Jones. See his, "Between Party Battalions and Committee Suzerainty," *The Annals* 411 (January 1974): 158-168.

12. For a somewhat more sanguine view of this rapid growth in transpartisan and intrapartisan caucuses as a means of expressing representation in an increasingly complex society, see Arthur G. Stevens, Jr., Daniel P. Mulhollan, and Paul S. Rundquist, "U.S. Congressional Structure and Representation: The Role of Informal Groups," *Legislative Studies Quarterly* 6 (August 1981): 415-438.

13. Norman J. Ornstein, "The House and the Senate in a New Congress," in *The New Congress,* ed. Thomas E. Mann and Norman J. Ornstein (Washington: American Enterprise Institute, 1981), p. 379.

14. See, for example, Charles Jones's classification of modes of executive-congressional relationship and the time periods they characterize in Charles O. Jones, *The United States Congress: People, Place, and Policy* (Homewood, Ill.: The Dorsey Press, 1982), p. 9.

15. For an illuminating discussion of these issues, see Paul Allen Beck, "A Socialization Theory of Partisan Realignment," in *The Politics of Future Citizens,* ed. Richard G. Niemi (San Francisco: Jossey-Bass, 1974), pp. 199-219.

16. For instance, see Paul Allen Beck, "The Electoral Cycle and Patterns of American Politics," *British Journal of Political Science* 9 (April 1979): 129-156; David W. Brady, Joseph Cooper, and Patricia A. Hurley, "The Decline of Party in the U.S. House of Representatives, 1887-1968," *Legislative Studies Quarterly* 4 (August 1979): 381-407; David W. Brady, "Critical Elections, Congressional Parties and Clusters of Policy Changes," *British Journal of Political Science* 8 (January 1978): 79-99; and Walter Dean Burnham, *Critical Elections and the Mainsprings of American Politics* (New York: W. W. Norton, 1979).

17. Benjamin Ginsberg, "Critical Elections and the Substance of Party Conflict: 1844-1968," *American Journal of Political Science* 16 (November 1972): 603-625, esp. p. 614.

18. See Jerome M. Clubb and Santa A. Traugott, "Partisan Cleavage and Cohesion in the U.S. House of Representatives, 1861-1974," *Journal of Interdisciplinary History* 3 (Winter 1977): 375-401, and Shade et al., "Partisanship in the United States Senate."

19. See Clubb and Traugott, p. 381.

20. Clubb and Traugott, p. 397.

21. Brady, "Critical Elections, Congressional Parties and Clusters of Policy Changes," p. 80.

22. Brady, "Critical Elections," pp. 86-98.

23. With regard to the Court, see Richard Funston, "The Supreme Court and Critical Elections," *American Political Science Review* 69 (December 1975): 795-811. In regard to the executive, see John H. Glascock, "Realignment and Public Policy: The Executive Connection." Paper presented at the 1981 Annual Meeting of the American Political Science Association, New York.

24. Burnham, *Critical Elections and the Mainsprings of American Politics,* p. 98.

25. Brady, "Critical Elections," p. 99.

26. Nor would they necessarily reappear in the same form. For interpretations suggesting that the political system is in the process of a complex realignment, see Steven H. Renten and James A. Stimson, "Events and Alignments: The Party Image Link." Paper presented at the 1982 Annual Meeting of the Midwest Political Science Association, Milwaukee, Wisconsin; and Paul Allen Beck, "Realignment Begins? The Republican Surge in Florida." Paper presented at the 1981 Annual Meeting of the American Political Science Association, New York.

27. Brady, "Critical Elections," pp. 96-97.

28. I acknowledge using two seemingly contradictory terms to describe the New Deal realignment, "limp" and "earthquake." Both are accurate, however. The "earthquake" feature of the New Deal realignment is a symptomatic reference to the displacement of national party majorities. This phenomenon has not occurred in the present period and even proponents of a "realignment" thesis are uncertain that it will. At the same time, the characterization "limp" also seems applicable to the New Deal realignment because, relative to earlier realigning periods, its cleavage structure was less clear and, to some extent, it overlaid rather than fully displaced prior cleavages. The cleavage base of the New Deal realignment threrefore was less straightforward than earlier ones and weaker in its apparent effect among elites for whom partisan divisions were less sharp than in the earlier realigning eras. On the other hand, Sinclair argues, the interparty differences were *ideologically* sharper than they had been. See Barbara Deckard Sinclair, "Party Realignment and the Transformation of the Political Agenda," *American Political Science Review* 71 (September, 1977): 940-953.

29. David S. Broder, "Budget Vote Game: 'Positioning' for November," *Washington Post,* May 26, 1982, pp. A1, A5.

30. Donald E. Stokes and Warren E. Miller earlier argued that because the public has little awareness of what goes on in Congress congressional party indiscipline owes to factors other than public awareness. See Donald E. Stokes and Warren E. Miller, "Party Government and the Saliency of Congress," in Angus Campbell, Philip E. Converse, Warren E. Miller, and Donald E. Stokes, *Elections and the Political Order* (New York: John Wiley, 1966), pp. 194-211. I do not quarrel with this contention because, as stated, "public awareness" implies a consistent programmatic cognition of, and interest in, politics on the part of mass electorates and a comprehension of detailed information regarding a member's policy behavior in Congress. These are steep assumptions. But Stokes and Miller also claimed that "by plying his campaigning and servicing arts over the years, the Congressman is able to develop electoral strength that is almost totally dissociated from what his party wants in Congress. . . ." (p. 210.) Nothing in more recent evidence effectively denies this point.

The growth in visibility of members of Congress even if nonprogrammatic, however, has had consequences since Stokes and Miller wrote. As Michael Robinson astutely notes, expanded coverage of members of Congress comes at the expense of the institution. The expansion, particularly of local coverage, is rarely policy-focused, but it has meant that members need to buy more and more insurance in the form of image management. Ironically, enhanced visibility means they are both safer and more anxious. Not surprisingly, tactical flexibility (opportunism if one wishes) is prized in such an environment. See Michael J. Robinson, "Three Faces of Congressional Media," in Mann and Ornstein, pp. 55-96, esp. p. 95.

31. Renten and Stimson, "Events and Alignments."

32. See Donald R. Kinder and D. Roderick Kiewiet, "Sociotropic Politics: The American Case," *British Journal of Political Science* 11 (January 1981): 129-161.

33. Kinder and Kewiet, "Sociotropic Politics," p. 158.

34. See George C. Edwards III, *The Public Presidency* (New York: St. Martin's, 1983), esp. pp. 251-253.

35. For evidence of politically inspired efforts to pep up the economy, see William D. Nordhaus, "The Political Business Cycle," *Review of Economic Studies* 42 (April 1975): 169-190, and Edward R. Tufte, *Political Control of the Economy* (Princeton, N.J.: Princeton University Press, 1978). For evidence, however, casting doubt on the ability to achieve that which Nordhaus and Tufte claim presidents aspire to, see David G. Golden and James M. Poterba, "The Price of Popularity: The Political Business Cycle Reexamined," *American Journal of Political Science* 24 (November 1980): 696-714. Golden and Poterba contend that:

Politicians may *try** to exert discretionary control over monetary and fiscal policy. Whether their efforts meet with success in either implementation or in result is another question completely. . . . The extent of this economic manipulation is inconsequential in the overall scheme of economic policy. (p. 713.)

*emphasis is in the original.

36. "The optimal partisan policy," Nordhaus concludes, "will lead to a political business cycle with unemployment and deflation in early years followed by an inflationary boom as elections approach." Nordhaus, p. 185.

37. Charles Tilly, "Does Modernization Breed Revolution?," *Comparative Politics* 5 (April 1973): 446.

38. Lee Sigelman, "A Reassessment of the Two Presidencies Thesis," *Journal of Politics* 41 (November 1979): 1204.

39. See Jeffrey E. Cohen, "The Impact of the Modern Presidency on Presidential Success in the U.S. Congress," *Legislative Studies Quarterly* 7 (November 1982): 528-529.

40. Aaron Wildavsky, "The Two Presidencies," in *The Presidency,* ed. Aaron Wildavsky (Boston: Little, Brown 1969), pp. 230-243. For two critiques of Wildavsky's thesis that, by stressing its overgeneralization, nevertheless highlight the accuracy of Wildavsky's thesis for the time period he studied, see Donald A. Peppers, "'The Two Presidencies': Eight Years Later," in *Perspectives on the Presidency,* ed. Aaron Wildavsky (Boston: Little, Brown, 1975), pp. 462-471, and Sigelman, "A Reassessment."

41. See Sigelman, "A Reassessment." For a view claiming that it is the variation in domestic support rather than in foreign support that makes for "the two presidencies," see Harvey G. Zeidenstein, "The Two Presidencies Thesis Is Alive and Well and Has Been Living in the U.S. Senate since 1973," *Presidential Studies Quarterly* 11 (Fall 1981): 511-525.

42. See Cohen, "The Impact of the Modern Presidency."

43. A former member of Congress takes note of the increased level of activity in the House regarding foreign affairs. In 1969, thirteen foreign policy bills reached the floor of the House; by 1979, thirty bills had done so. The increased roll call activity, it is claimed, exposes members and requires them to take positions on issues on which they had previously not had to record a stand. The consequence, according to this argument, is that by members taking positions so as to protect their electoral chances, foreign policy making has become ever more splintered, and its substance ever more unpredictable. See Charles W. Whalen, Jr. *The House and Foreign Policy: The Irony of Congressional Reform* (Chapel Hill, N.C.: University of North Carolina Press, 1982).

44. Cohen, "The Impact of the Modern Presidency."

45. See, for instance, James W. Ceaser, "Political Parties and Presidential Ambition," *Journal of Politics* 40 (August 1978): 708-739; Martin A. Levin, "A Call for a Politics of Institutions, Not Men," in Davis, *The Post-Imperial Presidency,* pp. 39-70; Bruce Miroff, "Monopolizing the Public Space: The President as a Problem for Democratic Politics," in *Rethinking the Presidency,* ed. Thomas E. Cronin (Boston: Little, Brown, 1982), pp. 218-232; James Q. Wilson, "In Defense of Separation of Powers II," in Cronin, *Rethinking the Presidency,* pp. 179-182; James W. Ceaser, Glen E. Thurow, Jeffrey Tulis, and Joseph M. Bessette, "The Rise of the Rhetorical Presidency," in Cronin, *Rethinking the Presidency,* pp. 233-251; and Nelson W. Polsby, "Against Presidential Greatness," in *American Government: Readings and Cases,* 7th ed., ed. Peter Woll (Boston: Little, Brown, 1981), pp. 417-424.

46. Anthony Downs, "Up and Down with Ecology: The Issue-Attention Cycle," *The Public Interest* 28 (Summer 1972): 38-50.

47. *Ibid.,* p. 44.

48. *Ibid.,* p. 42.

49. The dilemma is crisply stated by Charles O. Jones:

Public policy, generated despite limitations of knowledge and organizational capability, stands very much alone when a public, once concerned about certain consequences, dissolves.

Charles O. Jones, "Speculative Augmentation in Federal Air Pollution Policy-Making," *Journal of Politics* 36 (May 1974), p. 463.

50. David Braybrooke and Charles E. Lindblom, *A Strategy of Decision: Policy Evaluation as a Social Process* (New York: The Free Press, 1963), pp. 81-110.

51. See, in this regard, Steven Kelman, *Regulating America, Regulating Sweden: A Comparative Study of Occupational Safety and Health Policy* (Cambridge, Mass.: MIT Press, 1981), esp. pp. 221-237.

52. See Richard Rose, "The President: A Chief But Not an Executive," *Presidential Studies Quarterly* 7 (Winter 1977): 5-20.

53. *Ibid.,* p. 19.

54. An instructive example of this phenomenon is analyzed by Entman and Paletz. See Robert M. Entman and David L. Paletz, "Media and the Conservative Myth," *Journal of Communication* 30 (Autumn 1980): 154-165.

55. The label has fortuitous origins, the result of a typographical error in a memorandum prepared for a conference which the author attended. Without hesitation the conferees agreed that this "typo" was, in fact, a brilliant conceptualization of the management style within the Carter White House.

56. Campbell, "The President's Advisory System Under Carter." A similar view is offered in Thomas E. Cronin, "'Everybody Believes in Democracy Until He Gets to the White House . . .': An Examination of White House-Departmental Relations," in Wildavsky, *Perspectives on the Presidency,* pp. 362-392.

57. See Juan Cameron, "The Management Problem in Ford's White House," *Fortune* 92 (July 1975): 74-81.

58. Bruce Miroff, "After Consensus: The Dilemmas of Contemporary American Leadership, a 1979 View," *Presidential Studies Quarterly* 11 (Summer 1981), p. 411.

59. John Herbers, "The President and the Press Corps," *New York Times Sunday Magazine,* May 9, 1982, p. 75.

60. See Paul J. Quirk, "What Must a President Know?" *Society* 56 (January/February 1983): 55-62.

61. Valerie Bunce, "Changing Leaders and Changing Policies: The Impact of Elite Succession on Budgetary Priorities in Democratic Countries," *American Journal of Political Science* 24 (August 1980): 373-395.

62. Valerie Bunce, *Do New Leaders Make a Difference? Executive Succession and Public Policy under Capitalism and Socialism* (Princeton, N.J.: Princeton University Press, 1981), esp. pp. 222-256.

63. Bunce, *Do New Leaders Make a Difference?* p. 255.

64. For a discussion of the timing of these various features, see John H. Kessel, "The Seasons of Presidential Politics," *Social Science Quarterly* 58 (December 1977): 418-435.

65. Bunce, *Do New Leaders Make a Difference?* p. 255.

66. See James A. Stimson, "Public Support for American Presidents: A Cyclical Model," *Public Opinion Quarterly* 40 (Spring 1976): 1-21.

67. Richard E. Neustadt, *Presidential Power: The Politics of Leadership from FDR to Carter* (New York: John Wiley, 1980), pp. 64-79.

68. See George C. Edwards III, *Presidential Influence in Congress* (San Francisco: W. H. Freeman, 1980), pp. 86-115.

69. *Ibid.,* p. 110.

70. *Ibid.,* pp. 92-99.

71. For similar arguments, see Valerie Bunce, "The Cycles of the Presidency." Paper presented at the 1981 Annual Meeting of the Midwest Political Science Association, Cincinnati, Ohio.

72. For evidence of this proposition, see Edward R. Tufte, "Determinants of the Outcome of Midterm Congressional Elections," *American Political Science Review* 69 (September 1975): 812-826, and Samuel Kernell, "Presidential Popularity and Negative Voting: An Alternative Explanation of the Midterm Congressional Decline of the President's Party," *American Political Science Review* 71 (March 1977): 44-66. The impact of presidential approval on midterm congressional losses is a matter of some controversy, and the statement of its contribution to those losses is *not* a statement of its relative importance. See, especially, Lyn Ragsdale, "The Fiction of Congressional Elections as Presidential Events," *American Politics Quarterly* 8 (October 1980): 375-398.

73. Neustadt, *Presidential Power*, p. 149.

74. Paul C. Light, "The President's Agenda: Notes on the Timing of Domestic Choice," *Presidential Studies Quarterly* 11 (Winter 1981): 67-82.

75. Evidence of this decline can be seen in a reduction of the number of pages in *The Federal Register* and in decreased public service employment. See T. R. Reid, "Reagan's Register Sheds 25% of Its Pages," *Washington Post*, January 1, 1982, p. A21, and David Treatwell, "For First Time Since World War II, Public Service Jobs Decline," *Washington Post*, January 1, 1982, p. A2.

76. One analysis, comparing the congressional fortunes of Carter and Reagan to an expected level of performance, concludes that Reagan (thus far) has fared better because he more effectively exploited his partisan base. See Richard Fleisher and Jon R. Bond, "The Influence of Personal Skills and Political Structures on Support for the President in the House: A Comparison of Reagan and Carter." Paper presented at the 1982 Annual Meeting of the Midwest Political Science Association, Milwaukee, Wisconsin. Why this is so, however, may depend less on presidential political skills and more on the nature of presidential agendas.

77. See Steven J. Wayne, *The Legislative Presidency* (New York: Harper & Row, 1978), pp. 8-28.

78. Neustadt, *Presidential Power*, pp. 190-192.

5

"Modern Times": Contemporary Trends and Presidential Leadership

If the Civil War had been fought in the television age, I have no doubt there would be an independent Confederate States of America today, because that was a mismanaged, bungled operation (by the Union) almost until the end.

(Austin Ranney as quoted in the *Washington Post,* April 4, 1982.)

At the individual level rationality appears to be on the increase. Political interest is increasing, the electorate is becoming more educated, and habitual voting . . . is declining. Along with this pattern, people make decisions later and switch parties more. . . . They are probably subject to influences of opinion waves, mass media, and even personality politics much more than the Swedish electorate of the past.
(John D. Stephens, "The Changing Swedish Electorate," *Comparative Political Studies* 14 [July 1981]: 200-201.)

In recent years . . . the process of agenda setting has become steadily more open and competitive. Under these circumstances, with ambitious sponsors and an active press hungry for news, it has become next to impossible to deny a hearing to "an idea whose time has come."
(Jack L. Walker, "Setting the Agenda in the U.S. Senate," *British Journal of Political Science* 7 [July 1977]: 445.)

The dramatic expansion of the role of government in the United States in the 1960s and 1970s has made more visible the problems for reaching agreement that self-assertive values and adversary institutions create.

(Steven Kelman, *Regulating America, Regulating Sweden,* p. 232.)

After the speech, President and Mrs. Reagan . . . walked the length of the gallery. . . . And then several dozen of the audience [British MPs], instead of vacating the hall with the rest of the crowd, rushed forward instead for a look at the electronic prompting device that had enabled the President to appear to be speaking without

notes. . . . Although the technique is commonplace for the White House, it is virtually unknown in Britain. And to an audience of politicians, who make speeches all the time, it had exciting possibilities. The group on the stage afterward, which included former Prime Minister Edward Heath, pressed the White House technician who runs it to explain again and again how it works.
(Story in the *New York Times* of June 9, 1982 following President Reagan's speech to Members of the British Parliament in the Royal Gallery at Westminster.)

In the film "Modern Times," Charlie Chaplin portrays a worker ensnared by the inventions of modernity. Surrounded by sophisticated machinery, he is befuddled by it. Although the impact is undoubtedly less comical than Charlie Chaplin's ill-fated efforts to master his "brave new world," the principal effect of modern times on governance and political leadership is also paradoxical. In its most austere form, the paradox can be stated as follows: centrifugality amidst centrism.

Nearly everywhere (including the United States), government has become a more central agent in society. Nearly everywhere, the prominence of central authorities has risen. Nearly everywhere, there has been a growth in organization, an extension of its scope, and a phenomenal expansion of communication, information, and transportation networks. And everywhere, there has been an expanding attentiveness to national horizons. At the same time, there has been a remarkable growth in social and organizational complexity—an expansion of individualism and a diminished commitment to collectivities (a growth, in other words, of individual rationalism). Along with that have come increased opportunities for, and tendencies toward, participation within nearly all arenas. On the one hand, fluidity and uncertainty in the political environment are induced by factors such as these, while, on the other, the growth of government brings with it a growth in the power of its parts and the interest networks formed around them. The comments of one political scientist, though directed to the Netherlands, are appropriately generalizable: "With this interwovenness we also come upon the paradox that if the concept 'governmental' is used *grosso modo,* it appears that its influence on events in society is overwhelming, while in fact its steering capacities are quite limited."[1] In short, we have "centrifugal centrism."

In both the United States and Europe, the media penetrate the consciousness of superficially attentive publics. Similarly, in all of the industrialized societies, larger proportions of the public are becoming better educated (a phenomenon more shockingly sudden in Europe than in the United States), and thus less dependent upon traditional forms of political organization. New issues, unassimilated by older cleavages, are finding novel organizational forms, sometimes inside and sometimes outside existing political parties. The growth of environmental and antinuclear movements, for instance, often has been outside of existing party structures. Further, in Europe as in the United States, mandated expenditures linked to inexorable demographic trends also are taking larger chunks of present and future government allocations, thus reducing the latitude available to leaders while increasing pressures on them. All of these trends are common to the industrialized democracies, and though it is easier to spot them than to demonstrate their precise effects, the composite impact is to heighten expectation and attentiveness, and to decrease the discretion of governing authorities.

Though these forces have affected governance everywhere, they have not done so in precisely the same manner. Societal contexts—political culture and political institutions—accommodate similar trends somewhat differently and may produce somewhat different reactions. However destabilizing the tendencies, much depends on the nature of the chemical compound with which we begin. Since each society is a somewhat different compound, the effects of the new and usually volatile elements will generate somewhat different chemical reactions in each.

Systems begin at different thresholds in regard to such trends. In the United States, for instance, the very real growth in the center, in the integration of the society, and in national attentiveness must still be contrasted sharply with the more statist, more compact, less diverse, and less localized societies prevalent in Europe. On the other hand, the participation revolution, as Tocqueville undoubtedly would have noted, has been less shattering of prevailing norms and organizational modes in America than in Europe, while nonetheless accentuating the American problem of competent governance.

In all cases, however, it is true that governing has become harder, but that is because the standard for governing has shifted sharply upward. Governments do more: There are more interdependencies in society, and there is, concomitant with democratization, a vast increase in demands and expectations. Governing is harder because the governors do more, to be sure. But a simple linear extension of that proposition to the assertion that governing would be easier if governments did less is not necessarily warranted. For while the level of activity does imply convolution, and that, to be sure, is important in inhibiting coherence, what complicates governing so much is less the size of government, *per se,* than the exposure and visibility of the governors and the expectations of the governed. Convolution follows from the growth of public policy while expectation follows from a belief in its omnicompetence.

The growth in centralization and national awareness, then, expands the role of top political leadership by expanding its visibility and, therefore, expectations regarding its performance. The growth in complexity, however, also increases fragmentation in organization and society, decreases consensus, and erodes certainty. Individual rationalism and uninhibited egoism have unleashed ambition, assertiveness, and pressures for participation and democratization—unhinging intermediate organizations contingent upon loyalty while bolstering those based upon ideology and purpose.[2] Complexity, too, has meant that governments are often less than the sum of their parts, and that they are threaded through with claimants from past treaties and bargains. Modern interest groups burrow into governments. How they do so varies with the structures they wish to influence, but that they do so is now commonplace.

In the United States "modern times" mainly have reinforced persistent inhibitions on the possibilities of sustaining direction. In contrast to other political systems, the American system always has been more fluid, more loosely organized, more individualistic, less deferential, and more accessible. It has become even more so. But these qualities have grown in importance on a canvas of vastly greater proportions—a contribution, as well, of modern times.

In the pages that follow, I focus on six broad trends that challenge the capacities of leadership. They are: (1) the expansion of the public space; (2) the growth of rationalism; (3) the related growth of independence in the public sphere; (4) the expansion of subgovernments and of interest networks within government; (5) an environment of economic stagnation and, thus, of lessened policy slack; and (6) the expansion of political contest and the disjuncture thereby fostered between the politics of campaigning and the processes of governing.

"Trends" is a word with the ring of inevitability and determinism about it. I do not know how manipulable these trends are, if at all. Some, I suspect, are more manipulable than others. The laws governing political campaigns, for instance, are obviously more easily altered than the conditions governing the distribution of wealth among nations. The composite effect, however, is what is especially important—and thus, the impact of each acting alone is less than their interactive effect.

These "trends," assuming this is a correct designation, are not inherently good or bad. Any such evaluation of that issue rests upon due consideration of a complex of values, and not with just any single one. It is, however, a single value that I am mostly concerned with here, namely the capacity of governments to generate sustainable direction. This need not be the preeminent value for a policy. It is one, however, that depends ironically upon the legitimacy accorded both leadership and leaders. The tendencies discussed here, for the most part, do make sustainable direction more difficult to generate; they do so partly because they also erode the legitimacy necessary to leadership. While perhaps generative of other "goods," the trends discussed here tend to make more problematic the fulfillment of the leadership value.

THE EXPANSION OF THE PUBLIC SPACE

Who can doubt that the state has grown as a central agent in society? From the number and types of cabinet departments[3] to the bulging storehouse of administrative interpretations[4] and the disproportionate increase in public expenditure,[5] the evidence is overwhelming. In the tangible sense of what it is that governments do, the answer, almost logarithmically, throughout most of this century has been "more." Some "Tory" views of this expansion see in the "extravagance" of the state an inevitable extravagance of promises made by those seeking to gain or to hold political office. In this view, an enlarged assumption of "rights," of demands for public goods, and of politicians' responsiveness to those demands provide the core explanation for the growth of government.[6]

Whether "good" or "bad," the growth of government is a spur to, but not the equivalent of, the expansion of the public space. What I mean by the growth of the public space is principally a growth in public consciousness fostered by the enhanced visibility of public figures. There is no single explanation for this growth, but the technologies of the twentieth century, especially those of recent years, have helped trigger it. In the more parochial and limiting world of premodern technology, it would be virtually impossible to imagine the extent, however superficial, of public awareness induced by modern technologies. In fact, the expansion of the public space is a consequence of the integrating tendencies of modern society; their potential is centristic. Precisely how they interact with prevailing norms and structures, however, is another question, for in that they often promote centrifugal effects.

What are these new technologies that spark public consciousness and promote the visibility of the governors? They involve transportation, communications, and the media.

Transportation Systems

Transportation technology has made it possible to go long distances in a short space of time. Having done so, the jet airplane especially has also made it possible, as bleary-eyed campaigners know too well, to be in several distant places within a short time span. What enables presidents to travel abroad with dispatch and mind-numbing fatigue, also makes it possible for members of Congress to touch base at home with some frequency, no matter how distant their home base is from Washington. Between 1970 and 1977, for instance, members' allowances for round trip visits to their districts had tripled in the House of Representatives, an indication of both the relative ease with which such travel could be undertaken and the increased sense of urgency for protecting one's turf from would-be competitors.[7] Richard Fenno notes, in this regard, that

> House members work hard to get the job and work hard to keep it. In the course of that effort, they expend a great deal of time keeping in touch with their various constituencies at home. . . . When a congressman describes his seat as "safe," he implicitly adds: "because, and so long as, I work actively to keep it so."[8]

Not all members, as Fenno's analysis indicates, feel an equal imperative to spend time in their home district or to allocate their resources toward propping up their home base. But technology has made it increasingly possible for them to do so, and to the extent that such attentiveness helps to shore up the electoral prospects of members, it increases their potential for independence from their party.

In brief, by increasing their visibility, members have become better able to make their constituents aware of their existence. This alone cannot account for enlarged tendencies toward the electoral preservation of incumbents or the concomitant diminution in partisan unity on the floor.[9] Nonetheless, it increases the levers that members have in their hands to determine their own political future apart from whatever policy and partisan tendencies may be at work nationally. Parker and Davidson thus argue that

> Whereas citizens' expectations for Congress are vague and anchored to generalized policy and stylistic concerns, their expectations for their own representatives are unmistakable. Legislators are judged very largely on the way they serve their districts and communicate with them.[10]

Like sales representatives, members of Congress too find it necessary to keep in touch with their "customers." This is not because they are threatened by competitors, but because many feel they will be threatened if they do not maintain contact.

Information Systems

Along with taking to the skies or to the interstates, members find other ways to communicate with their constituencies—other ways, in short, to promote their visibility. Between 1971 and 1979, for instance, congressional mailing costs, unadjusted for inflation, increased six-fold, and the amount of franked mail between 1954 and 1979 increased over eight-fold.[11] These are indicators, Walter Dean Burnham notes, of the growing resources that members of Congress have at their disposal to try to entrench themselves in their districts.[12]

One such important resource has been the introduction of computer technology in Congress. Although the introduction of computerized information systems is multifaceted and has been used more often by some types of members then others, and used to do a wider variety of tasks by some members than others, the one objective all incumbents have in common is to employ the new information technology on behalf of their political needs. "The computer," according to one observer, is employed "most often for . . . impressing constituents," and thus simply "becomes one more weapon in the incumbents' growing arsenal of re-election tools."[13]

As with developments in transportation, the spread and sophistication of information technologies is essentially integrative, but each development has been placed in the service of an essentially centrifugal politics. Indeed, each has been put to the service of a more responsive, but possibly less responsible, government. Former Democratic House Whip, John Brademas, an outspoken advocate of the use of new information technologies, claimed on their behalf that such "advances promise greater accessibility of senators and congressmen to their constituents, individually and collectively, and greater access of citizens to their senators and congressmen as well."[14] In a word, such advances in technology expand the public space by penetrating the consciousness of the governed and broadening awareness of, and access to, the governors.[15]

Information technologies, as well, have helped alter the nature of political organization, generally increasing its centristic character. Computerized information of the electorate and direct mailings, like the patrol car, have taken the beat away from the foot soldier. The voter mobilization tasks of local party organizations have withered as the scale of organization necessary to acquire systematized information has broadened. The impact has been to some degree fragmenting as evidenced by the personalized organizations of candidates, the ascendancy of the campaign consultancy industry, and the growth of special interest political action committees (PACs). But at the same time, it also has changed the task and elevated the functioning level of political party organization. While the local party organizations have waned in their traditional tasks of face-to-face campaigning, the national parties, if far more advanced at this stage on the Republican side than on the Democratic, have gained in vigor and sophistication, moving from an exclusively presidential focus to become a recruiter of congressional candidates. The resources of patronage and petty corruption once prominently held by local party organizations have nearly vanished, while the fund-gathering capabilities of national party organizations have grown spectacularly. In the process, the national parties also have decreased the variance among state party organizations and increased the interdependence of those organizations with the national party organizations.[16]

The growth of communications systems is also a boon to president-centric motivations. The rapidity by which information is gained and dispensed makes presidents more powerful, central, and visible. It makes them more inclined, other things being equal, to intervene in nooks and crannies within their administrations in ways that were technically impossible for premodern presidents. It enables them to become their own ambassadors and generals, and to exert command heretofore unknown. Such tendencies cannot avoid making all chief executive leaders more prominent. In the United States, they have helped induce in presidents a tendency to want to establish proprietorship over government, or at the very least over the executive. Like Adam's apple, the lure has proved well-nigh irresistible, as tempting as it is dangerous.[17]

Modern Media

As for the modern media, they above all have been a prime stimulant to an expansion of public consciousness. The media are not a single entity, but instead range from elite newspapers to provincial dailies and weeklies, from national newsweeklies to specialized trade journals, from national network radio and television to local affiliates. Effects are equally multiple. Yet, the modern media, more by imperatives than intentions, influence how both politics and government are conducted in the United States.

One effect is a close focus on the president. The retinue of Washington correspondents of both the print and electronics media particularly follow presidents and their administrations with close intensity. To some extent, through charm and personal cultivation, presidents can take advantage of this. Franklin Roosevelt, Kennedy, and Reagan all have been effective in using the media, particularly the electronics media, as their stage. Through the media, and especially television and radio, the president can seek to mobilize political support or try to prepare the nation for forthcoming actions. Through the media, trial balloons may be floated and leaks purposefully perpetrated. It is, in short, hard to imagine a powerful executive without a massively available media presence lurking in the landscape.

If the instruments of modern media provide opportunities for presidents adept at manipulating them, they also engender troubles by exposure of delicate matters. The modern press is not strictly speaking an independent force in this regard, but is, instead, largely reflective of both the political culture of openness and its exalted constitutional status. Its opportunities are provided by the splintering of governmental interests. In all of these areas of which the media are reflective, they are also astonishingly reinforcing. The hovering role of the press, especially the national broadcast and print media, often makes governing difficult simply because its reporting of events becomes an event itself.

An interesting example lies in the tale of an intelligence report of a Soviet combat brigade in Cuba in 1979. Confided in by the secretary of state, the chairman of the Senate Foreign Relations Committee, Frank Church, took to the airwaves to denounce the threat posed by the brigade. Once having done so, the Carter administration and its secretary of state, Cyrus Vance, spoke harsh words and delivered ultimatums to expedite the removal of the Soviet brigade. Whatever the actual nature of the Soviet brigade—combat or, as the Soviets claimed, merely support forces—media exposure placed the administration in an untenable position. The Soviets claimed that the unit was not a combat force and would not be removed, and by later admitting, in essence, that U.S. intelligence concurred, the administration was caught in a bind, partly of its own making. By hollering publicly for removal of the brigade (which it would not otherwise have done), its credibility was further weakened and its image of indecisiveness reinforced.

In other words, as revealed by two authors of an extensive study of how the media portray the president, "Events frequently become problems for the president because they are reported in the media."[18] Without the hovering presence of cameras, the bevy of Washington correspondents, and the onset of a strong electoral challenge, Senator Church, assuming the legitimacy of his publicly voiced concerns, likely would have had a private tête-à-tête with the secretary of state to express his misgivings. The media, of course, did not create the incident. They only reported it. Their omnipresence, however, made it tempting for Senator Church to go public, thus forcing the administration to go public, thus creating an event.

As Presidents McKinley and Madison might have testified, this was hardly the first time that presidents have been pressured into doing things they seemed otherwise resistant to. The media have always provided a sounding board for disgruntled officials and politicians, and government in Washington has always been open. There are now, however, more media reaching far more people in a far shorter space of time. It is an environment discouraging of intimacy.

If appearance fosters reality, then how the press reports happenings and the images it portrays also becomes crucially important for presidents. Presidents and their associates work hard to ensure that the right image is portrayed. In an environment saturated with appearances, imagery and appearance can become powerful considerations in decision making. Avoiding negative stereotypes colors the responses of all presidential administrations.

The image of indecisiveness, for example, emerged from the Carter administration rather early. Whatever the accuracy of the stereotype, one official in the administration later confessed that after a while there would be times when there was a consensus to change a course of action on its substantive merits, but a reluctance to do so because it would play to the image of indecisiveness. Two scholars who have closely followed the relationship between the media and the president note also that

> reporters . . . influenced by their friends on the Hill . . . tended to emphasize Carter's words and deeds that showed him alternately as too demanding or too surrendering. . . . The emphasis . . . suggested that the President displayed qualities of indecisiveness. This picture of Carter represented the prevalent view in Washington. . . . But if the story was a reflection of the reality, it also contributed to the reality of the story. Carter's reputation, as shaped and hardened by the media, contributed to his difficulties in getting control of his office.[19]

Of course, a prying press, as earlier noted, is itself not a new phenomenon. The relationship between press and president, beginning with George Washington, Max Kampelman concludes, has always been adversarial.[20] Yet, there is a difference today. Coverage by the elite press is intimate. It makes the small deals, the petty flattery, and other tools of bargaining a matter of public domain. Robert Entman asserts in this regard that:

> Leadership has both public and private dimensions. One of a president's major tasks is to inspire the public. But publicity alone does not propel policies through the bureaucracy and Congress into action. Leadership also entails private communication. . . . Presidents and their staff deploy the . . . whole repertoire of persuasive tools—*in private*. Publicity vitiates these tools. Media coverage of the tactics, their rationales, and different actors' reactions adds an extra dimension of strategic complexity into a president's already Byzantine political calculus.[21]

In short, the fishbowl effect constrains bargaining strategies, makes government look disorderly (which it inevitably is), and heightens tendencies for personality and organizational clashes. It is a good setting for the disgruntled to voice their disgruntlement, but a problematic one for a president. Although the fishbowl has always been there, more observers now look into it.

In contrast to members of Congress (as distinct from Congress institutionally), the modern media have impacted on the president in a singularly disadvantageous way. In a fascinating essay, Michael J. Robinson shows us why.[22] Robinson's analysis emphasizes the diversity of the media, particularly contrasting the hard-edged elite and national component with the softer-tinged local elements. While more and more media technology has become available to the members of Congress for reaching their constituents from Washington, they also have been subject to two very different types of media exposure. While the national press tends to cover the institution, the local press tends to cover the incumbent. The bite of the former is hard and often hostile, while the latter tends to feature incumbents in a less critical light. In other words, as Glenn Parker and Roger Davidson have observed, members of Congress can divest themselves from the performance of their institution and derive benefit therefrom.[23] No such luck for the president, however. Unable to avoid responsibility for performance, but at the center of media visibility, the president suffers when things do not go well.[24]

Robinson's conclusion is worth listening to:

> The *media,* by focusing so fully on the office of president and then inevitably on the inadequacies of any person holding the job, *may be producing an office that is more powerful but at the same time may be weakening the power of each individual president.* On the other hand, *the media,* by treating Congress poorly but its incumbents relatively well, *may be strengthening incumbents but weakening their institution.* This process has probably been at work since the advent of national radio.[25]

All in all, the effects are: first, a constant spotlight on the president; second, a growing emphasis on, with the increased importance of, public relations and image management by presidents and members of Congress alike; and third, a growing divestiture of individual from institutional fate within Congress. The result is unharnessed energy. A growth in a centristic focus on the presidency is countered by the centrifugal tendencies spawned within Congress. Never deeply endowed in collectivizing incentives, the dilemma of governance in the American system is heightened by the media rich environment that provides increasingly more opportunities to enhance individualizing over collectivizing motives. What is possible for members of Congress is not, however, for the president. Fundamentally, the president is *both* the institution and the incumbent. Members of Congress are free to run against their institution in the name of self-preservation. Presidents, however, are the prisoners of Pennsylvania Avenue—responsible for their own failings, and often those of Congress as well.

The electronics media, however, remain alluring for presidents to employ—to mobilize political support, and to educate publics to presidential policy designs.

Under some circumstances, presidents effectively have made use of the media by appealing to sentiments for which there is already receptivity. Rallying around the flag does briefly help presidential public standing. For certain, presentation of self before the media is helpful if only because not knowing how to present self can be injurious.

The expansion of the media, however, also presents presidents with the opportunity to be the nation's educator in regard to public issues. Putting aside the question of whether presidents are more in need of being educated than capable of educating, the electronics media, far from being an educating device, lend themselves to simple messages. The real problem of education, after all, lies in putting forth a complex message in the media when either the problem being addressed is not immediately pressing, or when the problem is linked to others, or when the solution cannot be definitive—that is to say most problems worth educating publics to. Setting forth a complex message in the media, especially television, is mostly preordained to failure because receptivity to complexity is quite low. Viewing habits "interact with the nature of television news coverage in ways that reduce the informational impact of the medium," and, thus, "television informs slowly, through repetition and familiarity."[26]

Less elegantly stated, television informs through sloganeering. Those urging presidents to "educate" us through this medium are already no doubt among the "educated." Probably, if indeed they mean educating rather than sloganeering, they are overly impressed with what it is that presidents have to say to us and underimpressed by the immensity of the task. The opportunities to impart understanding are fewer than meet the eye.

All news media thrive on hoopla, on contest and conflict, on the big event. Television is more drawn to this than any other medium because it requires photogenic circumstances and must sustain an audience—what Robinson calls "the hoopla imperative."[27] All media addressed to popular audiences inevitably suffer from the hoopla imperative, but the electronics media more so. Television especially is inclined to focus on simple targets and on personalities, and to avoid the perplexing thicket of processes, institutions, and substantive policy dilemmas.

Whatever the specific effects of the mass electronics media on presidential-public relations, there may be longer-term and deeper impacts on institutions, on political authority, and on the trust on which legitimate authority in a constitutional system must be based. The effects of the modern media in this regard are quite speculative. We have no definitive evidence that there is less trust today than say in 1890 or, more importantly, more disgruntlement now than then. Nor can we say for sure that there is more skepticism now than a century ago, because we do not have comparable measures of such things. We cannot say if there are changes in these relationships that they can be laid exclusively at the doorstep of the modern mass media. We can only speculate on the basis of analyses of those effects in the present, and draw conjectures from them. In this regard, Michael Robinson fears that "our communications system may centralize authority while rendering the authorities themselves less respectable."[28]

There is, of course, much diversity in the media, and it is by no means the case that large tendencies toward increased cynicism about political institutions can be traced to media effects alone. The media, after all, are a prism, rarely an independent determinant. In some ways, the media probably had a more direct influence on political opinion in the heyday of yellow journalism at the turn of the century and during the days of the party press than today. Moreover, distrust feeds on real discontents, not just invented ones. Fed by its populistic roots, discontent with the responsiveness of leaders has been a mainstay of American politics. But the advent of the modern mass electronics media has helped shape the processes of politics and of governance both, making each more public than it had been. By highlighting contest in the former, an already candidate oriented system of politics tends to become even more so and, from this, volatility follows. By highlighting conflict and policy failures in government, the cognitive base from which discontent may spring is enlarged.

In sum, the public space has expanded substantially over the course of time. It has been promoted by advances in transportation, information and communications technology, and by the dramatic impact of the mass media, especially radio and television, both on political processes and on government. The expansion of the public space centralizes our focus, and provides for a national political realm. But it also increases elite visibility, public accessibility, and mass availability. On the whole, the effects have been presidency-centric, but that is not to say that these effects have been presidency-enhancing. For, with the increase in public focus on them, there has been no commensurate increase in the power presidents hold to successfully exert political leadership.

THE GROWTH OF INDIVIDUAL RATIONALITY

Closely linked to, indeed dependent on, the expansion in communications systems and the widening of the public space is a growth in individual rationality. Information richness, in fact, is a precondition for the spread of individual rationality, and, in turn, increased levels of education among the population provide for greater receptivities to information. These receptivities often enhance the preconditions for volatility. Higher levels of information and awareness tend to reduce organizational control and weaken traditionally based ties, although weaker party allegiances need not be an inevitable result.

Rationality is one of the trickier concepts in the language of social science, and it has been invested with several different meanings.[29] Here I emphasize the breakdown of traditional identities and loyalties and the enlargement of opportunities to make choices; in other words, the preconditions of rationality. We have seen already some of the effects of individual rationality at the elite level. The expansion of opportunities for members of Congress to protect themselves from once unalterable electoral forces has led many to try to maximize their insulation from such forces. The ensuing price to be paid is often in collective purpose, organizational maintenance, and effective policy making.[30]

Members of Congress differ both in their motivations and in their perceived needs, but they all have enlarged opportunities to minimize their electoral uncertainties and promote their individual goals. When the structured stability of strong central leadership in Congress devolved into committee fiefdoms, normative stability took its place. The Senate "Club" and Speaker Rayburn's dictum, "to get along, go along," exemplified this. It may as yet not be fully the case that today, "to get ahead, go it alone" is the appropriate normative tone within Congress, but the traditional structures and norms of deference and collective responsibility have given way to a more voluntaristic and individualistic assemblage. These tendencies are to be more fully discussed later in this chapter.

For now, however, I want to focus on the implications of the growth of rationality for two issues dealing with links between the public and bases for presidential success. The first involves mass electoral behavior, and its contemporary tendencies toward destabilization and susceptibilities to short-term influences. The second has to do with the public evaluation of presidents and the erosion of deferential support for the presidency.

Electoral Volatility

Habitual voting in the United States has waned. Defections from partisanship grew substantially throughout the 1960s and 1970s. The proportion of partisans in the electorate declined throughout this period, and even among the identifiable partisans there was a weakening of voting predictability.[31] For a longer period of time trends toward ticket splitting, lower turnouts, greater disparities in turnout across elections, and more volatile swings in the party vote have been occurring.[32] Over the long term, the control of local party organizations has grown infirm. Local party organizations were once in control of ballot forms, in mobilizing turnout (and perhaps in fraudulently reporting it as well), in dispensing patronage, and in providing for social amelioration. These activities made the local party organization into a powerful instrument. The march of voter mobilization, however, seems to have peaked with the firmness of the grip held by the local party organizations. As the grip weakened, as dependencies on local party organizations declined, and as voters became both more educated and susceptible to penetrable information, voters' choices became more individuated and influenced by short-term stimuli. Party, nonetheless, remains a powerful predisposition, and the power of habit when reinforced by other socializing agents is also great. That voters are less dependent and their environment more open does not by itself mean less partisanship or less partisan stability. It does mean that voters stand on their own more than was once the case—and that, in turn, means an electorate less locked in to predictable party-based choices.

This fluidity (or flexibility if one prefers) in the electorate tends to be more exaggerated among younger age groups and is not exclusive to the United States. A study of the Japanese public, for example, shows that between 1953 and 1973 the proportion of those claiming no party allegiance increased by three-fourths to a full one-third of the public. Among those in their twenties, however, this increase was two and one-third.[33] In Britain, Ivor Crewe describes "the younger generation of the salaried professional middle classes [and] the modern labor aristocracy of skilled, secure, high-wage property-owning workers,"[34] as being especially fluid in their allegiances. Most everywhere, apparently, these are the populations up for grabs.

The relationship between information and voter rationality is presumed to be intimate, if uncertain, in its effects. Naturally, a great deal depends upon the kind of information available to the voter, and the voter's predispositions toward the information. One perspective emphasizes that information, especially from the modern mass media, has a destabilizing influence on the behavior of voters, corroding their traditional identities and loyalties. Modern communications systems, from this perspective, are viewed as kaleidoscopic in their pacing of events, homogeneous, and fundamentally unwedded to overt political allegiances. Television is the epitome of this. One student of modern communications thus observes that the partisan, newspaper dominated system of communications (prevalent in the United States in the nineteenth century and, to some extent, still so in Europe), by segmenting audiences, emphasized the continuity of voters' affiliations and hence reinforced the stability of the party system. Television, in this view, with its undifferentiated audience and its claims to impartiality, tends to erode party affiliations and partisan stability.[35] One important change in the network of communications, according to this perspective, is its tendency to permeate diverse populations with homogenizing influences. Diffusion, thus, tends to erode traditional bases of behavior as personal horizons shift outward. This is the premise behind the belief that information promotes rationality, and rationality destabilizes prior identities.

A different perspective is associated with the view that increased levels of information actually reinforce partisan stability. A recent study of the West German electorate, for instance, concludes that exposure to televised political communication tends to reinforce stability in electoral choice.[36] The highly partisan voter, in other words, either seeks out political information or selectively perceives it so as to reinforce personal political predispositions. Much evidence, in fact, reveals a close connection between political information levels and stable political behavior, lending credence to hypotheses of reinforcing effects. Still, there are also indications that voters with unstable voting preferences over time are moderately high in their use of media.[37]

The influences of media use and partisan stability are inconclusive, and no doubt depend considerably upon characteristics of the voter, the character of the media, and, above all, the nature of the political context. That information does not have the same effects in all settings is handsomely illustrated in research comparing the visibility of French deputies and American representatives to their respective electorates. For while French deputies attribute even more weight than do U.S. representatives to personal standing with their electorates as a factor in the vote, they also attribute far greater importance to their party than do members of the U.S. House. Accordingly, the behavior of the French legislators is more party conforming than that of their American peers.[38] What may be destabilizing in one environment, therefore, may fail to have similar effects in another.

The intimate yet inconclusive relationship between information and rationality may be analogized to the situation of shoppers in a contemporary supermarket and an old-fashioned country store of a century ago. In the country store, the individual was both information and supply constricted. Customers made their purchases from the limited choices in the country store. In the contemporary supermarket, its shelves abundantly stocked with apparent variety, one is nearly overwhelmed by the range of possibilities. Choice is certainly influenced by predisposition, peers, and habit, but also by advertising and product design. In an era of sparse communications and segmented social networks, voters were in an environment somewhat akin to the old country store. A shopper's purchases would be unlikely to be diverted by eye-catching displays. In the present era, however, voters seem closer to shoppers in the supermarket. Choice is everywhere, at least superficially. Even when disciplined by a shopping list, the contemporary voter has more opportunity to be diverted by the array of stimuli from which to choose.

Thus, information leads to expanded opportunities for choice. It enhances rationality and induces uncertainty. Inevitably, it means more attention is given to the short-term components of the vote such as candidate evaluation and issues.[39] Voting patterns are more dynamic and volatile, and more dependent on short-term considerations—the products of enhanced voter rationality. The impact of these conditions, *inter alia,* is to stress candidacies and escalate promises while de-emphasizing parties. Declines in party cohesion are one likely result, and dividing the partisan base of an institutionally divided government is another.

Presidential Approval

Rationality suggests that people are more apt to make discrete judgments rather than ones based on loyalty and identity. In other words, they are more apt to be influenced by events, or by how events are filtered through the media, than by long-term commitments. Along with increased voter sensitivity to short-run environmental influences, approval of presidents also tends to be attuned to alterations in the environment. Although, as we discovered in Chapter 4, presidential popularity tends to spiral downward, the inner dynamic for explaining the curve rests with events and judgments of them. Richard Brody and Benjamin Page, for instance, have concluded that shifts in presidential popularity tend to move in the direction of good or bad news. Long-term tendencies resulting in the plummeting of presidential popularity, therefore, are best explained by a net valence in judgments of newsworthy events.[40] In short, presidents, like George Steinbrenner's managers, had better produce. Judging by the shape of their approval curves, however, the evidence of late has been that they are unable to do so.

In this regard, another researcher comments that "While most observers focus on the president's expanded authority and capacity for leadership, the evidence . . . here reveals that with authority comes responsibility. . . . Public opinion makes the president personally responsible." Consequently, "Sensing that the public is holding him responsible, the president is encouraged to engage in active problem-solving."[41] That presidents have gained more prominence and, thus, also more responsibility is consonant with modern tendencies toward centrism. That they have gained authority commensurate with the prominence so achieved is disputable. That most presidents now engage in active problem solving increases their prominence while it strains the centrifugal forces at work in the American system.

It is possible also that increased levels of education among the population have diminished rather than strengthened reserves of diffuse support for institutions in general, and presidents in particular. A study conducted by three investigators in the Bay Area indicates that those elements of the population that tend to provide the greatest amount of diffuse support for the presidency are drawn from among "the least knowledgeable and nonparticipant segments of the population."[42] In other words, according to the investigators, diffuse support is elicited from an ever-declining segment of the population.

Although the design of this study and its questions have not been replicated in national survey data, surveys conducted by the Center for Political Studies at the University of Michigan indicate that the decline in diffuse support has been far more homogeneous in its distribution across the population. Regardless, the decline of diffuse support will likely place the system under increasing pressure to perform. Lest the moral of this analysis fail to be understood, the direct translation of this proposition is that presidents will be under growing pressures to perform.

THE GROWTH OF INDEPENDENCE IN POLITICS

Mass media and the growing rationality and education of publics have helped expand public awareness. An important consequence has been the stimulus provided to a less rooted politics; a politics that is unusually vulnerable to the currents of short-term forces. There is some destabilization of traditional loyalties, more centralization of focus and responsibility on the president, and, in general, a more demanding reaction to government performance (or lack thereof). This more fluid environment at once constrains leadership by denying it predictable bases of support while providing opportunities for the pursuit of both self-interest and value maximization among individuals within the political elite.

The relative decline of longer-term partisan forces gives politicians more reason to be responsive to the things they think will make a difference in their electoral success or failure. In such an environment, party loyalty *qua* loyalty is a residual—the remainder of a subtraction process in which more pressing considerations are first given attention. This unpredictability means that for governing it is possible, as Anthony King notes, to gain majorities but not to build coalitions.[43] These processes are given fullest play in the United States, but the underlying currents are more diffused.

Another set of tendencies that further splinter political organization and make governing more vulnerable to individualistic and ideological motives is the growth of self-assertion and value maximization in politics, and the decline of deference and diffidence—in short the growth of independence.[44] The symptoms are not everywhere the same, however, because institutions do matter and the same motivations may interact differently with them. Yet, there is sufficient similarity among the symptoms to suggest a common underlying stream of motivations.

Participation and democratization are the watchwords of this new ethos. Stirring up action and trying to get a piece of it are subsidiary themes. Inside organizations and institutions, democratization and participation run counter to the spirit of organizational discipline, and assertiveness runs counter to the spirit of self-discipline.

In representative assemblies and in party politics, politicians are now drawn overwhelmingly from among the professional strata in society.[45] The growing proportions of British members of Parliament drawn from among the expressive occupations within this stratum has been traced by Anthony King (Table 5.1a).[46] The reputed rise of this expressive professional substratum to the political elite has been referred to with a strong hint of disapprobation by some (who are themselves members of this very same substratum) as "the new class."[47]

In the U.S. Congress, Table 5.1b reveals that representation of this substratum in the backgrounds of members has been strong for some time, and while it now constitutes nearly a fourth of the members serving in the Ninety-sixth Congress it is most unlikely that changes in congressional mores can be attributed to background characteristics alone. The influence of background by itself is therefore ambiguous at best. Whereas Anthony King believes that the new professionals in British politics have been responsible for putting a sharper edge on politics in Britain and for intensifying and polarizing conflict,[48] the professionalization of members' backgrounds in the West German Bundestag is seen by another observer as leading to reduced interparty conflict, a developed professional etiquette, and a possible limitation on the range of legislative responsiveness. Despite this, it is also claimed that professionalization of backgrounds in the Bundestag has led to an increased self-confidence and assertiveness among the legislators themselves.[49]

TABLE 5.1. Occupational Backgrounds of British MPs and American Members of Congress

(a) Percentages of Conservative and Labour MPs in Politics Facilitating Occupations, by Election

	1935	1945	1950	1951	1955	1959	1964	1966	1970	Feb. 1974	Oct. 1974	1979
Barristers and Solicitors	14.0	14.2	17.5	17.0	17.4	18.0	18.0	18.1	17.4	16.4	15.8	15.6
Journalists, Writers, Publishers, etc.	5.0	7.3	7.4	7.6	7.1	6.7	8.9	9.5	8.9	9.0	8.4	7.2
Lecturers	3.3	4.1	3.8	3.9	2.6	3.2	4.3	7.1	6.3	7.4	9.2	4.4
Schoolteachers	1.2	4.6	3.9	3.9	4.4	3.7	4.8	5.0	5.5	6.5	7.2	7.7
Communicators (i.e., sum of above three categories)	9.5	16.0	15.1	15.4	14.1	13.6	18.0	21.6	20.7	22.9	24.8	19.3

(b) Percentages of Members of Congress (House and Senate Combined) in Politics Facilitating Occupations, by Selected Congresses

	78th 1942	83rd 1952	88th 1962	93rd 1972	95th 1976	97th 1980
Lawyers	45.6	58.8	58.5	54.0	52.3	42.6
Journalists, Writers, Publishers	7.0	8.7	7.5	5.2	8.0	10.8
Academicians	2.4	4.1	3.4	3.9	5.2	5.6
Schoolteachers	3.8	8.3	5.6	9.0	7.1	7.3
Communicators (i.e., sum of above three categories)	13.2	21.1	16.5	18.1	20.3	23.7

Source (a): Anthony King, "The Rise of the Career Politician in Britain—and Its Consequences," *British Journal of Political Science* 11 (April 1981): 261. (Reprinted with permission of the Cambridge University Press.)

Sources (b): *Congressional Directory, Congressional Quarterly Almanac.*

Whatever its causes, there can be no mistake regarding the fundamental effects of membership assertiveness in legislative bodies (or for that matter in other organizations). A member of the Canadian cabinet comments on the motivations for the thrust toward self-assertion and its probable impact:

> . . . for other members of Parliament the most pressing necessity is to enlarge the role of backbenchers. This is a common aim of backbenchers in all parties. . . . Any great expansion in backbench activity would necessarily have to be in parliamentary committees. . . . Real improvement in the functioning of the parliamentary committees depends upon the possession and exercise of power by the standing committees: more control over their agenda and budget, the right to specialize, smaller membership . . . and increased status for chairmen, and the loosening of party bonds in both government and opposition. . . .
> . . . The greater independence that the Member of Parliament came to exercise in committees would be reflected in his general role in the party, and would lead to a greater diffusion of decision making. . . . The way to participatory democracy is . . . through a more obvious sharing of power in parliament among all members.[50]

The matter could hardly be stated more certainly. The diffusion of parliamentary and party caucus power and the constituency-tending behaviors of legislators have become notable in sites where they previously have seemed alien, and far more enlarged in the site (the U.S. Congress) where they have always seemed natural. There are stirrings in Canada and Britain, and West Germany, to be sure. But they have been far deeper in the United States where both structure and tradition are highly accommodating to the diffusion of power generated by self assertion.

The revolt of the formerly docile and intraparty fractiousness and indiscipline are linked events. Observers of the British Parliament have noted both a rise in the level of party cross-voting and a clamor among party backbenchers for increased participation through committees; in other words, a growing dissatisfaction among backbenchers with government by "the Government."[51] Throughout the 1970s, at least, there were backbench pressures for a diffusion of parliamentary power and an enhancement of the real power of Parliament. The result would be to decrease the authority of the parliamentary party, and hence the government, and (within Labour at least) to stiffen the powers of the constituent party organizations.

Structural or procedural change, influenced by recruitment, is at the heart of longer-term changes in legislative norms and behavior. One analyst of the British parliamentary scene, for instance, argues that "change in the underlying procedures by which a legislature has been presumed to operate may be critical to bringing about significant change in the behavior of incumbent members."[52] Even more importantly, in the words of another:

> The greater independence in voting behaviour in the Parliaments of the 1970s and the resulting Government defeats have meant not only that important precedents have been set, but their incidence has been such that many Members have ac-

quired new habits. The realization of the weakness of the constraints presumed previously to operate has meant that Members may maintain their habits in the current and future Parliaments.[53]

If I dwell here on changes in other parliamentary settings, it is because the events of the 1970s in the U.S. Congress resonate elsewhere. Always, local political conditions are the precipitant for reform and changed patterns of behavior, but their impetus is created by a newer political style, influenced partly through recruitment and partly through altered institutional socialization processes. The composite features of the newer style are more demanding and individualistic, more ideological in tone and yet less cohesive in partisan unity, more power diffusing and action oriented, and obviously less deferential and leadership sustaining.

The reforms of the U.S. Congress, of course, set it at a level of magnitude on each of these variables far greater than in any other legislative body, but that is because it has nearly always been that way. In some respects, the changes, though they nowhere attain the same level of magnitude as in the United States, are even more difficult for leaders in parliaments and in the executive in other settings to adjust to.[54] Even in a legislative institution renowned for its centrifugal effects, however, the change in Congress has been profound in terms of its power dispersing impact. "The degree of power dispersion now present," comment Joseph Cooper and David Brady, "is explicable in terms of present weaknesses in party unity or coherence both in absolute terms and relative to an organizational stucture that has grown far more complex in the past two decades."[55]

The diffusion of power fortified by the legislative reforms of the 1970s simultaneously increased legislative energy and decreased the capacity of Congress to act as an institution. New avenues for promoting special agendas were developed, and these have come to serve as vehicles for the promotion of the values and interests of members.[56] The multiplication of arteries, like the unintended effects of highway engineering, solidified rather than relieved legislative gridlock. As highway planners often belatedly discover, the highways they build do not so much relieve existing traffic as expand demand for more highways by increasing the traffic load. Similarly, the influence of legislative reform was to expand the sum of legislative energy, to enlarge the role of junior members, to activate commitments to specialized legislation, and to make committee chairs increasingly accountable to members. In so doing, it diminished arbitrariness, but also engendered messiness. Where once committee chairs arbitrarily could suffocate legislative proposals they didn't like, today specialized proposals are given new opportunities to survive, while large-scale ones may be more likely to suffer death by a thousand cuts. The activism of more members means more amending activity; the plethora of subcommittees means more hands wielding a scalpel (or voices trumpeting a proposal); and the result is often familiar—obstruction—but more obstreperously arrived at than previously.[57] There should be little wonder, therefore, at the trepidation of party leaders and executives elsewhere in contemplating similar trends in their systems.

Nowhere are these tendencies as far advanced as in the United States. And nowhere are they the result exclusively of younger and more ambitious and less deferential politicians. But everywhere parliaments are on their way to becoming more complex organizations, and not just simple extensions of "the Government." Everywhere, therefore, but obviously most extensively in the United States, executive leaders are operating in an environment of greater legislative unpredictability than in the past, an environment in which executive dominance in policy making is increasingly subject to challenge.[58]

In the United States, the consequences for the president have been stated with remarkable precision:

> The role of the President as "chief legislator" has been diminished. Members of Congress are increasingly independent from executive influence due to the weakening of political parties and the strengthening of Members' informational and representational resources.[59]

The growth of this **independence is partly** fostered by, while it further induces, the spread of ambition and the decline of deferential norms.

THE GROWTH OF INTERESTS

The growth of government is a growth also in its complexity and, thus, in its built-in resisters to centrally directed change. The more complex the pattern of growth and the more entangled the trail of bargains, the more points of resistance to central direction are capable of being engaged. "Complexity," says Richard Rose, "is central to the concept of organizational size." Therefore, "A big government is organizationally a complex government."[60] Complexity of structure inevitably makes central direction and coordination difficult even where party government gives the illusion of its attainability. Based upon his experience in the cabinet, a former British minister observes, for example, that "governments attempt to exert influence not power." In other words, "the government must consult, even negotiate, with other powerful factors in society."[61]

Among other things, then, big government makes central direction more problematic. It does so in at least three ways. First, by its long term spending commitments it decreases the generally available range of budgetary discretion. Second, it increases points of resistance to coordination. Third, and relatedly, it increases the vulnerabilities of governments to organized interests. These are tendencies, of course, not inevitabilities. The growth of governments in the post-World War II era, however, has been mainly in the form of expenditure commitments and of programs. Growth in sheer numbers of personnel has been less impressive than growth in the administrative units that have arisen both to administer programs and to oversee administration. Consequently, upper layers of officialdom and the funds they administer have been the real loci of growth.[62]

The Budgetary Barrier

It is best to begin with money because this is the most obvious way in which governments have grown, and, perhaps equally important, the most obvious way in which they constrain future direction. While the growth of governmental expenditures has proceeded less meteorically in the United States than in Europe, the growth rate still has been quite substantial. Between 1951 and 1976, Richard Rose and Guy Peters document real growth rates in public expenditures as being 179% in Britain, 254% in France, 188% in West Germany, 590% in Sweden, and 124% in the United States.[63] Much of this increase, in effect, is programmed, the result not of yearly discretionary judgments but of long-term commitments that in the United States are referred to as mandated or noncontrollable expenditures. In the United States, these account for an estimated 75% of the federal government's budgetary commitments.

To some extent, "noncontrollable" is a misnomer. There is nothing to prevent political action from changing laws that commit the expenditure of public funds automatically, and there already has been some tinkering on the margins of such commitments in the United States. To alter such commitments in a major way, however, takes great political will. That will must resonate throughout the political system, though, and not simply emanate from its executive center. It is clearly difficult to generate that will even where political structures are more favorable for doing so than they are in the United States.

One of the major reasons for this difficulty lies with factors that make political intervention costly. For one of the great areas of expenditure growth has been in transfer payments to individuals, especially in the form of pension and medical insurance benefits. And where pension and medical benefits are concerned, demography is nearly destiny.[64] As populations grow older, more must be expended on social provision, barring changes in existing expenditure patterns. Ironically, as populations age and more of the population therefore becomes dependent on pension benefits and uses more health services, the political prowess of the beneficiaries could well be further enhanced.

To central leaders bent on restrictive budgetary policies, the capacity to *limit* expenditures will be affected by the transpartisan nature of the interests arrayed against them, and the capacity to *reshape* the pattern of expenditures will be especially influenced by the nature of the affected interests. Existing expenditure patterns create stakeholders in the programs, and the stakeholders inhibit two different sets of initiatives: (1) alteration in the *overall level* of expenditure (downward), and (2) alteration in the *distribution* of expenditures. The former is likely to affect those leaders pursuing a program of budgetary retrenchment. The latter (the shifting of resources across sectors) may affect leaders of any political orientation. Where money is spent, then, interests are sure to follow. Thus there is, as the authors of a study of federal government transfers to states and communities argue, a tendency toward prodistributive rather than redistributive funding—stability in the structure of expenditures and dynamism in terms of new demands.[65]

To some extent, the resistance of government expenditure patterns to straightforward executive manipulation represents a triumph of the organic continuity of government over the efforts of its momentary leaders. It represents the institutionalization of past policies and their implicit present acceptance against the ambitions of temporary rulers. Whether interpreted with hope or with pessimism, President Reagan is fond of remarking that "the mistakes of fifty years cannot be undone in just a few years." A powerful impetus from the executive center means that change cannot be wholly thwarted, but comprehensive aspirations will be steadily tempered. The flip side, however, is that the tension between the accumulated claims (and claimants) from the past, and the capacity of governments to steer a course beyond them is also steadily mounting.

Subgovernmental Obstacles

The growth of the state also means the proliferation of subgovernments. With liberal democracy comes the legitimacy of autonomous interest groups. With growth and complexity of government comes an intimate relationship between interests and government. Lord Armstrong, former head of the British civil service, noted that in Whitehall "there is now almost certainly somewhere in the government a little unit of people whose job it is to acquaint themselves with what is happening in each industry and, as far as they can, watch over its interests."[66] This sort of segmentation is everywhere, and is nearly everywhere accepted as an appropriate norm. The dilemma of reconciling effective governance of the whole with responsiveness to its parts is a continuing concern of modern representative governments. Because there is always a struggle between the whole and the parts, both the form of government and beliefs about governance influence how the struggle is waged and the means by which bargains are reached.

While the form of the relationship between interests and government is not reducible to any single or comprehensive definition across an entire policy system, and may even vary over time within the same policy domain, some modalities can be spotted. Interest formation tends to reflect the structure of governmental authority, and the splintering of American governmental authority is thus conducive to the formation of many voluntary associations.[67] The fragmentation of governmental authority not only begets many groups likely to represent narrower constituencies than European interest groups, it also begets interest-government relations that are splintered, segmented, and reduced to virtually molecular level. Despite this, the politics of semiautonomous small groups intimately nuzzled into the bureaucracy is no more predominant in the United States than it is in Europe. In some ways, it is less predominant because it is seen as less legitimate and more conflictual with democratic ideals than in Europe. It is true, however, that the politics of small groups in the United States is paradigmatic of significant amounts of policy (or policy-deterring) activity, and that its form is typically more microscopic than in European contexts.

Small group politics in the Unitd States often consist of what has been labeled a "cozy little triangle" of dominant but narrow-based interests, bureau level officials, and congressional subcommittees. Under such circumstances, segmented attachments between interests and governmental agencies tend to become relatively secure niches. The relationship in the United States between interests and government is often at such a molecular level, however, that there is a natural resistance to central control or even to centralized bargaining. The particulate form of these attachments, in other words, is linked to the relative weakness of central bargaining instruments, the relative narrowness of interests (which therefore have no need for, or interest in, central bargaining), and the division of authority (which makes it virtually impossible to define a central bargaining partner).

Political structure, in other words, influences forms of interest group-governmental relationship, processes of bargaining, and attainable outcomes. The Office of Management and Budget (OMB) is an administrative invention designed to enable the presidency to do that which the Constitution deigned not to, namely to provide a centralized bargaining mechanism with the parts of government. OMB does have impressive technical capacity and substantial organizational memory. Despite its technical capacity, however, OMB lacks what the British Treasury has—a political support system. "While the [British] Treasury," in the words of one scholar, "by no means wins all the battles with departments, it does through the cabinet have a mechanism for endorsing bargains and enforcing decisions. Such a centre of authoritative decision making is lacking in Washington."[68] In contrast, the cabinet in the United States is merely a collection of department heads, not a collective entity.

Comparisons, of course, also invite romance. There is some temptation to overestimate the role of the cabinet in British government and to underestimate the will and ability of presidents to gain administrative compliance with their general directives, thus cutting through subgovernmental formations.[69] It may be, however, that subgovernments more often are broken up by forces operating beyond the range of presidential intervention. The cozy triangles, after all, can be made less cozy through the glare of public exposure. Dramatic incidents also may change the status of interest group links as evidenced by the altered relationship between the nuclear industry and the Nuclear Regulatory Commission after the Three Mile Island accident. Charles O. Jones comments that such events transform "cozy little triangles" into "sloppy large hexagons," involving and engaging interdependent interest segments.[70] Certainly, the enlarged capacity for drama and the upsurge of public interest groups in America makes it more difficult, rather than less so, to sustain "cozy little triangles." Yet, from the vantage point of central coordination such conditions may escalate rather than ameliorate presidential problems in getting a handle on government.

The Swirl of Interests

The metaphor of "cozy little triangles" connotes a system at rest rather than a system characterized by restlessness. It suggests an image of scattered, highly stable, and autonomous policy systems rather than entrepreneurial energy and advocacy. It suggests certainly the notion of structurally definable subsystems and of limited and clearly demarcated sets of actors. According to Hugh Heclo, however, "cozy little triangles" may no longer be the right nomenclature for the level of disaggregation (and penetrability) that has occurred in Washington.[71]

The segmentation, semiautonomy, and enclosed circle of participants characteristic of the cozy triangles image have been supplemented, if not partially supplanted by the emergence of more fluid networks of policy experts; of single issue interest groups; and of specialists in the bureaucracy, in the Congress, and from interest groups and other levels of government. Whereas the stable small group politics of cozy triangles was independent, according to Heclo, the new buzzsaw of issue-interest networks is interdependent.[72] These purported networks both integrate functional specialists and, by making policy endlessly debatable, dissolve consensus and certainty.

While resistant to central direction, subgovernments (the image of cozy triangles) represented points of stability and insulation. In Heclo's view, the growth of policy creates issue publics, mobilizes them, and creates interdependencies among them. "Activist policies," Heclo claims, "greatly increase the incentives for groups to form around the differential effects of these policies, each refusing to allow any other group to speak in its name." Moreover, Heclo continues, "if the current situation is a mere outgrowth of old tendencies, it is so in the same sense that a 16-lane spaghetti interchange is the mere elaboration of a country crossroads. With more public policies, more groups are being mobilized and there are more complex relationships among them."[73]

These "spaghetti strands" reach into Congress in the form of the growing array of specialized caucuses and the proliferation of organizational entities demanding specialized staff personnel.[74] They have even slipped into the White House, according to Heclo, complicating its management. Counting no less than ten divisions devoted to special groupings in the Carter White House before the beginning of the 1980 campaign, and noting the existence of over eighty advisory committees on the Reagan transition staff, Heclo concludes that presidential power has become "more extended, scattered, and shared," and thus "less unilateral and closely held by the man himself."[75] Why has this happened? In Heclo's view, it has happened because of a growth in policy constituencies and a decline in stable political and governing reference points. Presidents, therefore, must establish their own outreach to constituencies. The staffing necessary to do this, Heclo claims, perpetuates an interest in continuing to deal with these constituencies and their problems.[76]

Disaggregation and, as James Wilson notes, the American penchant to think of government largely as a focal point for representation are constraints.[77] What seems to be new is the growth in participants and the fluidity of once familiar bases of organization.[78] Following this course of reasoning, what once existed in the form of stable particles has been turned into a high-energy whirlwind. From stability and disaggregation have come fluidity and further dissolution. The imagery of issue networks—subsystems of policy entrepreneurs which heighten the ability to raise issues and impair the ability to resolve them—contrasts with the notion of subgovernmental monopolies formed around the protection of narrow but stable interests. The tendency, in other words, is toward freewheeling advocacy, and the result is not so much stalemate or autonomous fiefdoms as it is unmanageability at any level. Although thresholds certainly differ across political systems, these tendencies toward policy diffusion may be spreading. A British scholar, for instance, comments that while in the United States, "one can . . . see more of the qualities of issue networks than formerly . . . for Britain one can similarly identify movement . . . in the direction of issue networks."[79]

Subsystem politics, whatever its form, is always a problem for central leadership. But the base line of aggregation remains important, and while the locus of decision making in the United States has become increasingly centered in Washington, there is little evidence that decision making itself has become more centralized. In some ways, the more decision making has been centered in Washington the less of a center of gravity there seems to be. A contrast between the more decentralized yet less diffuse Canadian government and the more centralized but also more diffuse American government makes this clear:

> Canadian and U.S. political decentralization are vastly different. National government in the United States is unrivaled in its authority to set social policy, but this "central" government is itself divided into competing institutions, making agreement dependent on transitory coalitions. The system gives special opportunities to interest groups and to entrepreneurship by public officials, bureaucrats, and outside experts. In Canada, responsibility for social policy is shared between national and regional governments. . . . [But] The tightness of the policymaking circle is increased by the centralization of power within federal and provincial governments.[80]

No single description of interest relations with government is adequate, of course. There are "cozy little triangles" *and* "sloppy large hexagons"; there are transpartisan issue networks *but* also ones wired into partisan boards.

If Hugh Heclo is right, however, subsystems are becoming harder to track and to neatly identify. This has made them even more resistant to being harnessed. The growth of government has helped proliferate interests; the age of television has helped dramatize issues; and the era of computerized mailing lists and deepened public attentiveness has helped to mobilize new constituencies around them. Moreover, the rise in attentiveness and the decline in diffidence implies that governments are increasingly becoming focal points for representation, not simply instruments of governance. Like most other central leaders, the American president will be expected to cut through the Gordian knot of pressures. His knot, though, will be more entangled than those of most other governing heads, and his experience at such tasks unusually rare. Much like the system he represents, he will be skilled more at advocacy than at bargaining, more at representing than at governing.

If the relative quiescence of small group politics as semiautonomous subsystems has given way in certain respects to the swirl of more complicated and open subsystems (and whether it has, or how conclusively it has, remains to be researched), it is not self-evident that these are insoluble in the presence of strong aggregating or command mechanisms. Surely, a government that sets out to do less, by definition, will create fewer constituencies, although it may continue to be hemmed in by those already in existence, especially those that are interpartisan and well-levered. It also remains unclear to what extent the apparent cross-circuitry of issue networks can be plugged into a party switchboard. To what extent, in other words, can interests be linked to parties—and, if linked, which becomes the dog and which the tail? The Democrats' emphasis on government as a problem solver makes them especially inclined to be an interest creator. By their diversity they seem unusually susceptible to becoming the appendage of their agglomerated issue publics.

Messiness is inherent in the demands for representation and participation that seem endemic now to the industrialized democracies, but the extent of seeming indissolubility will reflect foremost the features of governmental authority itself and those of governing coalitions. Cutting through the "mess" is possible for presidents of steely purpose and of single mind; those focused on the contraction of government and accompanied by substantial legislative majorities with a shared perspective. Blessed with the legislative majorities that Republican presidents of the 1920s enjoyed, for instance, a president such as Ronald Reagan, bent on shrinking the governmental reach, would reduce much of the "messiness"—indeed, this, in some degree, already may be happening.

The costs of "cutting through" are also very real, however, and they can mean polarization and intensified conflict. Governing in a system of separated institutions and multitudinous points of authority, as Lester Salamon aptly points out, is a shared responsibility and depends as deeply upon the strengthening of capability among other institutions as it does in the presidency.[81] "All power" to a plebiscitory president might well enable presidents to cut through the "mess," but this gain is apt to be only short-lived while perhaps purchased at a frightful cost in legitimacy. Strengthening the collective governing power of institutions to balance their representative propensities, on the other hand, might help government to function with both heart and mind. Abstractly put, there is nothing to prevent a strengthening of governmental institutions, but also nothing in the trends heretofore discussed to encourage it.

WHEN THE BLOOM IS OFF THE ROSE

The proliferation of interests and of policy subsystems results not exclusively but inevitably from the growth of governmental activity and intervention. As numerous interests are the product of the interventionist tendencies of the modern state, so too is the modern state dependent in some measure on the interests it has fostered. Anthony King claims, therefore, that "each dependence . . . reinforces the others" with "their cumulative effect" being "to make the enterprise of government more difficult to carry on."[82]

These dependencies have grown, and our attitudes toward them have changed even more remarkably. A once common view celebrated both pluralistic diversity and the capacity of governments under skillful governors to manage it.[83] But such a view seems now to have faded, and to have been replaced by fears of governmental "overload" and concerns about the paralysis of authority. Overload, roughly defined, is the disequilibrium between the degree to which government is held responsible and the degree to which it is granted authority.[84] Lest the views of an earlier period be excessively romanticized, it is worth recalling that over thirty years ago David Truman wrote that interests "that must operate through the governmental mechanism and whose functions of stabilizing relationships in a complex society require a measure of coordinated treatment of group demands will, in the absence of stable and integrated lines of access, disrupt the political system."[85] Still, the earlier view seemed more salutary regarding the manageability of dispersed power. Now, the question of who governs has been replaced by the question, Can anyone govern?

There are a number of factors making the problem of governability and, thus, the manageability of interests seem more pressing. The central factors already have been discussed in this chapter. These need, however, to be set against the backdrop of the more limiting circumstances that have afflicted all of the Western economies throughout the 1970s (especially the late 1970s), and which have grown worse thus far in the 1980s. The data in Table 5.2 show that in all of the seven economic summit countries unemployment and inflation increased. These figures, in fact, understate the harsher realities on the economic front since relatively good times in the early 1970s mask the effects of stagflation prevalent from the mid-decade of the 1970s nearly to the present.

The increment of real growth has been too constricted to provide for much public slack. Instead of adding to the net beneficiaries of public goods, subtracting from them has become the calculus of the present. The stakes have become more obvious and, by becoming more obvious, also have become more conflictual.[86] Indeed, in some quarters, the growth of interests and the stagnation of Western economies are seen as being more than coincidental. A British analyst of jeremiad outlook, for instance, contends that "a society where legislation can be enforced only if it enjoys the tacit long run acceptance of all major groups, including those on the losing side" will place "an *excessive burden . . . on the 'sharing out' function of government.*"[87]

Now that the economic bloom is off the rose, the inevitable tension between governability, on the one hand, and interest and value maximization, on the other, has become more salient. New agendas are being imposed, and such agendas are

TABLE 5.2. Unemployment and Inflation in the 1960s and 1970s in the Economic Summit Countries

	Unemployment Rate 1960s	Unemployment Rate 1970s	Increase in Consumer Price Index through 1960s	Increase in Consumer Price Index through 1970s
Canada	5.1	6.7	+14.1	+67.9
France	1.8[a]	3.9[a]	+18.1	+79.3
Germany	1.0	2.9	+15.0	+41.7
Italy	5.2	6.4	+15.7	+122.5
Japan	1.3	1.7	NA	+59.1
United Kingdom	1.9	4.1	+8.2[b]	+116.9[b]
United States	4.8	6.2	+13.1	+62.9

[a]Unemployment rates in France adjusted to approximate U.S. measurements.

[b]Consumer prices in United Kingdom incomplete. Increase in United Kingdom is measured in wholesale price index.

Sources: OECD, Main Economic Indicators: Historical Statistics, 1960-1979 (Paris: OECD, June 1980), U.S. Government Social Indicators (Washington, D.C.: U.S. Department of Commerce, December 1981), OECD Observer (Paris: OECD, March 1981).

less apt to meet with acceptance. Faced with low growth rates, high inflation and unemployment, and continuing (if now lessening) concerns over the availability and price of raw materials and energy, demands for leadership likely will be issued in the abstract but retracted in the pinch. The problems of making decisions in governments, and then making them stick will be felt in all systems.

Bad times are not new, and those of recent times pale dramatically in contrast to the 1930s. At that time, however, government was small and knowledge was scarce. In the 1930s the absence of knowledge may well have strengthened a consensus for solutions predicated on faith, a precondition for followership. In an environment marked by uncertainty, however, presidents will be under pressure to provide clear vision and ultimately "favorable results." But despite the ready availability of "experts" in and hovering around government, expertise itself is no balm since its appropriate application is retrospective and not prospective.[88]

Now thoroughly marbled with interests, the steering capacity of government is increasingly limited as its activities have expanded. Responsibility is now centralized but power remains diffused. More leadership will be asked for and less followership given. So, while leadership from the White House frequently will be urged, supporting resources will as frequently be withheld by other elites. All in all, such conditions should not be inhospitable to the growth of cynicism.

THE ENDLESS CAMPAIGN

Our elaboration of trends affecting leadership and governability thus far has focused on those that are both universal and not highly manipulable. A trend, however, that is often seen as widening the gap between the processes of presidential selection and the possibilities of presidential governance is both unique to America and, for the most part, manipulable. It is the self-constructed labyrinth to the presidential nomination.

The multiplication of primary elections, as Table 5.3 shows, has been substantial just between 1968 and 1980. The number of primaries has more than doubled on the Republican side and almost doubled on the Democratic side. As a further glance at Table 5.3 reveals, the percentage of delegates chosen through the primary election route also has about doubled. This long-haul process of nomination places a premium on candidate organization instead of party organization, and emphasizes candidate financing rather than party financing. It advantages non-officeholders as office seekers and, by its sheer length, makes the politicization of government itself virtually ceaseless. This last, and probably most neglected, point may in fact have the farthest reaching implications. Before addressing it, I want first to focus on the more commonly discussed impact of the "new" processes of selection on the relationship between nominee and party, and, most particularly, the reputed implications of this relationship for governing. The implications of the relationship between selection process and nominee, and between selection process and governance, are not at all straightforward, however, though they often have been overstated.

TABLE 5.3.   Proliferation of Presidential Primaries, 1968-80

Party and Coverage	1968	1972	1976	1980
Democratic Party				
Number of states using a primary for selecting or binding National Convention delegates	17	23	29[a]	31[a]
Number of votes cast by delegates chosen or bound by primaries	983	1,862	2,183	2,489
Percentage of all votes cast by delegates chosen or bound by primaries	37.5	60.5	72.6	74.7
Republican Party				
Number of states using a primary for selecting or binding National Convention delegates	16	22	28[a]	35
Number of votes cast by delegates chosen or bound by primaries	458	710	1,533	1,482
Percentage of all votes cast by delegates chosen or bound by primaries	34.3	52.7	67.9	74.3

[a]Does not include Vermont which held a nonbinding presidential preference primary.

Source: Austin Ranney, ed., *The American Elections of 1980* (Washington: American Enterprise Institute, 1981), p. 369. (Reprinted with permission of the American Enterprise Institute.)

It is true certainly that the processes of presidential selection have been subject to a surfeit of participation, democracy, and also penetrability from forces with little involvement in organizational maintenance and continuity. But it is not at all clear that such processes produce better or worse nominees; that is, persons more or less fit for office. Closed processes, after all, produced Warren G. Harding and Calvin Coolidge, whereas Dwight Eisenhower and John F. Kennedy had to establish their appeal initially to mass electorates before convincing a number of important party insiders.

No process, however, guarantees that if elected nominees would be able to rely on their party's support in governing. Even when selection was made at the conventions rather than merely ratified during them, the separability of presidential and congressional party existed. Among other things, therefore, a lot depends on the state of internal party cohesion, and on the oportunities given to members of Congress to maximize their electability independent of their party. So long as the latter is permitted, the former will be in doubt. The difference, for instance, between Italy's Christian Democrats and America's Democrats is hardly in their surface propensities for cohesion; it lies instead in what behaviors are sanctioned.

The drawn out process of campaigning for the nomination and the ultimate increase in the influence of primary electorates, of course, does weaken the organic integrity of the parties as decision makers. National conventions are no longer decision-making arenas. They largely ratify decisions that have been made elsewhere. Undoubtedly, the parties can reduce the amount of time spent in contesting for nomination, but whether shortening the lengthy string of primaries and party caucuses would produce nominees better able to govern if elected is a good question with an unknown answer. The real question is whether the nominee may rely on party support if elected.

There is generally, I think, a good bit of confusion on the subject of party control in selecting the presidential nominee, and the effects that this presumably will have in improving governability. A key assumption is that necessary pacts will have to be reached between the nominee and sets of party intermediaries. An additional assumption is that a more party controlled selection process will eventuate in the selection of insiders—candidates familiar with the ropes in Washington. Although there turn out to be a number of different and noncompatible ropes to be learned in Washington, experience at governing is frequently at odds with partisan enthusiasms. Conclaves of party enthusiasts push goals and ideological nostrums. But much in Washington, even in the face of other changes we have discussed, still revolves around smoothing out rather than polarizing relations.

The Washington insider, at least on the legislative front, is a tag applied to those able to bring about interpartisan agreements and, in general, to bring agreement from diversity. Good credentials though these may be for governing, there is no indication that such persons would be particularly likely nominees by design under a system of selection dominated by party officials. Robert Kerr, Richard Russell, and Lyndon Johnson, for instance, failed to make it in a more controlled environment than now. Qualities for exercising influence in Congress are one consideration for presidential selection, but not necessarily a central one. It might be helpful if this were the case, but there is no indication that it is. Nor that it ever was. Moreover, the qualities needed for effectiveness within Congress are not necessarily the same as those demanded for effectiveness in the White House, much less for gaining title to it.

An even more central assumption about the value of promoting greater party control over the nomination process rests upon the idea that parties must provide the organizational means for governance, but that governance itself must be facilitated by extensive brokerage activity within the party. Nominees, therefore, should be products of the power-brokerage and intermediary functions of the parties. A nominee who emerges from such a process presumably will be obeisant to his party rather than a commander of it. Such a notion is implicit but prevalent in the appeals of those who scorn "activists," "amateurs," and ideological enthusiasts. Yet it is almost antique in conception. It assumes that there are power brokers to be had and bargains to be made among them. And that assumption rests on a further one, namely, that power brokers command continuous organizational resources. There is no longer any evidence to suggest this is so in an era when the power brokers are themselves ephemeral. So, from just precisely where the resources of these power brokers are to be derived on a continuing basis remains enigmatic.

A key presumption, further, is that power brokers have their feet on the ground rather than their heads in the clouds, and thus a selection process in which their preferences dominate, or are bargained over, will encourage moderation in the candidates so chosen. It is, in the first place, unlikely that power brokers, so described, are to be found, and, in the second place, to the extent that they can be found, they are likely to be drawn from amidst the congeries of citizen and issue groups that have sprung up in recent years—an insubstantial base, one might think, for encouraging moderation. The lengthy process of primaries and caucuses and the hoopla surrounding them does tend to encourage the entrance of candidates of less political seasoning than those once selected by party insiders, but not ones more or less moderate. Ironically, one of the most forceful and articulate proponents of the power brokers school, James Ceaser, claims that Carter's nomination in 1976 held "the Democratic coalition together in a way that would have been the envy of any power brokers." He finds it difficult, however, to accept the logic of his own claim, asserting instead that Carter was an outsider whose "unique accomplishment was to have been an insurgent of the middle."[89] One, I assume, could be an "insurgent" of the middle only because the space was vacated by candidacies perceived as being more fractious of the loose bindings holding together a remarkably diverse political party. Ceaser is right. It is difficult to imagine a set of power brokers doing better—at least from the standpoint of winning elections.

If not on grounds of political moderation, then, is Ceaser's concern more nearly justified on grounds of political seasoning? That is, would a conclave of party insiders select someone they did not really know? The answer appears to be yes. How else, after all, did the array of outsider candidacies of former military heroes get pushed to the top in eras not subject to the present methods of mass involvement in the nomination process? Moreover, a good many Democratic insiders were perfectly willing to press for General Eisenhower's candidacy in 1948, even though his basic party sympathies were unknown! And, obviously, some Republican insiders were willing to press his candidacy in 1952, although they barely knew him better. Whatever General Eisenhower's political seasoning by virtue of his command posts in the army, by conventional definitions he was also surely a neophyte.

One must distinguish, of course, between party insiders. Some may have national vote maximizing criteria in mind. But a good many more have in mind local vote maximizing criteria, and that can mean something entirely different. Increasingly, but consonant with other trends discussed in this chapter, many also employ value maximizing criteria. This third group, and in some respects the second as well, are less apt to encourage moderation than they are rabid partisanship. Taft, not Eisenhower, was their preference.

Under the present plebiscitory system, Ceaser argues that the problem is that successful candidates think they "own" their party, and need not answer to specific persons who can hold them accountable.[90] It is hard to imagine a less apt image, not to mention what "specific persons" Ceaser might have in mind. Richard Nixon and Lyndon Johnson (the latter, ironically, the ultimate insider) undoubtedly influence Ceaser's view. Nixon, however, ignored his party rather than asserted proprietorship over it. More fundamentally, it is implausible that Nixon's behaviors or policies would have been moderated by greater accountability to his party, however his party might be defined. Greater accountability to "his party" no doubt would have stifled the Moynihan inspired family assistance proposal and the Kissinger inspired diplomatic initiatives with both China and the Soviet Union. Possibly, greater accountability to "his party" would have deterred the involvement of some of the fringe characters and operations associated with Watergate and the "Plumbers." But corruption and scandal in the presidency didn't originate with Nixon. In fact, they were particularly prevalent during the presidencies of Grant and Harding when party brokers were much more in control of things.

Johnson did attempt to assert proprietorship over his party, and though he won most of the battles he ultimately lost the war. Mostly, Johnson appealed to party stalwarts, such as they were. As in Nixon's case, there is no evidence that he was opposed in any significant way by party leaders until sharp declines in public confidence set in. Even then, what remained of the power brokers continued to support him. In Johnson's case, his policies and style simply divided an always potentially fractious party. No party leaders were known to be moderating his course, however. In foreign policy, at least, that role fell to individuals of impeccable establishment credentials in foreign policy and finance, hardly constituencies that Democratic power brokers would be engaged in brokering.

In the cases of Gerald Ford and Jimmy Carter, the image of either "owning" his party is mildly amusing. Neither, it is true, had a center of gravity in his party, which in Ford's case, with his congressional insider credentials and repute as a partisan, is especially astonishing. Basically, however, this had less to do with their behavior,[91] and much more to do with the steady rightward drift of the Republicans and the dazzling diversity of the Democrats.[92]

As the cases of John Tyler and Andrew Johnson demonstrate, the problem of connecting president to party is now new. There is also a need, however, to connect party to president in the process of governing. If presidents need to be bound to their party and to coordinate their electoral efforts more,[93] there has to be an identifiable party core which must face up to the responsibilities of governing. No president can overcome, nor should we expect any to, messianic impulses within the parties that constrain policy by radicalizing it. Nor can a president overcome deep internal party division.

Discontinuity between presidential campaign organizations and party organizations has been going on for a long time now (Reagan in 1980 excepted)—too long to be attributed exclusively to the dramatic upsurge in primaries or their plebiscitory character.[94] It has been going on because in an era of mass communications the unpredictability of the nomination process will necessarily be more drawn out and more public. For unless American parties are to be truly Europeanized (an event of highly improbable proportions), securing the nomination will require candidates to have their own personal organization in place which, understandably, they will be reluctant to part with at later stages.

Since the advent of the New Hampshire primary as the premier winter season sporting event (challenged now by the Iowa caucuses and numerous "straw polls"), early *de facto* organization and candidacy have been important because good early showings are deemed to be critical.[95] The introduction of federal money into the nomination process since the 1976 campaign simply forces the *de facto* to become *de jure*. Rather than the long string of primaries, federal election money is the chief encouragement to the proliferation of candidacies which, in turn, contributes to unpredictability. The more candidacies there are, one analysis of the process suggests, the greater the role played by expectations and, consequently, the more early front runners tend to suffer.[96]

The longer the process, as well, the more officeholding candidates are affected as larger amounts of their time must be spent campaigning. Every fourth year, the Senate usually is quieter by several voices. Running for the presidency has become a full-time occupation in itself, and the irony in that, as Lyndon Johnson must surely have known in 1960, and Howard Baker in 1980, is that public officials with large responsibilities are disadvantaged. The length of the process seems most destructive particularly to the prospects of the Washington insiders—those holding leadership positions or otherwise playing prominent roles on Capitol Hill. It does provide opportunities, on the other hand, for those seeking, but not presently burdened with, responsibility. The process also enables candidates to throw verbal brickbats in the direction of Washington while noting their own lack of responsibility for the evils apparently lurking therein.

The most profound impact of the ceaseless campaign, however, has been its extensive overlap, and therefore inevitable competition, with governing. "To everything there is a season" with perhaps two large exceptions—American professional sports and American campaign politics. Both need to grab attention and money. The spread of the political season implies also the spread of politicization, and a tendency for incumbent sensitivities to anticipated reactions to become hyperactive. "The weight which will be given public opinion in presidential decisions," asserts a former presidential adviser, "increases in inverse ratio to the number of days remaining before a presidential election."[97] There now being more points of electoral contest and more specialized publics, there is also likely to be more attention to the immediate political impact of policy choice. Governments elsewhere soon come to recognize that in at least one out of four years it is difficult to expect significant decisions to be made in Washington.

Incessant politicking—the consequence of an open selection process—tends to eclipse governance. Symbols, promises, and interests are the language of one; feasible policies the product of the other. The time span available to move the latter is foreshortened by the lengthening time span devoted to the former—the result especially of the equity in presidential campaign financing generated by federal campaign law and, more generally, of the openness of selection processes. The long political season compresses the time available for presidents to focus on governing. While Richard Neustadt thought the third year of the presidential term would be the one during which presidents could maximize their leverage, the third year increasingly is crowded out by preparations for campaign activity, as presidents no longer can count on anticipating a struggleless renomination. Whatever the intrinsic merits of the process (it is greatly democratic) or the quality of the candidates produced (probably not greatly different from other processes), its sheer length detracts from the business for which politics is waged, the process of policy making.

CONCLUSION

Of the several trends discussed in this chapter, all but the endless political campaign can be generalized across the industrialized democracies. Because they impact at different times and across different political contexts, however, the effects on governing and politics are not always precisely the same or of the same magnitude. The main feature though stands out as a paradox: growth in the centrality of leadership and a dispersion of power to effectively govern. An attentive observer of British government, for instance, claims that while "the Prime Minister has much greater power within the political system . . ." that outside "the institutions of government, the modern Prime Minister may be weaker than his nineteenth century predecessors." This is because "governments have undertaken responsibilities which their Victorian predecessors would never have contemplated; responsibilities which are intrinsically harder to achieve and which require the support of powerful pressure groups, thus conceding to such groups considerable veto power."[98]

The trends discussed are more interactively powerful than the sum of each alone. Indeed, it is hard to imagine some in the absence of others. Without a rich communications environment, for example, it is difficult to imagine the enormity of the growth in political rationalism and individuation or, obversely, the breakdown of traditional organizational bindings. The net effect is an environment that is more fluid and dynamic and in which less can be taken for granted. Volatility produces centrifugal tendencies and, ironically, such tendencies occur both in the midst of a growth in government and in the expectations held toward central leadership.

In absolute terms, central authority in democratic settings is everywhere today more powerful than it had been, but is nowhere as powerful as it needs to be in order to meet the escalation of expectations. Governments have grown bigger and more prominent while their central steering capacities seem to have become ever more tentative and dependent. These are tendencies, of course, and not absolutes. Resolve to carry forth substantial change have been apparent recently in Britain and the United States, although resolve alone cannot call forth favorable outcomes. As with Hotspur in Shakespeare's *Henry IV,* the resolve to call forth spirits from the deep is mocked by their unwillingness to come.

Nostalgia induces romance, making us think that there was a golden age in which things were better. But it is difficult to deny that governing is more difficult today if for no other reason than because government attempts to deal with more difficult problems. Ultimately, it is the belief in the omnipotence of policy, a matter which is independent of the size of government, that is the culmination of many of the tendencies we have observed. Reformist or restorationist, governments will continually fall below the expectations held of them until their leaders first convince themselves, before they can convince others, that much lies beyond the grasp of solubility. To modern politicians, this is a request alien to their calling, one not apt to ring with resonance. For politicians in modern democracies most often get where they are by escalating promises of what ought to be done rather than dwelling on the limits of "doing."

Modern trends seem to engender policy escalation while splintering political power. They have made presidents more central figures in our political and governing constellation, central enough to publicize agendas, to articulate visions and ideals, to command presence, and to be magnets for criticism. Trends have made more difficult for presidents that which was always difficult but less aspired to—command of the instrumentalities of government and control over policy. Centrism of expectation amidst fragmentation and volatility in the governing and political base generally has been growing. And that makes presidents responsible without much opportunity for making them effective.

Trends everywhere seem to have simultaneously deepened dependencies on leaders while weakening the basis for leadership, but these have been felt especially strongly in the United States. Partly that is because the basis for leadership normally has been weak, and partly it is because of the long-standing democratic penchant to hold leaders accountable. In our disinclination to ponder institutional bases for leadership, we have given full expression to its personal bases. The next chapter explores those personal bases, their role in the equation of governance, and the extent to which, if at all, they may be systematically evaluated.

NOTES

1. Ilja Scholten, "Neo-Corporatism and Public Policy Making in the Netherlands: Institutional Sclerosis and Coercion," Paper presented at the 1981 Annual Meeting of the American Political Science Association, New York, p. 20.

2. Peter B. Clark and James Q. Wilson distinguished inducements for organizational participation as being material, solidary, or purposive. Roughly translated this respectively means money, community, and ideology. Insofar as the second of these is concerned, it is probably as an overall matter on the decline. Insofar as political party organizations are concerned, purposive incentives loom larger now than they once may have, while the others appear to have declined. See Peter B. Clark and James Q. Wilson, "Incentive Systems: A Theory of Organization," *Administrative Science Quarterly* 6 (June 1961): 129-166.

3. See Richard Rose, "On the Priorities of Government: A Developmental Analysis of Public Policies," *European Journal of Political Research* 4 (September 1976): 247-289.

4. Between 1936 and 1979, for instance, the U.S. Federal Register grew by thirty-three fold! See John F. Bibby, Thomas E. Mann, and Norman J. Ornstein, *Vital Statistics on Congress* (Washington, D.C.: American Enterprise Institute, 1980), p. 93.

5. See, for instance, Richard Rose, "What if Anything Is Wrong with Big Government?" *Journal of Public Policy* 1 (February 1981): 5-36.

6. For an exemplar of this view, see Samuel Brittan, "The Economic Contradictions of Democracy," *British Journal of Political Science* 5 (April 1975): 129-159. Put bluntly, Brittan states that "electorates tend to expect too much from government action at too little cost." (p. 139.) Alternatively, Alt and Chrystal concluded that "public expenditure . . . grows roughly in proportion with national income." See James Alt and K. Alec Chrystal, "Electoral Cycles, Budget Controls and Public Expenditure," *Journal of Public Policy* 1 (February 1981): 37-59, esp. p. 56.

7. See Bibby et al., *Vital Statistics*, p. 78. Office accounts were consolidated into a lump sum figure in 1978.

8. Richard F. Fenno, Jr., "U.S. House Members in Their Constituencies: An Exploration," *American Political Science Review* 71 (September 1977): 915.

9. A clear statement of the visibility hypothesis (and its reputed effects on the growth of government) is found in Morris P. Fiorina, *Congress: Keystone of the Washington Establishment* (New Haven, Conn.: Yale University Press, 1977). For another perspective that sees the tendencies of electoral preservation and party disunity as part of an historical drift in the decomposition of partisan coalitions, see Walter Dean Burnham, "Insulation and Responsiveness in Congressional Elections," *Political Science Quarterly* 90 (Fall 1975): 411-435.

10. Glenn R. Parker and Roger H. Davidson, "Why Do Americans Love Their Congressmen So Much More Than Their Congress?," *Legislative Studies Quarterly* 4 (February 1979): 60.

11. Bibby et al., *Vital Statistics*, pp. 77 and 94.

12. Burnham, "Insulation and Responsiveness," esp. p. 414.

13. Stephen E. Frantzich, "Computerized Information Technology in the U.S. House of Representatives," *Legislative Studies Quarterly* 4 (May 1979): 275.

14. As quoted in Frantzich, p. 273.

15. Indeed, such tools are offered by one theorist as a means of promoting a more democratic polity. See Michael S. Margolis, *Viable Democracy* (New York: Penguin Books, 1979), esp. pp. 158-170.

16. For a view, in this regard, emphasizing the growing vitality of the national party organizations, see Cornelius P. Cotter and John F. Bibby, "Institutional Development of Parties and the Thesis of Party Decline," *Political Science Quarterly* 95 (Spring 1980): 1-27. For a similar view emphasizing the technological base of party organization, see John H. Glascock, "Stages of Party Development: Extending Chambers' Taxonomy into the 1980s," Paper presented at the 1982 Annual Meeting of the Southwestern Social Science Association, San Antonio, Texas. For a more pessimistic view of the role

of information and communications technologies on party organization, see Michael J. Robinson, "Media Coverage in the Primary Campaign of 1976: Implications for Voters, Candidates, and Parties," in *The Party Symbol: Readings on Political Parties,* ed. William J. Crotty (San Francisco: W. H. Freeman, 1980), pp. 178-190.

17. For a good analysis of forces leading to this, see Hugh Heclo, "Introduction: The Presidential Illusion," in *The Illusion of Presidential Government,* ed. Hugh Heclo and Lester M. Salamon (Boulder, Colo.: Westview Press, 1981), pp. 1-17.

18. Michael Baruch Grossman and Martha Joynt Kumar, *Portraying the President: The White House and the News Media* (Baltimore, Md.: Johns Hopkins University Press, 1981), p. 320.

19. *Ibid.,* p. 317.

20. Max M. Kampelman, "Congress, the Media, and the President," in *Congress Against the President,* ed. Harvey C. Mansfield, Sr. (New York: Praeger, 1975), pp. 92-93.

21. Robert M. Entman, "The Imperial Media," in *Politics and the Oval Office: Toward Presidential Governance,* ed. Arnold J. Meltsner (San Francisco: Institute for Contemporary Studies, 1981), p. 86.

22. Michael J. Robinson, "Three Faces of Congressional Media," in *The New Congress,* ed. Thomas E. Mann and Norman J. Ornstein (Washington, D.C.: American Enterprise Institute, 1981), pp. 55-98.

23. Parker and Davidson, "Why Do Americans Love Their Congressmen," and also, Richard F. Fenno, Jr., *Home Style: House Members in Their Districts* (Boston: Little, Brown, 1978), pp. 232-247.

24. See Samuel Kernell, "Explaining Presidential Popularity," *American Political Science Review* 72 (June 1978): 506-522.

25. Robinson, "Three Faces of Congressional Media," pp. 92-93. Emphases are in the original.

26. Thomas E. Patterson and Robert D. McClure, "Television and Voters' Issue Awareness," in Crotty, *The Party Symbol,* p. 332.

27. Robinson, "Media Coverage," p. 184.

28. Michael J. Robinson, "Television and American Politics: 1956-76," *The Public Interest* 48 (Summer 1977): 22. Emphases are in the original.

29. One of the best analyses of several types of meaning given to rationality remains Paul Diesing, *Reason in Society: Five Types of Decisions and Their Social Conditions* (Urbana: University of Illinois Press, 1962).

30. See David R. Mayhew, *Congress: The Electoral Connection* (New Haven: Yale University Press, 1974).

31. For evidence, see Warren E. Miller, Arthur H. Miller, and Edward J. Schneider, *American National Election Studies* (Cambridge: Harvard University Press, 1980), pp. 31 and 383.

32. See Walter Dean Burnham, "The Changing Shape of the American Political Universe," *American Political Science Review* 59 (March 1965): 7-28. At least insofar as turnout is concerned, the 1982 midterm election runs counter to the general tendency of decreased voting participation.

33. See Kazuto Kojima, "Public Opinion Trends in Japan," *Public Opinion Quarterly* 41 (Summer 1977): 212.

34. Ivor Crewe, "Is Britain's Two-Party System Really About to Crumble? The Social Democratic-Liberal Alliance and the Prospects for Realignment," Paper presented at the 1982 Annual Meeting of the Midwest Political Science Association, Milwaukee, Wisconsin, pp. 37-38. For similar evidence in the United States, see Everett Carll Ladd, Jr., *Where Have All the Voters Gone?* (New York: Norton, 1978), esp. pp. 38-39.

35. See Anthony Smith, "Mass Communications," in *Democracy at the Polls: A Comparative Study of Competitive National Elections,* ed. David Butler, Howard R. Penniman, and Austin Ranney (Washington, D.C.: American Enterprise Institute, 1981), esp. pp. 173-178.

36. See Helmut Norpoth and Kendall L. Baker, "Mass Media Use and Electoral Choice in West Germany," *Comparative Politics* 13 (October 1980): 1-14, esp. p. 12.

37. See Douglas Dobson and Douglas St. Angelo, "Party Identification and the Floating Vote: Some Dynamics," *American Political Science Review* 69 (June 1975): 481-490, esp. pp. 487-489.

38. See Roy Pierce and Philip E. Converse, "Candidate Visibility in France and the United States," *Legislative Studies Quarterly* 6 (August 1981): 339-371, esp. pp. 363-366.

39. On the matter of candidate evaluation especially, see Donald E. Stokes, "Some Dynamic Elements in Contests for the Presidency," *American Political Science Review* 60 (March 1966): 19-28; and for an examination of links between issues and candidate evaluations, see Benjamin I. Page and Calvin C. Jones, "Reciprocal Effects of Policy Preferences, Party Loyalties and the Vote," *American Political Science Review* 73 (December 1979): 1071-1089.

40. Richard A. Brody and Benjamin I. Page, "The Impact of Events on Presidential Popularity: The Johnson and Nixon Administrations," in *Perspectives on the Presidency,* ed. Aaron Wildavsky (Boston: Little, Brown, 1975), pp. 136-147, esp. p. 145.

41. Kernell, "Explaining Presidential Popularity," p. 521.

42. Samuel Kernell, Peter W. Sperlich, and Aaron Wildavsky, "Public Support for Presidents," in Wildavsky, *Perspectives on the Presidency,* pp. 148-181.

43. Anthony King, "The American Polity in the Late 1970s: Building Coalitions in the Sand," in *The New American Political System,* ed. Anthony King (Washington, D.C.: American Enterprise Institute, 1978), pp. 371-395, esp. pp. 388-395.

44. A student of both Swedish and American political culture frets, for instance, that "the strength of deferent values in Sweden will erode further over time." This is apt to happen, first, because of "the democratic and participant ideology promulgated by the Social Democrats" and the policies they have introduced, and second, because of "the Americanization of Swedish culture." See Steven Kelman, *Regulating America, Regulating Sweden: A Comparative Study of Occupational Safety and Health Policy* (Cambridge: M.I.T. Press, 1981), p. 234. For similar observations, see Thomas J. Anton, *Administered Politics: Elite Political Culture in Sweden* (Boston: Martinus Nijhoff, 1980), esp. pp. 179-187.

45. W. L. Guttsman earlier noted the changing character of Socialist MPs in Britain; the steady replacement of the working class by university educated professionals among those MPs not sponsored by trade unions. See W. L. Guttsman, *The British Political Elite* (New York: Basic Books, 1963), esp. pp. 236-254. Documentation of these tendencies more generally may be found in Robert D. Putnam, *The Comparative Study of Political Elites* (Englewood Cliffs, N.J.: Prentice-Hall, 1976), pp. 21-28, and Joel D. Aberbach, Robert D. Putnam, and Bert A. Rockman, *Bureaucrats and Politicians in Western Democracies* (Cambridge, Mass.: Harvard University Press, 1981), pp. 46-83.

46. Anthony King, "The Rise of the Career Politician in Britain—And Its Consequences," *British Journal of Political Science* 11 (April 1981): 249-285, esp. p. 261.

47. In a summary of some of the literature discussing a "new class," they are referred to by Jeane Kirkpatrick as "a new elite highly trained in the use of ideas and symbols and skilled in their communication." See Jeane J. Kirkpatrick, "Changing Patterns of Electoral Competition," in King, *The New American Political System,* p. 280, passim.

48. King, "The Rise of the Career Politician," esp. pp. 279-285. As King argues, "the recent high level of vehemence in British politics is almost certainly associated with the fact that many more British politicians than in the past are now recruited from the ranks of journalism, public relations and teaching. . . . Such persons are likely to import into politics habits of disputation, generalization and abstract thought acquired in these other professions." (p. 284.)

49. Tony Burkett, "Developments in the West German Bundestag: 1969-1980," *Parliamentary Affairs,* 34 (Summer 1981): 291-307.

50. Mark MacGuigan, "Parliamentary Reform: Impediments to an Enlarged Role for the Backbencher," *Legislative Studies Quarterly* 3 (November 1978): 680-681.

51. Philip Norton, "The Changing Face of the British House of Commons in the 1970s," *Legislative Studies Quarterly* 3 (August 1980): 333-357. Also, see John E. Schwarz, "Attempting to Assert the Commons' Power: Labour Members in the House of Commons, 1974-79," *Comparative Politics* 14 (October 1981): 17-29, esp. pp. 22-27; and John E. Schwarz, "Exploring a New Role in Policy Mak-

ing: The British House of Commons in the 1970s," *American Political Science Review* 74 (March 1980): 23-37; and Norton, "The Changing Face," pp. 333-357.

52. Schwarz, "Attempting to Assert the Commons' Power," p. 28.

53. Norton, "The Changing Face," p. 353.

54. See, for example, the difficulties in adjusting to these new conditions on the part of British civil servants and ministers especially, as portrayed in David Lowe, "Legislative Oversight and The House of Commons' New Committee System." Paper presented at the 1981 Annual Meeting of the American Political Science Association, New York.

55. Joseph Cooper and David W. Brady, "Institutional Context and Leadership Style: The House from Cannon to Rayburn," *American Political Science Review* 75 (June 1981): 424.

56. See Jack L. Walker, "Setting the Agenda in the U.S. Senate: A Theory of Problem Selection," *British Journal of Political Science* 7 (July 1977): 423-445.

57. For a discussion of these tendencies and their impact on Congress, see Bruce I. Oppenheimer, "Policy Effects of U.S. House Reform: Decentralization and the Capacity to Resolve Energy Issues," *Legislative Studies Quarterly* 5 (February 1980): 5-29.

58. This point is developed further in my "Legislative Oversight and Legislative-Executive Relations." Paper presented at the Legislative Research Conference sponsored by the National Science Foundation, Iowa City, October 1982.

59. Daniel P. Mulhollan and Arthur G. Stevens, Jr., "Special Interests and the Growth of Informal Groups in Congress." Paper presented at the 1980 Annual Meeting of the Midwest Political Science Association, Chicago, Illinois, p. 9.

60. Rose, "What if Anything Is Wrong with Big Government?" p. 22.

61. Edmund Dell, as quoted in A. Grant Jordan, "Iron Triangles, Wooly Corporatism and Elastic Nets: Images of the Policy Process," *Journal of Public Policy* 1 (February 1981): 104-105.

62. See, for instance, Hugh Heclo, *A Government of Strangers: Executive Politics in Washington* (Washington, D.C.: The Brookings Institution, 1977), pp. 55-68.

63. Richard Rose and Guy Peters, *Can Government Go Bankrupt?* (New York: Basic Books, 1978), pp. 252-253.

64. See, for instance, Harold L. Wilensky, *The Welfare State and Equality: Structural and Ideological Roots of Public Expenditures* (Berkeley: University of California Press, 1975), esp. pp. 18-28.

65. See Thomas J. Anton, Jerry P. Cawley, and Kevin L. Kramer, *Moving Money: An Empirical Analysis of Federal Expenditure Patterns* (Cambridge, Mass.: Oelgeschlager, Gunn and Hain, 1980), pp. xv-xvi. "Viewed as a whole," the authors claim, "federal outlays to counties reflect a system driven by interest and constiuency accommodation, rather than centralized fiscal policy trade-offs." (p. 69.)

66. As quoted in Jordan, "Iron Triangles," pp. 118-119.

67. James Q. Wilson, *Political Organizations* (New York: Basic Books, 1973), p. 89.

68. Jordan, "Iron Triangles," p. 119.

69. For a critique of the cabinet as a decision-making instrument, see John P. Mackintosh, *The British Cabinet,* 3rd ed. (London: Stevens and Sons, 1977). For critiques of presidential impotence in dealing with the executive, see Graham K. Wilson, "Are Departmental Secretaries Really a President's Natural Enemies?," *British Journal of Political Science* 7 (July 1977): 273-299, and Ronald Randall, "Presidential Power versus Bureaucratic Intransigence: The Influence of the Nixon Administration on Welfare Policy," *American Political Science Review* 73 (September 1979): 795-810.

70. See, for example, Charles O. Jones, "American Politics and the Organization of Energy Decision Making," *Annual Review of Energy* 4 (1979): 99-121.

71. Heclo, "Issue Networks and the Executive Establishment," pp. 87-89.

72. *Ibid.*

73. *Ibid.,* pp. 96-97.

74. See, for instance, Arthur G. Stevens, Jr., Daniel P. Mulhollan, and Paul S. Rundquist, "U.S. Congressional Structure and Representation: The Role of Informal Groups," *Legislative Studies Quarterly* 6 (August 1981): 415-437, and Robert H. Salisbury and Kenneth A. Shepsle, "U.S. Congressman

as Enterprise," *Legislative Studies Quarterly* 6 (November 1981): 559-576. A survey by the latter two researchers revealed as of mid-1978, 990 separate congressional units that were staffed. (p. 575.)

75. Hugh Heclo, "The Changing Presidential Office," in Meltsner, *Politics and the Oval Office,* pp. 172-173.

76. Heclo, "The Changing Presidential Office," pp. 168-177.

77. Wilson, *Political Organization,* p. 82.

78. This is Heclo's point in his "Issue Networks." For a critique of the assertion that issue networks are unstructured, see Jordan, "Iron Triangles."

79. Jordan, "Iron Triangles," p. 98.

80. Christopher Leman, *The Collapse of Welfare Reform: Political Institutions, Policy and the Poor in Canada and the United States* (Cambridge, Mass.: M.I.T. Press, 1980), p. 136.

81. Lester M. Salamon, "Conclusion: Beyond the Presidential Illusion—Toward a Constitutional Presidency," in Heclo and Salamon, *The Illusion of Presidential Government,* p. 294.

82. Anthony King, "Overload: Problems of Governing in the 1970s," *Political Studies* 23 (June-September 1975), p. 170.

83. See, especially, Robert A. Dahl, *Who Governs? Democracy and Power in an American City* (New Haven: Yale University Press, 1961). Even though New Haven's celebrated mayor, Richard Lee, was accorded considerable skill as a manager of political diversity, his limits also were duly noted by Dahl:

> He was a negotiator rather than a hierarchical executive. He could rarely command, but he could apply his political resources and skills to the task of negotiating and bargaining. Given the distribution of political resources in New Haven perhaps he achieved about as much centralization as the system would tolerate. (p. 209.)

84. King, "Overload," p. 166. My definition is a liberal translation of King's.

85. David B. Truman, *The Governmental Process: Political Interests and Public Opinion* (New York: Alfred A. Knopf, 1951), p. 529.

86. See, for instance, Thomas L. Gais, Mark A. Peterson, and Jack L. Walker, "Interest Groups, Iron Triangles, and Representative Institutions in American National Government." Paper presented at the 1982 Annual Meeting of the Midwest Political Science Association, Milwaukee, Wisconsin, esp. pp. 44-45.

87. Brittan, "The Economic Contradictions of Democracy," p. 130.

88. James Q. Wilson, "'Policy Intellectuals' and Public Policy," *The Public Interest* 64 (Summer 1981): 31-46.

89. James W. Ceaser, "Political Parties and Presidential Ambition," *Journal of Politics* 40 (August 1978), p. 738.

90. *Ibid.,* p. 739.

91. According to an analysis by Jeff Fishel, in domestic policy 65% of Carter's legislative proposals were in accord with campaign promises. This compares with 63% for Johnson and 67% for Kennedy, his two Democratic predecessors. Jeff Fishel, "Presidential Elections and Presidential Agendas: The Carter Administration in Contemporary Historical Perspective," Center for Congressional and Presidential Studies, Working Paper #001, The American University, 1980, p. 44.

92. For evidence thereof, see John S. Jackson III, Barbara Leavitt Brown, and David Bositis, "Herbert McClosky and Friends Revisited: 1980 Democratic and Republican Party Elites Compared to the Mass Public," *American Politics Quarterly* 10 (April 1982): 158-180. As they claim (and their evidence shows): "The Republican elites are a rather homogeneous group taking consistently and clearly conservative stances on the issues" whereas the dominance of the Democratic party since the New Deal could be attributed to its heterogeneity. (p. 177.)

93. More and more, there is evidence that the Republicans are achieving this organizational coordination as evidenced by running candidate Ronald Reagan's campaign in 1980 through the Republican National Committee (RNC), and by the growing resources and organizational machinery of the RNC. On the latter, see Cotter and Bibby, "Institutional Development of Parties."

94. Ceaser, however, views the process as dating essentially from 1968. See his, "Political Parties and Presidential Ambition," pp. 708-709.

95. New Hampshire, for example, elicited in 1976 over 41% of the total news stories devoted to state selection processes. In fact, Massachusetts, the second primary, received only 28% of the New Hampshire total. See Robinson, "Media Coverage in the Primary Campaign," pp. 180-184. And, as Rhodes Cook asserts, "Iowa and New Hampshire underscored the premise that unlike general election politics where it is important to peak late in the campaign, in preconvention politics it is more important to score early." Rhodes Cook, "Media Coverage of the 1976 Nominating Process," in Crotty, *The Party Symbol,* p. 161.

96. See John H. Aldrich, "A Dynamic Model of Presidential Nomination Campaigns," *American Political Science Review* 74 (September 1980): 651-669. More formally, Aldrich proposes that the degree of instability will be positively related to the number of candidates. Definitionally, any candidate will do better the more resources he possesses and the fewer his opponents possess, but the availability of federal matching funds provides more candidates with resources. That federal funding provides more resources initially to several candidates than they would have had without it generates a larger probability of a deviation from expectations regarding the showing of the front runner, thus disadvantaging him in the acquisition of further resources.

97. John Erlichman, "The Effect of Elections on Doing the Work of Government," in *The Impact of the Electoral Process,* ed. Louis Maisel and Joseph Cooper (Beverly Hills, California: Sage Publications, 1977), p. 296.

98. Mackintosh, *The British Cabinet,* p. 630.

6

"Persona" and Presidential Leadership

If we want Presidents alive and fully useful, we shall have to pick them from among experienced politicians of extraordinary temperament. . . .
(Richard Neustadt in *Presidential Power,* 1960.)

[One potential basis for stabilizing and enhancing presidential power may be] television as a source at once of news and entertainment, and [finding] a presidential master of the medium. . . . We await the potential master: convincing, engaging, concerned, and alert. . . . The next decade [may be] quite likely to produce him. . . . If so, he might be able to attract, and hold . . . partisans for *him.* . . .
(Richard Neustadt in *Presidential Power,* 1976.)

A president or would-be president must be bright but not too bright, warm and accessible but not too folksy, down to earth but not pedestrian.
(Thomas E. Cronin, *The State of the Presidency,* 2nd ed., p. 14.)

Do leaders lead, or do they follow?
(Donald D. Searing, "Models and Images of Man and Society in Leadership Theory," *Journal of Politics* 31 [1969]: 10.)

Just precisely what is the role of the individual leader? To what extent, and in what ways, does the individual make a difference? These simple questions remain endlessly fascinating if utterly perplexing. Perspective influences how we look at these questions, of course. The more we focus on and are absorbed by individual variability, the more we shall come to think that individual leaders are indeed very important, although often we will be stymied in specifying "how" and "in what regard." If, however, we focus more on broader environmental factors, impersonal forces will loom larger and more determining. Still, individual differences (no matter how great our difficulty in precisely defining them) do exist among leaders, and they seem to have consequences (no matter how problematic our efforts to specify these and to causally link them to performance).

Would "it" have turned out differently is a question that the study of the individual in leadership roles cannot definitely answer, however insightful and informative many such studies may be for providing clues to persistent styles of behavior.[1] Obviously, one reason this question is so hard to answer lies in the incommensurable nature of the problem it addresses. It is extremely rare that leaders face similar situations in similar political environments with a similar stock of political resources at their disposal. The task of drawing exacting comparisons, in other words, is quite large, perhaps even insuperable. Scientific explanation rests upon the logic of controlled comparisons. Yet, intensive biographical studies of individual leaders' behaviors and operating styles are not likely to provide us with controlled contexts—the *sine qua non* for answering the "what if" question.

We are left then with a paradox. Individuals are too important to be left out of the leadership question. Yet, studying the individual in a systematic way so as to grapple with the question, What difference would it make if "X" rather than "Y" occupied a given leadership role? is remarkably frustrating. Ironically, while this scientific dilemma persists, modernity tends to magnify the centrality of the individual leader by virtue of the media attention now provided.

In this chapter, therefore, I begin with a brief discussion of the influences of the modern environment on the position of the individual leader. Subsequently, I turn to the effects of American culture, institutions, and practices on the individual leader in general, and the U.S. president in particular. Different perspectives on the role and nature of political leadership and its relation to history and to context are then set forth. A schema that links the individual leader to outcomes through a set of conventional, but often implicit, assumptions is sketched. Its elements and assumptions are then critically explored. Diverse meanings of success, and diversity in the styles and skills of leadership, also are noted and some potential contradictions between these analyzed. The expected link between "experience" and presidential "success" also is evaluated. In concluding, I find it safe to say that "answers" to the leadership question which focus on the role of the person remain still at the level of proverbial wisdom.

MODERN TENDENCIES AND PERSONA

The modern era focuses attention readily on national political leaders. The forces stressed in Chapter 5 make this focus nearly universal. Especially pertinent are modern mass communications which literally provide a lens through which to focus on leaders. Inevitably, the individual leader has been given much attention. One can find exceptions here and there. The collegial presidency operative in Yugoslavia after the death of Tito, and the traditional collegial leadership in Switzerland, purposefully undermine the role of personal leadership. Countries with nearly exclusive party list voting also are apt to be somewhat less prone to the cult of individual leadership since governments, by virtue of being the products of interparty bargaining, tend to emphasize party over leader. The visibility of personal leadership, then, can be tempered to some degree either by institutional arrangements or by other organizational features of a political system.

Nonetheless, the principal thrust of modern trends is to place the person at the top in sharp focus. Key personal traits are quickly latched onto: Giscard's imperiousness, Trudeau's temper, Thatcher's iron will, and Carter's indecisiveness. Most national leaders are subject to assessments of how they, not just their governments or parties, handle the tasks of political leadership. Their traits, their abilities, and their characteristics are subject to continuous exposure and, thus, to evaluation above and beyond their party's or government's programs. This exposure, by itself, is neither beneficial nor harmful to an incumbent, but simply exaggerates personal traits. What enlarges gaffes, after all, also enlarges the opportunities for public relations.

THE AMERICAN PRESIDENT

Insofar as these tendencies are concerned, America is not so much unique as it simply is in the forefront. It is affected far more deeply by trends that lead to an emphasis on the personality at the top because its resistances to personalized political discourse are so very low. These predispositions toward personalism in American politics are rooted in history, culture, and institutions.

First, the relative slack between the social system and the political system makes for a politics in the United States that is more personalized, and that condition is aided immensely by an electoral system that promotes individual entrepreneurship. More than ever, American politics is fluid and noncrystallized; not quite structureless but not immensely far from it. In the American system, therefore, leadership becomes an individualistic enterprise and is viewed as a universal solvent. Oddly, a system designed to frustrate leadership has spawned a great faith in its potential.

Secondly, there are cultural reasons behind the American emphasis on the individual leader. Individualistic achievement is prized by the American culture. The ethos of individual responsibility as well as that of individual entrepreneurship are important cultural influences in the American repertoire of belief. Bred of liberal individualism, the American culture is a source for emphasizing the role of the individual as leader.

Thirdly, institutions help to account for the emphasis given the role of the individual leader in America. The president is not the head of a group of senior officials but rather their overseer; not necessarily a party leader or notable but nonetheless his party's titular head. The victor of an election process that is both tortuous and seemingly endless, he will have had to showcase and sell his own qualities to arrive where he is. And his election, being separated from elections for the legislative branch, inevitably points up the unique qualities of the office and its holder. Having attained a commanding view of the field of action, however, the president generally has few troops to command. He will have to get by on his personal resources and his wits to an unusual degree. The popular process of selection means also that the talents and skills of prospective presidents will have been subjected to little peer review (which, however, does not mean that they will be more lacking, as the cases of Alec Douglas-Home in Britain or Warren Harding in the United States demonstrate, than those who have been subjected to such review).

A fourth and rather recent development adds, curiously, to an emphasis on personal aspects of leadership and governing—although it affects directly only a very tiny but select opinion-influencing sector of the population. This development is the enlargement of the Washington community to include outside policy and political analysts. The enlargement began in a perceptible way during the Kennedy administration, and, in some respects, traces to Franklin Roosevelt. Until very recently, the Washington community has grown enormously. The new members of the Washington community are mostly centered in the capital, but some stay only for a while, and others regularly dart back and forth from academic or research centers. The growth of the Washington intellectuals and of centers to accommodate them has been impressive. While the centers provide a nucleus, many more scholars and observers are in and out doing research, engaged in conferences, and mixing with government officials, politicians, staff personnel, and political writers. Some even become government officials themselves, if most often on a very temporary basis. The relevant population includes both policy specialists (experts in particular policy areas or analytic techniques) and political analysts (astute observers of the Washington scene, its inhabitants, and the workings of its institutions).

For political scientists, especially, Washington is a heady site. It is difficult to think of either the place or the actors in it as being a marginal element to the national well-being. The actors, therefore, are subject to tactical scrutiny and, thus, the newer intellectual elements of the Washington community add to those who measure a president's repute and assess his talents. These "newcomers" to the Washington community additionally serve as conduits of impressions to their less-immersed colleagues on university campuses.

The swarm of researchers and analysts has become a new, if fringe, element of the Washington community. These observers have contributed greatly to our knowledge of politics and policy making in Washington. They have helped us to understand the importance of detail, of management, and of tactics while perhaps inadvertantly, if simply by concentration of focus, reducing the scale of vision. One student of the presidency complains, "What is most unsatisfying about the state of presidential studies is not a deficiency in research . . . but a deficiency in vision."[2] There is an inevitable tendency to take on the focus of the Washington players themselves. The Washington focus tends to be short-term and immediate:

What is happening today? Who is doing what to whom? Who is adept? Who is inept? Who is in? Who is out? In many ways, Washington is as much a town made for gossip as is Hollywood—even if the occupations of the subjects only recently have converged.

Though the issue is raised, it is feckless to address whether it is most useful to focus one's attention directly on Washington or outside of it. That is much like asking whether it is most worthwhile to ingest protein or minerals; both are essential. Without tapping into the Washington scene, our thinking is apt to be airy, empty, and platitudinous. But without, as Bruce Miroff says, going "Beyond Washington" there is danger of losing perspective, a matter that those who study, write, and talk about politics are always susceptible to in any case.[3]

Tactics, organization, experience, and skill—the elements of leadership—are not unimportant or trivial, but they also are not foremost. Individual leadership skills are simply less important in shaping outcomes than the more primal factors discussed in earlier chapters. Capabilities are basic; agility in handling resources is secondary, though not insignificant. Possessed with the world's most superbly trained diplomats, it is perfectly evident that Upper Volta still could not be a major power, whereas even with very mediocre diplomats the United States would be one. Yet statistical importance ought not be confused with practical relevance. Elections, for instance, often turn on factors that are statistically trivial but, by definition, hardly irrelevant. Campaign tactics under select conditions can make a difference. So too, if not the most important factor, the quality of leadership is not unimportant.

In assessing the role of the individual leader, in comparing individual leaders, and in discerning what, if any, traits are useful in leadership performance, we need to ask a series of questions: Under what conditions are particular attributes pertinent? To what sets of outcomes, goals, and objectives are various attributes appropriate? To what extent are certain of these attributes likely to be incompatible? In other words, are the prescriptions provided for presidents to be successful much like the mutually exclusive "proverbs of administration" that Herbert Simon claimed were the product of traditional management science?[4] It remains worth asking as well, To what extent are the traits that enhance a president's probabilities for political success separable from those relevant to the interests of the nation—however these may be calculated?

PERSPECTIVES ON THE LEADERSHIP QUESTION

Leadership and Theories of History

The way we look at the question of leadership—the balance of nonmanipulables to manipulables—is in no small measure bound to a philosophy of history, or at least a theory of how societies function. This being the case, we can gain some appreciation for the particular emphasis given to leadership in the United States.

As the archetypical liberal society, the exercise of successful entrepreneurship by individual leaders is accorded rare importance in the United States.[5]

Why should this be so? No simple answer prevails of course, and intellectual traditions provide a misty and often distant source of explanation. At its core, however, liberalism emphasizes progress and individualism. Most important, Karl Mannheim argued:

> The deepest driving forces of the liberal ideas of the Enlightenment lay in the fact that it appealed to the free will and kept alive the feeling of being indeterminate and unconditioned. The distinctive character of the conservative mentality [and] . . . the central achievement of conservatism . . . in conscious contrast to the liberal outlook . . . gave positive emphasis to the notion of the determinateness of our outlook and our behaviour.[6]

In the conservative perspective, society is evolutionary and organically unified. The laws and institutions of the state are the concrete expressions of this organic, communitarian unity. Indeed, Clinton Rossiter claims that the American conservative (whose outlook is affected by the prevalence of liberal assumptions in America) is in substantial disagreement with traditional conservative notions—of the uncertainty of progress, of the fallibility and limited reach of human reason, and of contentment and prudence, and, above all, with the idea of the primacy of the community.[7]

In the Marxist tradition, systemic forces propel change. The exertions of individuals are fundamentally irrelevant (the emergence of both Leninism and some modes of neo-Marxism, notwithstanding). The tides of history are the product most distantly of the techniques of production, and most directly of the structure of social relations and the contradictions that emerge therein.

Obviously, Marxism and conservatism have little in common. But one can point to two things they do share. First, neither is an individualistic ideology. Second, neither planted roots in any significant way in American soil. The key elements of American liberalism, in fact, have influenced both the American Right and the American Left, while the American political culture has been largely oblivious to the deterministic currents of European conservatism and to those of its Marxist nemesis. While some recent neo-Marxist scholarship emphasizes the entrepreneurial role of leaders within a broader deterministic structure of social forces,[8] as philosophies of history and theories of society both traditional conservatism and classical Marxism dampen enthusiasms for the role of "the great leader" as a force in society. Untouched by these currents, the American spirit gives full reign to the ideas of progress, free will, and individualism embodied in the liberal idea. Within such a perspective, leaders count for much, while the leadership stratum and its systemic determinants are given little recognition.

Organismic and Mechanistic Models

Donald Searing, in an insightful essay, brings different organizing modalities to bear on the study of leadership. He distinguishes between studies of leadership that are system focused (organismic models as he calls them) and those which are subsystem focused (mechanistic models). The basic assumption behind the organismic image, according to Searing, is that "Society . . . grows and evolves while the institutions within it evolve in harmony with the larger organism."[9] Searing cites both Hegel and Marx as leading proponents of this perspective, and also the British Darwinist, Herbert Spencer. What they have in common, according to Searing, is the belief that "individual leaders were unable to manipulate the controls. . . . [and] that no leader was more than a catalyst for events . . . which . . . would have occurred with or without these heroic personalities."[10]

Counterposed to these deterministic perspectives is what Searing describes as the mechanistic image of leadership. The mechanistic image lacks the strong integration of the organismic focus. Instead of emphasizing interdependence, it seizes upon the shaping impact of leadership, and focuses on the traits that leaders possess to enable them to lead. A key assumption is that "Social events are sufficiently open-textured to permit semi-autonomous individual actions. . . ."[11] The mechanistic assumptions are viewed as being atomistic. In contrast to the organic and systemic thinkers such as Hegel, Marx, Spencer, Pareto, and Mosca, the exemplars of mechanistic thinking cited by Searing are Hobbes, Locke, and Mill.[12]

The two images for thinking about leadership—organismic and mechanical—are used by Searing for purposes of epistemologically classifying leadership studies. They connect, however imperfectly, to the basic premises of liberal, conservative, and Marxist thought. For it is the liberal conception that sees the free will of individuals moving society along the path of progress. Society is malleable and changeable (at least in its parts) and capable of being influenced by determined action. The mechanistic image and the liberal theory of society are not completely coincident, but they greatly overlap in their essential premises. To the question that Searing raises, Do leaders lead or do they follow?, the mechanistic image and the liberal theory of society with which it is allied respond that leaders can and do lead. Employing the language of Chapter 2, leaders can be directors.

The conservative and Marxist theories of history, however, are linked to organic and systemic premises about the evolution of society and each is inclined toward holistic and deterministic perspectives. Leaders follow from their contexts more than they reshape them. Social forces and social stratification, Searing notes, are the keys to the organismic model.[13] In the language of Chapter 2, leaders are more apt to reflect than to direct.

All theories of history, of course, see the problem of determinism and free will, of structure and opportunity, as being of relative rather than absolute proportions. As Betty Glad's biography of Jimmy Carter suggests, the boundaries between the impact of the leader on the system and that of the system on the leader are quite hazy. Carter's problems, she asserts, were to a great degree of his own making. Yet, she continues, his career reflects "aspects of the American political system and culture."[14] Except for the most vulgar interpretations of the determinist outlook, leaders are thought to be able to make a dent if they are so disposed. They can be manipulators, not merely puppets pulled by the strings of historical forces to enact predetermined roles. The relationship between power base and the exercise of opportunity is inevitably the focal point of students of leadership, and is next to engage our attention. Yet it is essentially the leader's power base that affects the magnitude of change that is possible.

Transactional and Transformative Models of Leadership

What are the possibilities for leadership? This presumably depends on one's definition of it—on the scope and magnitude of change one seeks to bring about, on the unit of analysis one focuses on ("decisions" say those holding the mechanistic perspective; "systems" say those holding the organismic perspective), and on the relationship between leaders and led. In James MacGregor Burns's encyclopaedic study of leadership, he distinguishes between *transactional* and *transformative* leadership.[15] Transactional leadership he defines essentially as an instrumental, bargaining, or exchange relationship, whereas transformative leadership is essentially based on an inspirational relationship. Transactional forms of leadership are seemingly incremental and discrete. Emphasis on this form of leadership comports well with the mechanistic focus on decisional subsystems and on decisions as an appropriate unit of analysis. Transforming modes of leadership, by definition, occasion larger, nonincremental outcomes. They do this, in part, by joining leadership and led toward a mutual consensus of goals and objectives. Precisely how this is done Burns does not make very clear, although he does note that party leadership may have the potential for producing it.[16]

If leadership is the product of resources "times" skill in their exploitation, then it is the nature of both the resources and the character of their use that concerns Burns. Is leadership used, among other things, to transform the nature of the resources by transforming the relationship between leadership and followership? That appears to be Burns's preoccupation.

Because the ability of government to act in a unified way is weak, the basic power resources of American presidents are also relatively weak. How to create sufficient unity to enable the achievement of purpose is the question that is at the heart of both Richard Neustadt's analysis of presidential leadership and that of Burns.[17] Each emphasizes the exploitation of opportunity and each is concerned with presidential vigor. At the same time, different means are stressed and apparently different aspirations of what is possible are put forth.

How to maximize the opportunities available to the president in the face of constraints on presidential leadership is central to Neustadt's concerns. How may a president optimize points of leverage in a system not designed for presidential direction? Neustadt's fundamental premise, of course, is that the most natural director is the president. Neustadt's analysis of presidential power fits nicely with the mechanistic image of leadership. It emphasizes conflict among the parts of the system: the inner drives, skills, and traits of the leader in sensing and manipulating opportunities; and the importance of the decision as the unit of analysis.[18]

Consonant with Neustadt's mechanistic emphasis on conflict between the parts of the system, a president's capacity to bargain and to persuade is at the core of his ability to bring forth favorable outcomes. To be successful in the arts of bargaining and persuasion, presidents also must take care to manage their reputation, to control and shape that which must necessarily be delegated to others. They must be busily interventionist, yet also judicious of temperament and reflective of their power stakes in the decisions they make. These are the key ingredients of presidential power in Neustadt's formulation. The question with which he is concerned, the maximization of presidential leverage, however, does not ask, as Thomas Cronin has noted, the succeeding question, "to what ends" other than the president's own?[19]

Neustadt's seeming obsession with the means of wielding influence is denigrated by James MacGregor Burns, who sees it as a lesser form of leadership. The virtually *ad hoc* character of power wielding—the personal skills employed to maximize one's tactical opportunities for increasing bargaining power—in Neustadt's view is the main source of adhesion in the American political system. But from Burns's perspective, it is a decidedly inferior form of leadership. Instrumental and *ad hoc* bargains are necessary, yet limiting. From these instrumental transactions, Burns concludes that because "no enduring purpose" holds the parties to a bargain together, dissipation of the leadership act inevitably will occur as nothing effectively "binds leader and follower together in a mutual and continuing pursuit of a higher purpose."[20] In Burns's view, this transactional form of leadership constitutes the central element of Neustadt's theory.

Thus, in contrast to the entrepreneurial style emphasized by Neustadt, Burns claims that a higher form of leadership (transformative) needs to be emphasized.[21] If cutting deals is the essence of transactive leadership, then the transforming leader is described by Burns, without apparent embarrassment, as one who engages others "in such a way that leaders and followers raise one another to higher levels of leadership and morality."[22] What this formulation means, in fact, is rather hard to say. It is apparent, however, that Burns believes that it, and not Neustadt's perpetually dickering president, is the key to generating the necessary political adhesion required to achieve far-reaching public goals. Burns questions whether Neustadt's emphasis on bargaining is really executive leadership or whether it is merely adroit management and effective application of the techniques of manipulation.[23] Burns's fear, as well, is that an emphasis on transactional forms of leadership implicitly begs the question, to what ends? Presidents, after all, may build up their own leverage without pursuing more general purposes, according to

Burns. In a more general way, this particular distinction also has been made by Lawrence Mohr who, in discussing the concept of organizational goals, differentiates between "reflexive" goals (inward or maintenance ends) and "transitive" goals (mission objectives).[24]

Accordingly, the maximization of presidential leverage, in Burns's view, unaccompanied by an articulation of larger purpose, is mere power aggrandizement, and thus under the normal conditions of American politics unlikely to be sustained. At the same time, transformative leadership is both directive and visionary, and of broad scale. A transformative leadership, therefore, must alter the existing parallelogram of forces, as Burns puts it, and, in doing this, sustain its impetus and followership. Purpose and power must be welded together. To accomplish this, Burns is skeptical of the powers of executive leadership alone. Put another way, Burns sees individual entrepreneurship and individual skill as means ultimately ineffective for the accomplishment of great ends, indeed, sometimes diverting, even corrupting those purposes. Acting alone, the executive will make great exertions on behalf of small goals, while large and transformative goals will be thwarted altogether.

This is not to say that Burns denigrates the role of the individual leader. For in Burns's scheme the individual leader who seeks transformative change must guide followers with a clear vision. But other instruments will be needed. Foremost are political parties, which Burns sees as normally engaged in the transactional business of maneuvering and horsetrading, but which have, he asserts, "vast transformative potential."[25] Visionary and skilled individuals are necessary but not sufficient. Elsewhere, Burns makes this abundantly clear. In his book, *Deadlock of Democracy,* Burns argues first that presidential leaders must be more than skillful leaders; they must reshape the forces around them. To accomplish this an energized party system that can establish party government will be required.[26]

We are left, then, mainly with incantations for presidents to do good and to be high-minded, yet also to be vigorously partisan. In Chapter 1, I am equally critical of both the simple suppositions of the party government model and of the notion that leadership is an undiluted good. Transformations produced through direct and overt clashes of political will neither happen with great regularity nor, more important, are a harmless way of bringing about change. Nebulous definitions of general purpose (to be divisively arrived at via adversarial partisanship) are hard to be critical of, but also exceedingly difficult to pin down.

What, then, is the relationship between the president's power base and presidential opportunities? Neustadt, it seems evident, sees the American president as having a weak power base. His powers, for the most part, will come through a vigilant attentiveness to his power stakes. Plasticity exists in the presidential role and, to some extent, its shape comes from the role occupant. Even so, possibilities are constrained by conditions in the broader political environment that simultaneously increase presidential exposure and shape presidential opportunities. Burns, however, sees the test of leadership as not merely seizing what opportunities are provided, but altering the structure of opportunities themselves by transforming both the base for exercising power (through responsible parties) and the purposes for which it is exercised.

Controlling the Agenda

To what purposes do leaders attempt to lead? This is the question posed by the transformative notion of leadership. This notion is at heart goal-directed, and the president usually is assumed to be the chief director of goals. As time wears on, however, presidential agendas become susceptible to alteration. The unforeseen consequences of past policies—those of previous occupants of the White House and those of the incumbents—conspire along with unprogrammed events and with changes in the composition of political majorities to provide new problems requiring reaction. Some of these will not be consistent with earlier elements of the presidential agenda. Fishel comments in this regard that

A pattern of early attempts to redeem much in the campaign agenda, followed by *selective* reversals, drift, or displacement . . . was . . . characteristic of the Johnson and Nixon administrations (as well as the Carter administration). Only Kennedy avoided this, partially because of his assassination, but more importantly because the agenda Kennedy was seeking, later incorporated into the "Great Society," was perceived by Kennedy staffers as politically viable, in fact central to his reelection.[27]

Fishel's excellent analysis of presidential agenda setting concludes that agenda unpredictability is a function of new forces in the environment whose causes and effects are uncertain, and for which, therefore, there is no consensus. When the assumptions of the past no longer hold, the prescriptive formulas on which they are based have reduced acceptability. The break between older assumptions and formulas and newer ones, however, is rarely clean. Remnants of the old coalitions vie with the embryonic forms of new coalitions. Sometimes presidents are caught between them.

In the Carter administration, for example, Fishel reveals that while the first two years brought forth a fairly high degree of consistency between issues on the campaign agenda and those on the presidential agenda, the last two years generated several new issue clusters not previously stressed in the campaign. As with Ronald Reagan's reluctant acceptance of a tax increase package in 1982 (standing in contradiction to his 1981 tax cut proposals), issue responses over the course of an administration are increasingly addressed to problems unforeseen at its outset. These are, of course, strategic retreats—necessary concessions to reality.

The president's partisans typically provide some inhibiting counter against adjustments in the presidential agenda. Party "ideology" is an anchor. It stabilizes a presidency and provides for consistent expectations by emphasizing adherence to party platforms and campaign rhetoric.[28] In the absence of broad consensus, however, party stalwarts tend to inhibit adaptation to new courses. In President Carter's case, Fishel points out, the play of issue currents set him apart from significant sectors of his party. Democratic presidents do not generally stress inflation and budgetary constraint as priority problems. Double-digit inflation, however, had not been a pressing problem since the New Deal (except briefly after World War II). A continuation of past Democratic policies in regard to social programs and expansionary economics, while acceptable to party activists, was much less acceptable to opinion leaders beyond the party.

Some elements of a traditionally expansionary Democratic agenda remained even into the 1980 election year, but Carter was (and had been) clearly putting forth an agenda that failed to resonate with Democratic dogma. The percentage of spending programs that Carter put forth during his administration in relation to his total proposed program agenda, for example, is a bit higher than that reported for his Republican predecessors Nixon and Ford, but quite a bit lower than that reported for the Democratic presidencies of Kennedy and Johnson. The latter two presidencies, according to data collected by Paul Light, averaged 57.5% spending programs on their agendas while the Nixon and Ford presidencies averaged 31.5% across theirs. The figure for the Carter presidency is 39%, a profile closer to the Republican than the Democratic presidencies. In terms of the projected start-up costs of these programs, Carter falls between the Nixon-Ford Republican and Kennedy-Johnson Democratic poles. The Nixon-Ford presidencies averaged $2.27 billion in estimated start-up costs, while the estimate of the Kennedy-Johnson program start-up costs was $6.95 billion. The estimated start-up expenditure for Carter administration programs was $4.5 billion.[29]

To those stricken with the crucial importance of purposive drive, the Carter presidency seemed peculiar because of its unfamiliarity to Democratic partisan activists. It seemed, therefore, to lack a unifying theme. Without theme, there could be no inspiration. To those more taken by the role of political tactics, Carter's maladroitness was legendary. To be sure, there is plenty of evidence that Carter did not seem overwhelmingly possessed of oratorical skills that would inspire. Nor did he possess the tactical qualities so prized (and perhaps idealized) in Franklin Roosevelt by Richard Neustadt in the latter's *Presidential Power*. The fact is, however, that Carter was an active president (like other Democratic presidents) but his agenda ventured into unfamiliar terrain for a Democratic president, especially later in his administration's tenure. Of presidencies since Kennedy's, for instance, Carter is tied with Lyndon Johnson at the top in regard to the percentage of large, new issues proposed—one of the few indicators on which Carter does sharply contrast with the Republican presidencies.[30] Increasingly, the Carter picture comes into clearer focus: an expansive agenda of not traditionally expansionary programs.

In Carter's case, the play of issue currents set him apart from significant sectors of his party. Buffeted by countercurrents (the result of problems that seemed intractable, lacked familiar solution, or imposed costs without immediate or clear benefit), a middle-road presidency inevitably would be thought of as a "muddled" presidency. With the exception of Richard Nixon, whose early agenda also contained elements not normally associated with traditional Republican party issue postures, Carter fared less well with members of his own party in Congress during his initial year than did any president since Eisenhower.[31] To Carter's supporters who claim that it was the issues that did him in (a lament voiced by the former president himself), there is much to be said. But to Carter's detractors from within his own party, it was less "the issues" than the issues he chose that failed him. Each perspective turns out to have some validity.

It is hard to specify with much exactness the extent to which presidents may keep control of their original agendas, though that seems to be at the heart of the idea of purposeful direction. Much depends on how strongly committed individual presidents are to their proposed programs and perhaps how driven they may be to accomplish a great deed.[32] At least for a while, presidents are well placed to control both the flow and the face of issues on the public agenda. Their policy "solutions" will take prominence, and keeping those "solutions" clear and simple is relevant to establishing "a theme." Set against the idea that presidents are rational directors of their agendas is the notion that alterations in the context of choice are a continuous source of constraint on the fulfillment of initial agendas.[33] The idea that fulfilling initial agendas is the test of directive leadership is a notion that gives no credence to the values of adaptation and learning that are essential to judicious decision making. Is it possible, ironically, for a president to have control of his agenda without having command of the job?

This question leads to a focus on the nature of the skills and attributes often, although frequently in contradictory ways, thought to be important to mastering the presidential role. What are some of these skills? How may we select them? What behavioral consequences flow from having them? Can we effectively sort them out from the context of choice? The next section of this chapter deals with these questions.

PRESIDENTIAL SUCCESS, SKILLS, AND BACKGROUND

The Meaning of Success

Prior to embarking on answering the question, What skills should presidents have?, there is an even more basic question that needs to be addressed: What outcomes should presidents strive to achieve? Put another way, What are the different meanings of success? Following upon Clinton Rossiter's classic discussion of the many hats the American president wears, Fred Greenstein observes that two of the roles the president performs tend to collide. The role of head of state embodies the unity of the nation, whereas the role of head of the executive branch embodies both the aspirations of the president's political followers and his own ideals.[34] The tension between these roles brings us to a new familiar theme—that of balancing legitimacy with purpose.

Gaining direction and maintaining legitimacy are not the only meanings of success, however. Another consideration that must weigh in a definition of success is that of policy competency—a willingness to absorb and use knowledge, to inquire, and to plan for the future.[35] These criteria frequently conflict with both the generation of political direction and popular approval, each of which, broadly conceived, can be thought of as a political function. Technically "correct" proposals may be, indeed often are, politically infeasible. In the hands of extraordinarily astute leadership, by definition, it is possible that policy competency can be given politically accepted direction—accepted by partisan enthusiasts and broader publics both. While not impossible, it is rare.

Ultimately, policy competency is not merely an attractive luxury; it is, instead, at the core of long-term legitimacy. However uncertain is the link between policy and its effects on the public condition, policies designed to appeal to the passions of political supporters or to the short-run popularity of the mass public at the expense of the criterion of effectiveness ultimately will weaken legitimacy as problems mount and the costs of meeting them multiply.

In the face of these complications, the idea of "success" in relation to the presidency is a troublesome concept. It is troublesome, moreover, in at least two respects. The first is the problem of identifying the different dimensions on which we evaluate presidencies and presidents. The second lies in specifying causal antecedents, personal and otherwise, of success.

Dealing with this second problem first, Figure 6.1 presents a schematic linking the personal attributes of the president to the probability of successful outcomes. It posits, in the first instance, a link between personality and temperamental attributes, on the one hand, and experiential or role related ones on the other. This link, for the most part, probably runs from temperament to the nature of one's experiences, but there also is room for causation to be generated in the opposite direction. If, in other words, our temperaments lead us to select certain roles, the roles we experience also tend to have some influence in shaping our temperaments. Filtered through selection processes that may promote or discourage particular sets of traits (interpersonal skills, for instance), the amalgam of experience and temperament should lead to the presence or absence of a given repertoire of skills.[36] (If one does not like politics, for example, it is hard to imagine that entrepreneurial bargaining and skills associated with it will abound.) A given repertoire of skills should then lead to characteristic behavior patterns; patterns that can affect the probability of success along specific dimensions.

The general schema set out in Figure 6.1 is disconnected from environmental and situational forces. Moreover, its links are not empirically derived, but merely a set of common hypotheses about getting the right individual into office and the consequences of doing so. The left-hand side of the diagram asserts a relationship between the process of selection and the probability that persons with the right assortment of skills, deriving from past experiences and temperament, will be selected. This putative link, as I argue in Chapter 5, is problematic. Later in this

FIGURE 6.1. **A Simplified Diagram of Links between Leader Characteristics and Outcomes**

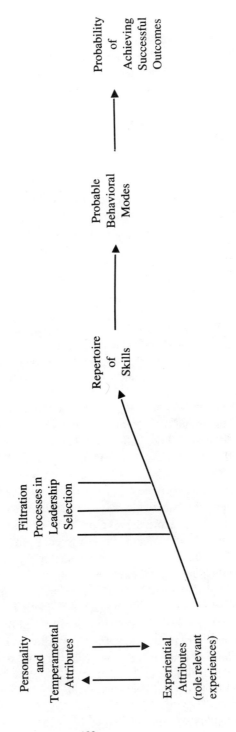

chapter, a partial test of another aspect of this link, namely that between a president's experience and reputed success, will be undertaken.

But what is success? Ultimately, that question is answerable only in judgmental terms. Although there are potentially many ways in which to consider the question, I concentrate here on four ways in which presidencies are judged as successes or failures: (1) retrospective reputation, (2) legislative performance, (3) public approval, and (4) decision making.

1. Retrospective Reputation

Certainly one meaning of presidential success is given through retrospective rankings provided by experts. Originated by the eminent historian, Arthur Schlesinger, the practice of ranking presidents seemingly has now become a tradition, at least as much (and probably with as much system and bias) as the wire press college football rankings. The most recent version of these rankings stems from a *Chicago Tribune* poll of nearly fifty presidential scholars. The case against taking these rankings very seriously is lucidly set forth by one of the participant scholars, Thomas Cronin, who observes that

> Several scholars will question . . . whether rigorous comparisons can be made among modern presidents and presidents in the early years. . . . Scholars [also] raise countless questions that suggest these surveys can only be considered as general rankings and that subjectivity necessarily enters. . . .[37]

Whatever the analytic status of such presidential ratings, presidential reputations seem to possess remarkable stability across various polls, populations of experts, and rating methods.[38] Like college football teams, past performance in the polls counts heavily toward present prominence in them. Unlike college football teams, however, past presidents are not subject to weekly reappraisals of their performance, and so reputations once solidified are rarely altered. Presidents of recent vintage, however, are somewhat more susceptible to reputational movement as interpretations of the record depart more or less from the prevailing contemporary view. Such interpretations, and thus retrospect itself, are influenced inevitably by the conditions of the present, and the leadership styles that come into demand.

Despite the numerous dangers of getting carried away by rankings of possibly incommensurable presidencies, and despite the inevitable variability of interpretation, we cannot resist judgment altogether. For whatever reasons, Hoover couldn't inspire confidence in his administration while Franklin Roosevelt could; Madison couldn't (or didn't try to) develop effective political support in Congress while Jefferson did; Harding could bring no sense of purpose to his leadership while Wilson most eloquently could.

The principal point, of course, is not that individual leaders are all similar, but that the situations they face are contingent and so are their resources. Equally important, as Cronin notes, the evaluators themselves bring significant biases to their task, and one of those biases generally has been a preference for both eloquence (which appeals to people who use language for a living) and activism. In this regard, President Eisenhower's legacy fared poorly until Fred Greenstein's rather recent revisionist interpretations of the Eisenhower mode of leadership.[39] Indeed, Greenstein's analysis reveals the problem of interpretation itself. Eisenhower's "hidden-hand" style of leadership, by definition, could reveal itself only retrospectively, but also only under the closest scrutiny. Moreover, were it not for the succeeding rash of one-term presidencies and a common belief about failures of the presidency, the seemingly tranquil Eisenhower presidency doubtlessly would not have stood in such sharp contrast to earlier judgments of it.

Then, too, it is hard to ignore the fact that historically well-regarded presidencies also tend to be associated with particularly challenging times. If the Republic was to last, would not virtually any first president have been its legitimating symbol? It is not surprising, therefore, that George Washington is always in the select group of those at the top of the rankings. So too, it is not surprising that Lincoln consistently would be rated at the top. If the Republic was to be maintained in the midst of civil strife, would it not be probable that the president who served in such times would be granted the most prominent place in the presidential pantheon? In short, the "great leaders"—"great events" conundrum hovers over retrospective judgment.

2. Legislative Performance

Building a legislative record of success is certainly one indicator of a president's capacity to achieve his goals. Yet, it is abundantly clear that the most important factors attached to presidential success with Congress are beyond a president's immediate control. To the extent that legislative success is measurable (roll-call votes are only a partial measurement), the partisan distribution of seats and the internal cohesion of the president's party are the most critical variables influencing the success of the president's legislative agenda.

Whether the partisan composition of seats and internal partisan cohesion within Congress are primarily parameters a president faces or variables a president may influence is inevitably a matter of some dispute. To the extent, for instance, that presidential interventions, bargaining skills, and programs help promote partisan coherence, the latter is a condition susceptible to influence and not simply a rigid parameter. That circumstances facing presidents and presidential responsibility for them often cannot be disconnected from one another is true enough, but pushed too far such a proposition becomes nearly tautological, i.e., presidents make their own beds and lie in them.

There is precious little evidence, however, to indicate that presidents can be sorcerers when it comes to either shaping or dealing with Congress. There is, on the other hand, more compelling evidence to suggest that broad-scale legislative success is both rare and the product of larger political currents.[40]

If legislative success is principally the product of forces that are at least not directly manipulable, can a benchmark be established by which we can assess presidential legislative succeeess? Two political scientists, Richard Fleisher and Jon Bond, have made an effort to disentangle the presidential elements of this equation from those owing to parameters such as the distribution of seats in Congress.[41] Fleisher and Bond seek to establish for a president of a particular party and a particular distribution of seats an expected level of support. The objective of their exercise is to isolate presidential factors from those that are either a simple function of legislative seat distribution or of ideological compatibility.

Their analysis reveals that internal cohesion of the president's party is especially critical to how the president will fare. In other words, the key determinant of legislative performance is how the president fares with his own party support base. What, in turn, influences this is less clear. It could be, among other things, a result of a president's political astuteness (stroking and bargaining skills), but it also could result from greater party discipline in one party than the other, or from changing agendas and new issues that disturb or exhaust existing coalitions. In brief, there is no evidence to permit us to deduce that presidential skill (or lack thereof) is the (or even a) principal causal attribute.

Lastly it needs to be underscored that legislative success by itself says nothing about the nature of the proposals being legislated, or the care taken in thinking through their implications. The president who is successful with Congress, however, does acquire an image of a vigorous head of the executive branch, able to push his party's agenda ahead.

3. Popular Approval

A modern barometer of presidential success is the level of approval provided presidents in mass surveys. Although popular reactions to a president are greatly determined by party, popular success tends to reflect a president's role especially as chief of state or as vigorous and effective national leader. President Eisenhower, according to Greenstein's recent account, was especially astute at playing the chief of state role—a role, however, that tends to come more easily to those who enter office with the stature of national heroes.[42] Others, however, have given an aura of public presence to the office through their articulateness, charm, and skills of communication. Modern presidents especially endowed with such skills have been Franklin Roosevelt, John Kennedy, and Ronald Reagan, though these skills provide only limited resistance to erosion of popular support.

According to Greenstein, it was Eisenhower's rare talent (or simple good fortune), that he was able to achieve both popularity (legitimacy) and purpose. The former is indisputable. Eisenhower, after all, won election by a wide margin, and reelection by an even wider margin. His approval ratings with only one substantial dip remained consistently high, and he left office as well thought of as when he entered—a formidable feat. More skepticism exists, however, on the achievement of presidential purpose. Neustadt remarks, for instance, that while Eisenhower left office in the heroic state in which he entered it, he did so with his essential strategic aims unfulfilled.[43]

Whether or not sustained approval is consonant with the attainment of purpose is as yet still unclear from the Eisenhower example. In Neustadt's original formulation, prestige (popularity) was the necessary but not sufficient ingredient to the attainment of presidential purpose.[44] It was capital to be invested. But without investing it, no gains could be had. On the other hand, improper investments of presidential prestige could deplete the stock of capital.

The conditions under which presidential approval lasts are also rare. Since the inception of the modern presidency, only Franklin Roosevelt and Dwight Eisenhower remained unscathed in prestige. But it is hard, as Neustadt's struggle to do so attests, to find any clear lessons across those two chapters of American history. The two men (Roosevelt and Eisenhower) seemingly could not be more unalike, nor did their times or political conditions seem to have much in common. Nor, for that matter, do there seem to be many clear personal-based lessons to be drawn from the far larger proportion of presidents whose approval has plummeted. Why presidential popularity tends to plummet owes to many forces—the most powerful of which may be beyond presidential control. To the degree that approval is influenced by the qualities of the leader, however, those qualities remain largely enigmatic.

4. The Management of Decisions

The Cuban Missile Crisis of 1962 is now popularly accepted as the prototype for how presidential decisions ought to be managed. Accounts ultimately portray a decision-making process that was judicious, questioning, and nonbureaucratic in the face of strong propensities for both particularistic advocacy among organizational heads and bureaucratic routine in the implementation of decisions.[45] It would be overstated, to be sure, but yet not unfair to say that much of the reputation John F. Kennedy gained as an astute decision maker derives from the handling of this most portentous crisis of the nuclear age. Neustadt sees from this episode, for example, a president who evidenced "a deliberate reaching down for the details, hard questioning of the alternatives, a drive to protect options from foreclosure by sheer urgency or by *ex parte* advocacy, and finally a close watch on follow-through."[46]

Such prototypes are subject to revisionist tides, however. A recent analysis of the EXCOM decision-making process during the Cuban missile crisis suggests that it had much in common with other decisions whose outcomes were adjudged less favorable.[47] In fact, this analysis suggests that decisional outcomes were evaluated more for their feasibility than their influence on the state of events, and that decisional alternatives were posed sequentially (not synoptically) and evaluated mostly for their negative implications. This is a logic familiar to students of organizational decision making, and it suggests that the process of deciding is fundamentally more similar than different across events. By this logic, what tends to distinguish successful decision making in our minds from failures is our evalua-tion of the outcome rather than the process. Relatedly, Herbert Kaufman notes the dilemma we have in reconciling the idea of being governed by forces beyond inten-tion (Searing's organismic model) with the more culturally familiar notions of vol-untarism and rationality. As Kaufman argues: "The idea that a system could have a life of its own . . . rather than merely serving human purposes and calculations clashes with many assumptions about intelligence, leadership, management, and democracy. . . . The model does not sit well with cherished beliefs."[48]

Outcomes, of course, are not randomly associated with attentiveness to de-tail, planning, and strategic integration, but neither are they guaranteed by such. The more contentious point suggested by the above reevaluation of the decision-making process in the Cuban Missile Crisis is that decisions rarely entail these qualities because to do so would interfere with the prospect of arriving at any deci-sion. The transaction costs incurred in optimizing decisions, in other words, are too great.

Whatever the mix of fate, inertia, or adeptness, the critical point in viewing decision making as one guide to presidential success is that the outcomes them-selves be viewed as successful. Failed decisions are rarely thought to have pro-ceeded from "right" principles of decision making. Similarly, "correct" decisions are often viewed as the product of judiciousness, whatever the process.[49]

Herbert Simon noted that the classic literature of management rested on non-contingent principles that were essentially proverbial—as likely, in absolute and unspecified form, to produce a "bad" as well as a "good."[50] For the most part the state of management prescription in the White House is not far from this proverbial status. A recent book by two members of the Carter administration illustrates the problem. Doubtlessly chastened by their experiences and by the perceived failures of the Carter administration to manage its priorities, the authors provide a number of suggestions on behalf of what they call a "strategic presidency." Ultimately, the strategic presidency is a Carter antidote. Stick by your goals, but adapt to events may be derived as one of the book's major integrating maxims.[51] It is not abun-dantly clear that we have pushed much beyond Machiavelli.

Presidential Styles, Skills, and Outcomes

The scheme presented earlier in Figure 6.1 makes the commonplace assump-tion that success is the offspring of skill. Yet, the influences of the unforeseen and the limits of cognition and of intent compromise that assumption. Nonetheless, those who focus on leadership are apt to emphasize the volitional role and the im-pact of the leader. They are, in brief, apt to take what Searing has called the mechanistic view. The relationship between a leader's talents and behavior on the one hand, and outcomes on the other, of course, is a matter of lengthy historical de-bate—indeed, as noted, of a theory of history itself.

Broadly conceived, I divide the realm of skills, like the brain, into two hemispheres—a "political skills" hemisphere and a "policy skills" hemisphere. Each of these "hemispheres," of course, contains functions that can be elaborated further. And like the hemispheres of the brain, the idea is that politics and policy functions are complements rather than inhibitors of one another. Heineman and Hessler state it thusly: "Policy is where you want to go. . . . Politics is how you get there."[52] Yet, there is inherent tension between "policy" and "politics." For "The increasing professionalism of both the political advisors and the policy advisors," Heineman and Hessler also admit, "has served to widen, not narrow, the gap in language and approach."[53] Politics, then, is both instrumental, and at times antagonistic, to policy. Politics is the vehicle through which policies come to fruition, but politics frequently is the inhibitor of policy "rationality."

In Figure 6.2, four sets of presidential styles and skills are broadly set forth. The first two are further subdivided into two clusters of apparently distinctive traits. Both of these general traits, "public presence" and "intra-elite relations" are political but represent different aspects of politics. The third set of traits, "organizational and managerial," straddles a fuzzy boundary line between technical talents and political ones. Organizational and managerial skills, in Neustadt's view, flow inevitably from a president's sense of power and attentiveness to sources of leverage and information.[54] Whether or not managerial skills are simply a subspecies of political skill, it is probably the case that they have become increasingly central to the conduct of the modern presidency. Simply coordinating the flow of routine so as to avoid political embarrassment has become a task of substantial proportions. A president's management skills, of course, are necessarily different from those of a middle-level manager. A president's talents for management inevitably must be generated from a sense of politics, not just a reading of organizational charts or a sensitivity to detail. How the president attends to detail, but particularly how he handles and meshes personnel responsible for the details, makes management virtually synonymous with politics. As noted below, however, there are several different types of objectives to be managed, and contradictions exist across the particular managerial styles called for by these different objectives.

The fourth set of traits, however, more distinctly falls into a different hemisphere of functions, one having to do with policy making. Policy skills are based on a capacity for detachment and knowledge, and on analytic ability. None of these are traits that tend to be cultivated by a career in politics. These traits are least likely to be appreciated since care taken in arriving at policy judgments is almost always paid less attention than the substance of the policy decisions themselves.

To be made effective, policy skills must be linked to other sets of skills—the organizational and political ones just discussed. To move decisions along effectively, to coordinate them, and to have a sufficient informational base to make them, presidents need to have some managerial propensities. To gain political support for them, presidents need to have entrepreneurial and mobilizing abilities.

FIGURE 6.2. Types of Presidential Traits and Their Expected Consequences

Traits	Forms of Success	Outcomes Generated
1. Public Presence		
(a) Unifying Traits ———▶	Popularity ——————————▶	Legitimacy and Prestige of Presidency
—warmth, chemistry —articulateness —symbol of nation		
(b) Mobilizing Traits ———▶	Partisan Support ———▶	Partisan Cohesion and Enthusiasm
—articulateness —ideological fervor		
2. Intra-Elite Relations		
(a) Conciliatory Traits ———▶	Trust, Persuasion ———▶	Nonpartisan Agreement
—rapport, accommodativeness		
(b) Entrepreneurial Traits ———▶	Political Reputation ———▶	Promotion of Program and Legislative Enactments
—risk-taking, manipulativeness, bargaining skill		
3. Organizational and Managerial ———▶	Coordination Rationality Control ———▶	Consistency and Integration; Appearance of Competence; "Good Decisions"
4. Policy Knowledge and Analysis ———▶	Appearance of Wisdom and Soundness ———▶	Prudence

196

And to provide a larger base of policy and political support, presidents need to have conciliatory skills and some capacity to generate a magisterial public presence.

Skills are specialized, linked to particular forms of success, and presumably to particular kinds of outcomes. Yet, if skills are specialized the presidency compels their interdependence. In fact, though, it is rare, perhaps impossible for all these traits to be integrated in one person.

The crux of the leadership problem is inherent in this dilemma. How can diverse traits be combined? Of course, all top leadership positions require a repertoire of skills, some of which inevitably are in contradiction to others, and all top political leaders are engaged in a multiplicity of games requiring different emphases. The U.S. president, like leaders elsewhere, is engaged in multiple games, but is apt to be engaged in more of them, in more contradictory ways, and to be facing more formidable obstacles to achievement than leaders in most other industrialized democracies. The skill factor, thus, becomes so especially crucial for American presidents, not because they are inevitably less talented than their peers in Europe or Japan, but because they must play in so many competing games requiring vastly different sets of talents. Like football players of another era, U.S. presidents must have skills appropriate to all phases of the game. But they, in turn, face specialists on all fronts.

Numerous studies of the concept of leadership produce large lists of associated traits—all of them contingent upon situational and other contextual variables.[55] After listing an extensive inventory of political leadership traits, Glenn Paige reduces them to their essence. "Taken as a whole," he argues, "these concepts suggest that political leadership comprises decisional initiative, pacific and coercive persuasion, the exacerbation or reduction of conflict, follower need satisfaction as related to task accomplishment, and action within an influencing but partly influenceable situational context."[56] These overlap substantially, though not stated in exactly the same ways, with the traits set forth in Figure 6.2. Each of these "leadership traits" needs to be elaborated on in order to see both its possibilities and limits.

(1) Public Presence

Public presence has two important, and quite divergent, characteristics. On the one hand, public presence provides a leadership symbol of the whole of the political community, a role that Greenstein believes Eisenhower fulfilled superbly. Another sense of public presence, however, as Greenstein also claims, seemingly requires diametrically opposite tendencies. This is the role of partisan head of government. The first emphasizes unity; the second emphasizes partisan leadership. The first emphasizes a reaching out to (or at least a symbolic representation of) the community at large; the second emphasizes a stoking of the partisan fires, an appeal to the ideals (and interests) of a faction. The two appear to be con-

tradictory, and the fulfillment of both roles, assuming they can be effectively fulfilled together, will require either unusual leaders or circumstances.

(a) A Unifying Presence.   Perhaps more than any other leadership value, providing an embodiment of the nation and its organic unity is dependent more upon the
prior achievements and status of the presidential role occupant than the cultivation
of a particular set of skills honed while in the presidential office. For a president to
enjoy the image of national symbol in more than perfunctory ways, it is likely that
both the situation that produced his ascent into office and his background are exceedingly important to his ability to carry off this particular aspect of the presidential role. To come into office as a national hero or otherwise unassociated with a
particular political faction is an advantage in fulfilling the unifier role, though it is
insufficient as a condition for determining successful fulfillment of this role. (An
indication that more than these circumstances is required may be gleaned from the
Carter experience—perhaps next to Eisenhower the modern president least identified as a partisan or factional representative.)

Possessing a background as a national but nonpartisan figure is a key resource
for laying claim to unifying leadership. How to hold on to this resource, however,
is a problem that requires political skill and good fortune. If the status of unifier is
nearly impossible to achieve by behavior in office alone, it seems easily enough
squandered there. The inability to compromise, to see the play of perspectives, or
to accept the satisfactory and feasible over the optimal and impossible are traits
that seem likely to squander such a resource. Drivenness, a quality seemingly
characteristic of Woodrow Wilson, destroyed his prospects for maintaining his
status as a reform president and wartime leader.[57] His opportunity to influence
American involvement in the postwar world was lost by the unwillingness to accommodate suboptimal positions. By contrast, Greenstein's portrayal of
Eisenhower emphasizes a leader concerned with goals but also with appearances; a
leader as concerned with the implications of "how" it is to be done as with "what" it
is that needs doing.[58]

Inevitably, though, the idea of a leader as both unifier *and* goal-seeker is hard
to imagine unless the leader is willing to defer the seeking and attainment of many
of his goals. It is on this score that Greenstein's portrayal of Eisenhower becomes
more debatable, although even Greenstein concedes that Eisenhower's domestic
program was incrementally (or decrementally) adjusted to the political circumstances he faced.[59] The unifying leader is likely to be oriented toward the
status quo, to be temperamentally conservative and incremental when there is no
great swell for change. When there is, on the other hand, a mood of dissatisfaction,
placidity may come into disrepute. It is, after all, worthwhile noting that
Eisenhower's low point in popularity was reached in the midst of the deep recession of 1957-58. The advantages of indirection are large; so too are its limits. A
hundred years prior to the Eisenhower presidency, both the advantages and disad-
vantages of indirection and of incremental compromise became evident as the sec-

tional fissures beneath the fragile American state were patched repeatedly in order to maintain the state itself. In the end, however, the patches could not hold.

At other times, the sheer urgency of action (or the appearance of it) may be so demanding and generally accepted that a president inclined to respond to it will be seen as a national leader rather than a partisan or factional one. Franklin Roosevelt in both the early and later days of his administration seemed to fit this mold. The depression crisis of the early years and the war crisis of the later ones were times allowing for the exercise of much leadership latitude. Collective problems, however, beget responses that ineluctably have distributive consequences. Thus, no matter how much early latitude is given, attempts to tackle them will appear increasingly driven by partisan outlooks and interests. Is this not, in fact, what the end of the fabled "presidential honeymoon" is mostly about? It is essentially a movement from the chief of state role (the unifying leader tackling common problems) to the partisan head of government role (seeking divisive solutions).

President Eisenhower, in the revisionist interpretation, is now accepted as the prototype of the national hero (the route most often being military leader) who takes advantage of this stature to enhance the legitimacy of the office he holds (partly by sacrificing some of the goals he wishes). While there is much in common here with the first general to hold presidential office, the generals in office between the first (Washington) and the last (Eisenhower) have failed to fulfill similar roles. Some (Harrison and Taylor) died in office at an early stage. But Jackson and Grant, two of the grander national heroes to attain the presidency, were more famed for their partisanship and favoritism (spoils) than their commitment to national unity in office.

To have a background that adds stature provides a firm pedestal, and to inherit a situation perceived as requiring "national solutions" enhances opportunities. Willingness to adjust goals to appearances and elevate equilibration to an exalted mode of presidential conduct, however, are the characteristics of presidential behavior that diminish the potential for enmity. Lacking stature, of course, a president with such a temperament is more apt to be ridiculed as equivocal and indecisive than to be honored. For better or worse, such a style of leadership also will not frontally attack problems that lack consensual solutions, nor will it tend to define direction or inspire vision. Moreover, for such a style of leadership to be thought successful, it will be dependent upon times in which few political passions are stirred and in which political divisions are weak (this of course may be the product, not simply the determinant, of such a style of leadership). This style of leadership, furthermore, is best distilled by those who are most widely respected and venerated. Heroes, ironically, are best positioned to legitimize antiheroic leadership.

(b) A Stirring Presence. A very different set of skills from those that help to generate a unifying presence are those that respond to (or help stoke) partisan appeals. Partisanship, of course, was in evidence long before the development of a partisan

mass public that was able to be communicated with directly from Washington. As president, Jefferson demonstrated the power of party to support the presidency. Jackson further exemplified this, and by his era localized party organization had begun to be established. By the 1840s, as we earlier noted, partisanship and cultural values had become closely linked.

Presidents have always symbolized the political forces that brought them to office, of course. And these forces must continually be appealed to. The instant and obvious irony, however, is that the more sharply presidents appeal to their partisans—not always these days coterminous with party—the more they are seen as being incapable of uniting the nation. Such charges have been leveled against President Reagan but also commonly unleashed against other presidents in the past.

The capacity to excite partisan or factional passions is often associated with the notion of leadership. Its essence is to reduce complexity to simplicity, and to appeal to those who define the situation similarly, i.e., partisans. We can easily think of candidates, of politicians, and of presidents who excel (or excelled) at partisan rhetoric—among others, William Jennings Bryan, Franklin Roosevelt during the heart of the New Deal years, Harry Truman, Hubert Humphrey, Ronald Reagan, and Ted Kennedy. Although the means by which rhetoric is carried have altered significantly over the years, the essential impulse remains much the same—to capture the hearts of partisan enthusiasts.

Without partisan enthusiasm there is no gyroscope, but with an excess of it there is no judiciousness or balance. Skills at promoting partisan enthusiasm need not collide with skills at generating national unity. They might operate at different levels, for example. Still their propensities are to collide. Moreover, problems are inevitably far more complex at any time, not merely the present, than are their partisan "solutions." The rhetoric of partisanship can be a help in sustaining the enthusiasms of activists and party workers for gaining nomination, though more inhibiting for gaining election.[60] It no doubt always has been such, regardless of the nominating process. Bryan was not the product of the same process that produced McGovern, no matter how similar some saw their candidacies to be. How much partisan enthusiasm and rhetoric can help a president govern successfully—the ultimate payoff—is uncertain. For partisan fire that appeals to party activists does not necessarily pay off in political support within Congress, especially if coalitions are slim. If rhetoric enlists support, it equally invigorates opposition. While no one can safely predict what the fate of Ted Kennedy would have been with Congress in 1980 had he rather than Jimmy Carter been president, his agenda sharpened on the abrasive of partisan enthusiasm would seem to have held even less prospect than Carter's. Partisan rhetoric, whatever else, is escalatory and reflexive rather than reflective. Whether or not the policies that flow from it lead to disaster, it is surely the case that the promises that flow from it can. Indeed, on a sobering note, what most distinguishes the era of Reagan from that of Bryan is not so much the rhetoric of partisanship as the speed with which flamboyant promises (and their premises) can be juxtaposed with their quite unflamboyant "effects."

2. Elite Relations

Thus far, I have focused on traits appropriate to the world outside Washington while recognizing some measure of connectedness between the two. For now, however, we turn to the capital and to the elites with whom the president, or presidential surrogates, must engage directly. In presidential relations with these elites, I draw a broad distinction between behaviors that tend to promote accommodation and those that tend to promote programmatic aspiration. No sharp line separates these activities, and indeed skills that produce trust and faith among bargaining partners are also a vital resource to a president's entrepreneurial aspirations. To the extent, however, that entrepreneurship implies risk taking, conciliation implies risk reduction and certainty for one's potential bargaining partners. First, we look at those traits that seem to promote conciliation and agreement.

(a) Conciliatory Styles. Under normal circumstances the environment faced by the president is one of fractionated authority with significant limits to party cohesion. Thus, the American system makes personal relations important (they are, of course, to some extent everywhere) because so little can be taken for granted. Interpersonal chemistry, warmth, and rapport, therefore, are helpful ingredients of a candidate's personality—ones that serve to provide public presence as well as to smooth dealings with other leaders. Remoteness and coldness are characteristics that weaken these bonds, as perhaps most sharply evidenced in recent times by the personalities of Nixon and Carter. Naturalness and charm, as seen most recently in presidents such as Ford and Reagan, are prized as in most other walks of life, requiring a good bit of interpersonal engagement. As a political capital, Washington glitters more than most with egoism. Its elite—official and unofficial—wants to be attended to, and is, in any event, aggressively independent. Presumably, therefore, as popular lore has it, gaining the ear and the trust of this elite is an important matter. A president's willingness to stroke those who write about him, or those who seal the fate of his proposals, is a sign of his political sensitivities. At least in cultivating the doyens of the press, the leading Washington-based columnists, President Kennedy was reputed to have been masterly—though being in Washington already he had a head start at this. Those arriving at the White House from outside Washington have some disadvantage in cultivating these relationships, especially if they have no large national reputation to begin with. Obviously, the combination of these circumstances plagued Carter. Presidents of either more earthy veneer than Kennedy (such as Johnson) or just simply less cosmopolitan tastes (such as Ford) are also less likely to be drawn to, and thus nurtured by, those in the opinion business.

Cultivating members of Congress is another very important means by which presidents can build trust and presumably gain assistance for those times they are most in need of it—at least, so says the conventional wisdom. Both the possibilities and, perhaps more starkly than intended, the limits of such cultivation are suggested by two scholars of American political institutions. In the first case, John Manley emphasizes the importance but especially the limits of building good will among members of Congress.[61] Favors cannot alter political arithmetic, as Manley puts it. They can buy, in his view, only a chance of success. The chance has no fixed probability of course; the odds may be very long, and the costs incurred in its purchase steep. Favors, Manley notes, beget debts.[62] In short, lobbying and building trust does more for atmospherics than for programs. In the end, such activities are justified on the principle that their absence is apt to hurt more than their presence is apt to help. Manley thus concludes two things of special note. First, the political arithmetic is primary—big changes can be pushed and accommodated only in the presence of big majorities. Second, presidents can learn from the past only those lessons relevant to forming strategies applicable to their present circumstances; judging which elements of the past are appropriate to the present is itself problematic.[63]

Appraising the relational styles of Presidents Johnson, Nixon, Ford, and Carter with Congress, Charles O. Jones observes that the emphasis given to diplomacy and cultivation has much to do with the nature of the president's agenda (how much he is asking from Congress) and the political arithmetic he faces in Congress (whether or not he has much opportunity for success).[64] In this view, Presidents Johnson and Carter shared similar ambitions and confronted similar situations. Johnson paid much attention to cultivation and Carter little if any, at least in the early reputation setting days of their presidencies. Where Johnson seemed aware of the importance of the stakes for those he sought to influence and to lead, Carter operated alone. Some of Johnson's skills in dealing with Congress, no doubt, derived from his intimate working knowledge of the institution, one of whose chambers he led. As well, his attention to accommodative dealings may have derived from his experience of being majority leader in the Senate under a minority president who, himself, emphasized consultation. Carter, on the other hand, had none of these experiences. For all that, Johnson failed to do appreciably better with Congress than did Carter, once the giddy days of the first session of the Eighty-ninth Congress had passed.

A politics influenced by mutual reciprocity and sensitivity to stakes is apt to spur accommodation and, in turn, to be deeply influenced by an accommodative climate. Students of Scandinavian politics have noted the centrality of such characteristics in the political culture of these countries.[65] There is much to commend a mode of politics that emphasizes these characteristics. It is, however, equally important to recognize the limitations a controversial issue climate places on this form of politics. The divisive circumstances of the Vietnam War and domestic disturbance ended Johnson's ability to deal with Congress in this accommodative mode,[66] and the midterm losses suffered in the 1966 elections put an end to the advantageous political arithmetic. The skills of conciliation and of cultivation, then, hinge on the existence of a largely consensual environment. If they are to produce success, they also require a favorable political arithmetic. Among the manipulable factors responsible for the loss of consensual atmosphere, most ironically, was a Johnson weakness of a different sort: weighting the short-term political values associated with policy over the consequences of imprudence.[67]

Entrepreneurial Styles. Entrepreneurship and conciliation can be synergistic rather than distinctive traits. Effective entrepreneurship often requires cultivation of those in a position to critically affect the success of a leader's goals. Whereas conciliatory skills especially require reducing the risk for others and enlarging their sense of self-importance (in essence, cooptation), entrepreneurial talents lie in risk taking, manipulation, bargaining, and in the picturesque phraseology of American politics and business, wheeling and dealing. Conciliators are respected for not leaving potential supporters in the lurch or for not leading them astray. Entrepreneurs are admired for their seeming capacity to cajole results and promote their aims. Effective entrepreneurs, when conditions call for it, are effective conciliators as well. "Let us reason together" was Lyndon Johnson's familiar biblical incantation. But if Johnson anticipated needs he also was equally famed and reputed for his application of "the treatment" and his ability to browbeat and intimidate those of lesser constitution. Entrepreneurship, by definition, is also risk taking. And risk taking normally produces aggressive behavior.

Greenstein's inquiry into Eisenhower's leadership style notes that Eisenhower was unlikely to be an effective promoter of broad-scale programs; that he was neither of partisan nor entrepreneurial bent.[68] The literature of political science is filled with the exploits of entrepreneurial leaders (a form that seemed more in vogue when there seemed more opportunities to exploit than elements of constraint), from the fabled Mayor Lee of New Haven to the more publicly obscure leaders of local and regional public authorities.[69] Among presidents, both Franklin Roosevelt and Lyndon Johnson in the modern era have been celebrated for ther keen sense of exploitation of opportunity, indeed of creating opportunity. Johnson's repute as an effective manipulator of congressional outcomes runs deep—apparently deeper than evidence warrants. A masterful political operator, according to a common supposition, works in the margins turning close calls into narrow victories, a characteristic that also was attributed to Ronald Reagan through his inaugural year in the presidency. An analysis by George Edwards, however, indicates the tendency to overestimate these manipulative powers.[70] On votes in Congress on which Johnson took a clear position and intervened directly in the legislative process, very few were close. In fact, according to Edwards's data, Johnson won very few marginal roll calls. Further, he concludes none of these marginal roll calls were of major importance.[71] The political arithmetic is clearly the dominant force. Much of Johnson's "magic touch," then, was simply predicated upon favorable political arithmetic, a seeming mandate derived from a landslide electoral victory over a foe of distinctly different outlook, and a reputation as a masterful practitioner of the arts of "wheeling and dealing" on Capitol Hill. As Manley shows, however, after the favorable Eighty-ninth Congress departed, Johnson was regularly humbled on Capitol Hill.[72]

Finally, just as the chief of state style normally leads to a *status quo* or incremental mode of conduct, the entrepreneurial style is associated with the promotion of change. The entrepreneurial style tends also to emphasize immediate results more clearly than consequences—getting the job done, rather than assessing the implications of what the job is. As a style of leadership, entrepreneurship seems especially appropriate for those times when opportunities maximally avail themselves. Ironically, the fragmented quality of the matrix of power in the United States leads to a maximum dependency on the entrepreneurial talents of political leaders. Such talents during normal circumstances often blossom at the intermediate ranges of formal power within the system—committee and subcommittee chairs within Congress, upper-level bureaucrats, and so forth. Their opportunities, however, are often presidential constraints. At the apex of the executive, opportunities are more limiting if only because aspirations are typically more comprehensive. A president's attempts to maximize the opportunities granted by the occasional moments when his resources also are at their apogee is indicative of his entrepreneurial flair. Consequently, entrepreneurial skills may be utilized to open wider the windows of opportunity that are made available, but rarely can entrepreneurs by their talents alone get the window to open at all.

3. Organizational and Managerial Styles

Notwithstanding incantations to the virtues of organizing things properly, prescriptions for appropriate organizational forms and sensibilities are wondrously diverse and ultimately proverbial. Though organizational and managerial skills have a technocratic timbre, these abilities also spring from one's sensibilities about politics, and, in turn, influence one's reputation for political aptitude.

The model of organization that Neustadt attributes to Franklin Roosevelt has nearly attained legendary status as a prescribed style for managing the White House. The idea is to perpetuate uncertainty among one's subordinates, to have them share responsibilities without definitive demarcations, and to maximize the flow of intelligence to the top by informal means of communication. This frenetic and informal organizational style was shared at least in part by Lyndon Johnson, and earlier by President Kennedy, who was a studied pupil of Neustadt's observations. What Kennedy learned, Johnson seemed to have an instinct for. But the Johnson personal style and his intimidating presence brought informality into disrepute. Fashions in presidential organization have come and gone, each new one (which, of course, is usually an old one) ultimately succumbing to vulnerabilities that provide the prescriptive base for its replacement. By the time Eisenhower's reputation was gaining scholarly rehabilitation, it became clear that his more orderly, less obtrusive, and more institutionalized style of White House management was regaining favor. The problem is that organizational style and the president are not separable commodities. The general esteem in which the president is held during his administration and in short-term historical perspective, obviously contributes mightily to the perceived virtues or deformities of his style of White House management.

While there is no single prescriptive mold into which all presidencies can be organizationally cast, there also is an inevitable tendency to believe that organizational process and structure is itself an independent variable influencing decision making. A recent account of presidential decision making in regard to escalating American involvement in Vietnam illustrates full well, however, that organizational processes are frequently epiphenomenal to the drives of the president. Rather than forming the boundaries in which decisions would take place, the advisory process served principally to legitimate those decisions.[73]

There is no single valid theory of White House management, only particular strands of managerial emphasis. This being the case, organizational styles are strongly contingent on precedent (what was perceived to work or fail) and on what precisely a president seeks to achieve. Three points of emphasis, frequently contradictory, are discussed below.

(a) Appearing Competent. Appearances in politics are especially crucial. A former U.S. cabinet officer with a background in business nicely contrasted the world of enterprise with that of government. In business, he concluded, "it was the reality of the situation that in the end determined whether we succeeded or not. In the crudest sense, this meant the bottom line. . . . In government there is no bottom line, and that is why you can be successful if you appear to be successful. . . ."[74]

While there is a variety of ways in which a president can look either competent or incompetent, one of the key aspects of developing such an image relates one way or another to the president's seeming ability to be in control of things. From a managerial standpoint, this commonly means avoiding unseemly public spats among administration officials or the appearance of dramatic policy inconsistency over a short span of time. Avoiding these pitfalls calls for some degree of coordination and policy reliability. It calls, above all, for maintaining some measure of control over the White House and the departments. The proximity of senior officials to the press and other convenient outlets makes it difficult to control the overtness of policy, institutional, or personal competition. Sealing off all of government (even the White House) often necessitates draconian measures that make a president look even worse.

At the most elementary level, however, presidents must appear able to competently manage their own immediate operations. Richard Rose claims this is the most a president can sensibly aspire to; to be a chief, not a chief executive.[75] Yet, like a good executive in any setting, the president must at a minimum do two things: (1) Have some system for keeping tabs of the different schedules attached to the many different things that must be done or be kept aware of; and (2) delegate authority to those with a reputation for competence, influence, and loyalty.

At the same time, from the standpoint of appearances, the more publicity attached to doing each of these things (it helps, in this regard, to have begun one's administration by doing them), the more detrimental they become. President Carter, who was tagged with the image of being a technocratic decision maker, had one of the least organized presidencies in recent times despite the president's intense involvement with detail. Once management science was put in the service of the Carter presidency in the person of Alonzo McDonald, the deputy chief of staff, the operation of staff work and tracking deadlines improved, but the exercise itself came in for ridicule as a technocratic game of musical chairs and synchronous charts.[76] The calling in of old standbys ("wise men") as trouble shooters tends to call further attention to an administration's plight, wherein the standing of the president is sufficiently reduced that he becomes visibly dependent upon the reputation of professional insiders. The moral is that it is better to start off with the Washington luminaries than to be forced later to admit the need for them. Unlike presidents, however, advisers or cabinet officials have the opportunity to get out at the peak of their powers and so add luster to their reputations—such that they are apt to be called on in a pinch by future presidents. President Reagan's much acclaimed head of the Office of Congressional Relations (OCR), Max Friedersdorf, who left after the first year, took advantage of his (but not his president's) opportunity to escape the consequences of his monumental legislative successes of 1981.

(b) Being Rational. Whereas "appearing competent" requires presidents to seem to be in control of their administrations, "being rational" requires a diversity of intelligence sources, vigorous debate and analysis of positions. Diversity, debate, and analysis are to be encouraged if a president chooses to maximize the range of decisional options so as to select optimal policies. Paradoxically, such a choice will encourage every tendency that contributes to an organizational and procedural dynamic that can make a president look "incompetent" and out of control. Diversity arises soon enough in any presidential administration. One that is staffed with the idea of accentuating diversity for the virtues it is reputed to bring to policy debate also will exacerbate the problems that diversity generates in an information leaky environment.

   In addition, a style of organization that encourages others to commit themselves while the president's cards are held closely also encourages fierce jockeying among the "petitioners" for the last word. For if the president is to maximize a range of well thought out options, it is virtually necessary that the presidential hand not be tipped, and that the president's patterns of preference not become reflexively predictable. Aside from the difficulties this style inevitably would create with a president's political constituency, the encouragement of others to pursue their angles and to gain the last word also would make for the appearance of chaos in an administration and inconstancy in the White House. To a considerable extent, especially in its earlier years, the Carter administration suffered severely from this syndrome.

(c) Being Omnipresent. Seeking to get hold of the operational details of government in order to gain control of the functioning of its parts is an organizational style

that springs from presidential aspiration to command all of the executive branch through the White House. A taste for defining all problems of government as problems with a White House tag accompanies this style of management, and requires what Richard Rose calls, "saturation tactics."[77] Rose distinguishes between the saturation styles employed by Johnson and Nixon and what he takes to be the self-consciously more limiting "free-enterprise" (Neustadtian—overlapping responsibilities) style employed by Presidents Roosevelt and Kennedy.[78] A less kindly view of the Kennedy presidency, however, sees its most influential organizational tendency to have been the deinstitutionalization of government, substituting informal and *ad hoc* White House centralization for bureaucratic and routine elements of government.[79]

However particular presidencies are characterized, the more important points here are twofold. One is the conflict between the pervasive presidential centrism implied by omnipresence, on the one hand, and knowledgeable decision making, on the other. The second is the potential danger of escalatory expectations associated with the "omnipresent presidency." In regard to the first of these issues, omnipresence implies centrism, and centrism suggests that it is the duty of the executive branch to fall in line with presidential wishes however these are communicated. In this style of organization, the bureaucracy itself is to be either short-circuited or penetrated by the White House but, in any event, subject to unhealthy disrespect. Whatever limited memory government possesses and whatever constraints this imposes upon rashness are treated as obstacles to be overcome. Berman's analysis of the Johnson administration's decision to commit combat troops on a large scale in Vietnam, for example, illustrates that "the problem was not necessarily one of information scarcity, but an insensitivity to how expert knowledge should be utilized."[80] In brief, a decision was imposed to be legitimized and accepted by experts rather than to be shaped by them or sharply debated between them.

The second danger, that of escalatory expectations presumably generated by the omnipresent presidency, is alluded to by Garry Wills in his critical analysis of the Kennedy presidency. Wills fears that "This personalization creates expectations of charisma in noncharismatic times, to be followed by inevitable disappointment."[81]

Whether these assertions are true or not, what I hope to have illustrated is that presidential organization can be developed around several different values, three of which—competence, rationality, and control—are emphasized here. Moreover, these different modes of organization are not often consistent with one another, points I also hope to have indicated here. In the end, of course, organizational style is the byproduct of a president's concept of the presidential role and, therefore, generally cannot be prescribed apart from that.

4. Policy Skills

Policy skill may mean several things. It may mean, for example, the capacity to think strategically, to see how the parts fit a larger vision; it may mean a sophisticated historical knowledge or background to a set of problems of either international or national importance; it may mean a capacity to see various angles of a problem and to stand back from it with elements both of empathy and of analytic detachment; it may mean a bent toward the reanalysis of assumptions when existing assumptions appear to fail tests of reality; it may mean a tempered capacity to put policy (and thus its limits) into a broader perspective; and lastly, in its most common form, it may mean a consuming interest in the "facts" relevant to policy making and a willingness to examine them in a nonreflexive way.

Just as presidents are not management scientists, however, they also are not staff analysts. Ultimately, they are political leaders. Yet, unless the role of political leader is defined solely in terms of the survival and good image of the incumbent, it must encompass wisdom—a term notoriously susceptible to subjective definition. Wise leadership, Robert C. Tucker asserts, is "foresightful, takes into account, in weighing what the response should be, the potential or probable further development of the circumstances that have already taken on meaning as a problem situation. It assesses the situation in its future dimension. This requires both the capacity to analyze the causation of circumstances and vision."[82]

Putting aside for the moment the troubling question of defining criteria by which to assess "foresight" (as well to extricate it from simple good fortune), Tucker's definition joins what may be very separable ideas: The ability *to analyze causation* and the capacity *to articulate a vision* based on that analysis, and inspire others to it. The latter, Tucker makes clear, is necessary for effective leadership. As he puts it: "The leaders of national governments are in default by failing to fulfill the first function of political leadership—the authoritative defining of the situation for the political community."[83] In other words, the political leader, in order to lead by this definition, will have to muster the skills of public presence and entrepreneurship on behalf of a situational definition arrived at through careful analysis.

Although these are not inherently mutually exclusive tasks, they are apt to be joined together mostly in dreams. While analysis of causation emphasizes the acquisition of knowledge, it also yields a high level of complexity, and complexity induces uncertainty rather than its opposite. Uncertainty, in turn, tends to promote inconsistency, awareness of contingency, and caution about prescriptions designed as comprehensive solutions. Conditionals lead to hems and haws, not inspired visions. And surely if one cannot inspire uninhibited confidence in one's own perspectives, it can hardly be communicated to others. In the more austere definition of the term, consistency and simplicity provide the essence of leadership.[84] Strongly held beliefs with a low level of complexity, under this definition, are key ingredients both for holding a clear vision and inspiring others on its behalf. The capacity to communicate complexity carries with it an obligation to de-escalate proposed solutions and to communicate their limits as well. Insofar as the rhetoric of leadership goes, this prescription sounds more soporific than inspiring.

Complexity and detachment, then, are likely to limit the capacity to emit clear and unequivocal postures, to define situations without ambiguity, and to galvanize others in and outside of government to a clear vision. More than likely, persons for whom complexity and detachment are central traits will be decried as wishy-washy, unable to provide direction, and incapable of leading. Such commentaries were not uncommonly made about a candidate such as Adlai Stevenson or a president such as Jimmy Carter.

Once knowledge was less abundant and faith more common. Now, however, political faith predicated on simple visions travels a shorter distance. More knowledge, faster feedback, and more skepticism diminish the latitude for direction based on heady visions. All of this works to hem in simplistic purpose, yet fails to provide a basis for other more limited or contingent directions. Simplistic courses of action are more frequently subject to skeptical reaction, but skepticism by itself cannot build political support for leadership. Complex estimates of causal forces and sober appraisals of courses of action are hard sells.

These observations are limited, to some degree, by the culture and forms of politics in different settings. In West Germany, a setting more conducive (if increasingly less so) to a bureaucratized politics, Helmut Schmidt could appear both knowledgeable and prudent and also politically popular—more so, it turned out, than the activist base of his party wished. In the age of skepticism, however, both knowledge and inspiration are desired from our leaders, both an awareness of complexity and an ability to generate direction. It may be that we are demanding impossible things.

For the moment at least, among the mass public, strong leadership is most valued.[85] Thus, the president must be "hot," appearing to be a strong leader, among mass publics. At the same time, the president must be "cool" and dispassionately analytic in regard to much smaller and selective but influential audiences. At times, decisions are made that generate the appropriate image for different audiences. During the Cuban Missile Crisis, President Kennedy gained the reputation of being cool and analytic, and of being skeptical and questioning of options that would eliminate further choices. The audience engaged in this evaluation was tiny but influential in making Kennedy's reputation as a cool and calculating and knowledgeable decision maker, especially in contrast to his successor's reputation for handling foreign policy decisions. But the missile crisis also made Kennedy look forceful to broader mass audiences. For a time, he basked in this remarkable confluence of favorable judgment. Just the obverse happened for Carter, however, as a result of the decision to rescue the American hostages held in Iran. Carter's decision seemed insufficiently calculating as to its consequences. Its failure added to Carter's ill-starred reputation for incompetence. But the need to appear forceful could well have been an underlying propellant toward rashness.

Background and Presidential Success

The message that Richard Neustadt left us with over twenty years ago was that masters at the helm were needed to steer amidst rocky shoals. They would be found, he warned, only from a select group within our political class. In his words, "we shall have to pick them from among experienced politicians of extraordinary temperament—an even smaller class."[86] In successive additions to his masterful analysis, Neustadt grew less and less optimistic of finding persons to meet the job description that he generated in the initial volume, and more dependent on the hope that caution might be had from leaders and realism from publics. Such reduced aspirations seem to stem from the belief that the navigable waters have narrowed as American politics has grown more fluid and its governing has grown more complex.[87]

As we recall from Figure 6.1, it is usually assumed that skills derive from experience and temperament. Thus, skill repertoires are expected to be associated with past roles. In Neustadt's portrayal, the presidency is a supremely political job requiring exceedingly astute political skills: Not the skills of a mere campaigner, however, nor exclusively the skills of those who run for (or run others for) office, but the skills of those who *both run for and run an office*. Skills in electoral politics get a candidate there, but skills in the politics of governing are presumed necessary for presidential objectives to be achieved.

During the Carter administration, and to a lesser extent at the midpoint of the Reagan administration, the disrepute of perceived amateurs and outsiders has run high. Along with it has come the belief that changes in the nominating process have unfairly advantaged the inexperienced—those whose repertoire of skills is weighted mainly to electoral politics rather than the politics of governing. The present early start-up dates of presidential campaigns do make it difficult for a nonincumbent candidate to hold a responsible position and devote full energies to organizing a political campaign, thus providing some credibility to the point. Whatever larger costs to the political system such incessant campaigning imposes, the prior issue of the relevance, if any, of past roles has to be resolved. For if the present system provides larger opportunities for the lesser known, it has yet to be shown how much, if any, difference experience makes to the presence or absence of success in the presidency.

Experience, unfortunately, is a word that can be shaped to mean nearly anything one has in mind. Is the requisite experience that of a chief executive? (Both Carter and Regan were state governors, as was Roosevelt.) Is it service on policy panels such as Jimmy Carter's Trilateral Commission that introduce the would-be candidate to complicated issues? Is it the intellectual experience that stems from a background such as Woodrow Wilson's? Is it experience on Capitol Hill? Or as a Cabinet officer? The contention of late (wherein "late" encompasses Carter and Reagan) is that the key test is experience in Washington and in knowing how its institutions work. Career lines in Washington, unlike those in many other capitals, however, are notoriously tracked to service in a particular institution (usually Congress). Even the most experienced, by this definition, will wear blinders because their experiences are usually institutionally limited. Are there, then, any clues to the credentials a president ought to have?

Apparently not. Table 6.1 examines the relationship between political/ governmental experience and presidential success. If experience is a word of malleable form, success, as we have discovered, is both multidimensional and frequently inextricable from dumb luck. Here, success is defined by its retrospective reputational meaning; more exactly, the survey of presidential scholars conducted by the *Chicago Tribune* in 1982. I test here several different forms of political experience—total governmental experience, congressional experience, congressional leadership experience, and federal executive experience—and only one of these, congressional experience, is substantially related to presidential standing, with the relationship being the obverse of the conventional expectation.

Despite a good many platitudes surrounding the subject, the evidence is that political/governmental background by itself is too crude an indicator to predict presidential success (at least as that is operationally defined here). This is not, however, to say that experience is irrelevant to the presidency. A former congressional leader may have a good understanding of what makes the legislative institution tick, though, by virtue of that, may also lack knowledge of what makes the country tick beyond Capitol Hill. Temperament, it would seem, is especially crucial if not at all easy to flag, and temperament is likely to vary some within any role. After all, if presidents vary individually, there is every reason to believe that incumbents of roles that are supposed to help predict presidential performance also vary individually. Lyndon Johnson and Mike Mansfield were both majority floor leaders in the Senate, for example; Cyrus Vance and Alexander Haig each were secretaries of state. Temperamental variation could not be greater. Thus, there being no special road to travel to achieve success, the hunt for leaders of appropriate temperament will have to continue without clear road signs.

CONCLUSION

Leadership has been made more important in exact proportion as it has been made more vulnerable. The conditions that bring us to long for leadership while we constrain its exercise stem in part from nostalgia generated by changes in accustomed patterns of life and by the ease with which "problems" emerge in modern sociey—problems that in an earlier era would never have been identified as such. "The fact that basic causes seem obscure and long range consequences dismal," one student of leadership contends, "may well extend the belief that things were better in 'the good old days' and that strong authoritative leaders might somehow restore the lost paradise."[88] In America, these characteristics are especially promi-

TABLE 6.1. Political and Government Backgrounds of Best and Worst Presidents (1982 *Chicago Tribune* Poll, expert panel of top ten and bottom ten presidents)

	Mean Years in Government (all levels)	Mean Years in Congress	Congressional Leadership Experience	Mean Years in Federal Executive (excluding military)
Top 10	15.1	3.7	only one for 4 years (Polk)	2.6 (4 presidents)
Bottom 10	16.9	7.6	only one for 11 years (Buchanan)	2.3 (7 presidents)

Sources: Background information compiled from Thomas A. Bailey, *The Pugnacious Presidents: White House Warriors on Parade* (New York: The Free Press, 1980), and Tim Tayla, *The Book of Presidents* (New York: Arno Press, 1972).

nent because they interact with an unpredictable degree of fluidity in our politics and with a strongly voluntaristic conception of human action.

The question of what, if any, difference a leader makes is both an analytic and an implied prescriptive one. The analytic question is of staggering complexity. It is, in fact, not a single question, but many questions. At the core of all these questions, however, is the issue of causation. Glenn Paige says it nicely:

> Political leadership takes place in, is conditioned by, affects, and is affected by its environment. Thus, a major challenge facing leadership studies is to determine which partial aspects of an environment or which total configurations of environmental characteristics are causally related to leadership behavior.[89]

The "challenge" Paige alludes to taunts us still. I confess, too, that in this chapter I have probably added to rather than subtracted from the complications that beset satisfactory answers to the analysis of leadership impact. I have tried first to link conceptions of leadership to conceptions of history, to theories of societal change, and to contexts of choice. Second, I have set forth in diagrammatic form a schema linking individual temperament and background, selection processes, skills filtered through these processes, behavioral patterns generated from these skills, and outcomes likely to be produced (or missing) when these patterns or styles of behavior are present (or absent). This schema is employed mostly to elucidate several points in the apparent causal chain. Thus, several different ideas of "success" are explored, several different types of skills and styles of leadership are analyzed, and finally, the reputed link between background characteristics and presidential success is investigated. It is fair to note also that implied prescriptions to the leadership question come more readily than either analytic clarity or empirical evidence regarding the suppositions behind them.

The tendency to fixate on political definitions of success and on political skills (notably given impetus after the Eisenhower and Carter presidencies) as much beclouds the issues surrounding leadership as it clarifies them. As Hargrove testifies, "The experience of Lyndon Johnson, a thoroughly political man, has caused us to think again. . . ."[90] Politics is a means, not an end. Political scientists (and much of the Washington cognoscenti), however, are best equipped to deal with questions of means, that is, how presidents relate to the political process rather than how they think about policy or "the good society." The reasons, of course, why attentive observers focus on means and tangible political results rather than societal consequences are twofold. First, we often are at loggerheads over questions of policy. Secondly, at any point in time, we can only dimly realize the distant, even the intermediate, consequences of present actions. If for no other reason than default, therefore, president watchers are mostly inclined to assess the incumbents from the standpoint of able political tactics, the consequences of which we are apt to exaggerate.

Even from an exclusively political standpoint, however, the president must play a variety of games, each defined by different rules and, thus, requiring diverse sets of skills and propensities. These, in turn, not only may come into conflict with one another, but some also may conflict with those tendencies most pertinent to judicious governance. The axioms of leadership, as earlier were the strictures of "management science," are largely reducible to proverbs.

How we define presidential skills and leadership styles, as argued in Chapter 4, is enormously influenced by immediate precedent and by the apparent needs of the times. Erwin Hargrove notes correctly that "Our evaluation of Presidents is greatly influenced not only by how we study them, but when we do so."[91] Even many of those opposed to Reagan's policy thrust could not help contrasting his amiable presence with his predecessor's stiffness and his flair in dealing with Congress with his predecessor's early setbacks, nor could they ignore his ability to make large (if simple) changes that so frustrated his predecessor. But all this was before the controversiality of that policy thrust set in. By mid-1982, Carter was reborn in some circles. His former antagonists on the Democratic party's left already were proclaiming that he had much to recommend him after all.[92] The inspired and directive leadership that was in fashion in 1981 had become less prominent by 1983, when the direction appeared less inspired. Clichés in regard to leadership and presidential skill, it seems, have a brief half-life.

By telling us that presidents who fail to "comprehend power" will fail equally to achieve anything they value, Richard Neustadt's analysis of presidential power ensured, whether intentionally or not, that we would focus on questions of means and instrumental skills.[93] While we (and Neustadt too) are still searching for the adroit few, and for the skills they will need, to shape the system to their ends, we have given inadequate attention to whether presidents themselves ought to be thought of as the appropriate units of analysis. Yet our clearest instincts tell us, despite all the conditions that seem more potent than their own designs, that presidents are remarkably different in all of the characteristics that influence decision making: temperament, flexibility, ideological stability, curiosity, and basic assumptions, to name a few.

While we conclude, therefore, that presidents are individually quite diverse, the influence of their individual styles remains elusive, the extraction of cause from event perplexing, and the answer to the "what if" question continually problematic. The ways in which presidents differ along various cognitive, evaluative, and behavioral dimensions seem capable of being identified. The differences these differences make, however, although commonly asserted, remain less commonly demonstrated.

NOTES

1. For a small sample of these, see Alexander L. George and Juliette L. George, *Woodrow Wilson and Colonel House: A Personality Study* (New York: Dover, 1964); James MacGregor Burns,

Roosevelt: The Lion and The Fox (New York: Harcourt, Brace & World, 1956); Betty Glad, *Jimmy Carter: In Search of the Great White House* (New York: Norton, 1980); Fred I. Greenstein, *The Hidden Hand Presidency: Eisenhower as Leader* (New York: Basic Books, 1982). Two studies that explicitly compare aspects of personal temperament, skill, and character among at least some presidents are Richard E. Neustadt, *Presidential Power* (New York: John Wiley, 1980 and earlier editions), and James David Barber, *Presidential Character: Predicting Presidential Performance* (Englewood Cliffs, New Jersey: Prentice-Hall, 1972 and subsequent edition). Still the best analysis of the theory and methodology of studies of the individual in politics is Fred I. Greenstein, *Personality and Politics* (Chicago: Markham, 1969), esp. chaps. 2, 3, and 5.

2. Bruce Miroff, "Beyond Washington," *Society* 17 (July/August 1980): 66.

3. *Ibid.*

4. See Herbert A. Simon, *Administrative Behavior: A Study of Decision-Making Processes in Administrative Organization*, 3rd ed. (New York: The Free Press, 1976), pp. 20-44. Simon comments in regard to the prevailing "principles of administration" that "like proverbs, they occur in pairs. For almost every principle one can find an equally plausible and acceptable contradictory principle. Although the two principles of the pair will lead to exactly opposite organizational recommendations, there is nothing in the theory to indicate which is the proper one to apply." (p. 20.) A quick glance at Thomas Cronin's "paradoxes of the presidency" indicates that the same holds true in regard to "principles of leadership." See his, *The State of the Presidency*, 2nd ed. (Boston: Little, Brown, 1980), pp. 3-25.

5. See Louis Hartz, *The Liberal Tradition in America: An Interpretation of American Political Thought Since the Revolution* (New York: Harcourt, Brace & World, 1955), and Clinton Rossiter, *Conservatism in America: The Thankless Persuasion*, 2nd ed. (New York: Vintage Books, 1962). The idea of entrepreneurial leadership, by extension, flows from a view of the political system as a market.

6. Karl Mannheim, *Ideology and Utopia* (New York: Harvest Books, n.d.), p. 229.

7. Rossiter, *Conservatism in America*, p. 200.

8. For instance, see Theda Skocpol, "Political Response to Capitalist Crisis: Neo-Marxist Theories of the State and the Case of the New Deal," *Politics and Society* 10 (1980): 155-202.

9. Donald D. Searing, "Models and Images of Man and Society in Leadership Theory," *Journal of Politics* 31 (February 1969), p. 9.

10. *Ibid.*, p.11.

11. *Ibid.*, pp. 15-18, see p. 16 for quoted material.

12. *Ibid.*, p. 9.

13. *Ibid.*, p. 27.

14. Glad, *Jimmy Carter*, pp. 505-506.

15. James MacGregor Burns, *Leadership* (New York: Harper & Row, 1978), p. 4.

16. *Ibid.*, pp. 308-343.

17. Neustadt, *Presidential Power;* Burns's most emphatic statement of this may be found in his, *Deadlock of Democracy* (Englewood Cliffs, N.J.: Prentice-Hall, 1963).

18. At the same time, elements of the organismic model filter through. At the end of *Presidential Power*, published in 1960, the thinness of the ranks of available leaders from which those of appropriate temperament and skill may be selected is cause for Neustadt's concern. The thinness of those ranks, however, is a consequence of features of the political system and the system of political recruitment it spawns. By 1980, Neustadt's despair is deeper, and the remedies even more uncertain.

19. Cronin, *The State of the Presidency*, pp. 119-141.

20. Burns, *Leadership*, pp. 19-20.

21. *Ibid.*, p. 20.

22. *Ibid.*, pp. 388-397.

23. *Ibid.*, p. 389.

24. See Lawrence B. Mohr, "The Concept of Organizational Goal," *American Political Science Review* 67 (June 1973): 470-481. Mohr puts it trenchantly:

Whereas to be exclusively transitive is hardly possible, to be exclusively reflexive may be suicidal; a society that does not honor the transitive roles of its members may not be viable. (p. 481.)

25. Burns,*Leadership,* p. 343.

26. Burns, *Deadlock of Democracy,* pp. 338-340.

27. Jeff Fishel, "Presidential Elections and Presidential Agendas: The Carter Administration in Contemporary Historical Perspective," Working Paper, Center for Congressional and Presidential Studies, The American University, Washington, D.C., p. 59.

28. This point is made from the president's perspective by Fishel, "Presidential Elections," pp. 50-61; it is also shown by Pomper and Lederman that, from the standpoint of party platform pledges (and therefore the president's accountability to his party) the norm is toward fulfillment. See Gerald M. Pomper with Susan S. Lederman, *Elections in America: Control and Influence in Democratic Politics,* 2nd ed. (New York: Longman, 1980), pp. 156-178.

29. See Paul C. Light, *The President's Agenda: Domestic Policy Choice from Kennedy to Carter* (Baltimore: Johns Hopkins University Press, 1982), p. 127. Data are derived from those in Table 14, though recalculated for this analysis.

30. *Ibid.,* p. 125. Data are derived from Table 13.

31. See Richard Fleisher and Jon R. Bond, "Assessing Presidential Support in the House: Lessons from Reagan and Carter." Revised paper originally presented at the 1982 Annual Meeting of the Midwest Political Science Association, Milwaukee, Wisconsin. A noteworthy item on Nixon's early agenda was the Moynihan inspired Family Assistance Plan (FAP). Another was the embrace of environmental protection which resulted in the Environmental Protection Act, expanding both bureaucracy and its regulatory compass.

32. A matter especially emphasized by the Georges's study of Woodrow Wilson. See their, *Woodrow Wilson and Colonel House.*

33. Light, *The President's Agenda,* pp. 172-186.

34. Clinton Rossiter, *The American Presidency* (New York: Harcourt, Brace & World, 1956), and Greenstein, *The Hidden-Hand Presidency,* p. 5.

35. This is what S. E. Finer calls the "futurity principle." See his, "Princes, Parliaments, and the Public Service," *Parliamentary Affairs* 33 (Autumn 1980): 353-372.

36. Greenstein particularly stresses the combination of temperament and roles experienced by Eisenhower as being central to an understanding of his style of leadership in the presidency. See, *The Hidden-Hand Presidency,* p. 233.

37. Thomas E. Cronin, "News Notes," *Presidential Studies Quarterly* 12 (Spring 1982): 292.

38. At least six separate "expert" polls have been taken; the original one was instituted by the historian Arthur Schlesinger, Sr. in 1948, followed by his survey in 1962, the Maranell-Dodder Poll in 1970, the mass-based Gallup Poll in 1975, the U.S. Historical Society Poll in 1977, and the *Chicago Tribune* Poll in 1982. Differences in timing make it impossible to gain exact comparability. So, too, do differences in the nature of the ranking and the manner in which votes are accumulated. However, since the U.S. Historical Society and *Chicago Tribune* polls are only five years apart, some comparability can be achieved at the top of each survey. Across the two surveys, nine of the top ten presidents remain intact, holding virtually identical standing. For a listing of the various polls, their results, and original citations, see Robert DiClerico, *The American Presidency,* 2nd ed. (Englewood Cliffs, N.J.: Prentice-Hall, 1983), pp. 332-333. For a more comprehensive and also disaggregated set of results from the 1982 *Chicago Tribune* Poll, see Cronin, "News and Notes," p. 293.

39. The culmination of this work is *The Hidden-Hand Presidency,* published only in 1982. But the direction this work was taking was evident a few years earlier in conference papers and published articles. Among these earlier works of Greenstein's, see his, "Eisenhower as an Activist President: A Look at New Evidence," *Political Science Quarterly* 94 (Winter 1979-80): 575-599, and "A Tory Theory of the Presidency: Eisenhower's Leadership Reexamined." Paper presented at the 1979 Annual Meeting of the American Political Science Association, Washington, D.C.

40. For a recent analysis of presidential limitations in regard to legislative success, see George C. Edwards III, "Presidential Influence in Congress Revisited: Narrowing the Focus." Paper presented at the 1982 Annual Meeting of the American Political Science Association, Chicago, Illinois.

41. Fleisher and Bond, "Assessing Presidential Support in the House."

42. Greenstein, *The Hidden-Hand Presidency*, esp. pp. 3-54.

43. Richard E. Neustadt, "Presidential Power: A Reflective View," *Presidential Studies Quarterly* 11 (Summer 1981): 362-363.

44. Neustadt, *Presidential Power*, see esp. chap. 5, in the original edition.

45. For a popular account, see Elie Abel, *The Cuban Missile Crisis* (Philadelphia, Lippincott, 1966); for an insider's account, see Robert F. Kennedy, *Thirteen Days* (New York, W. W. Norton, 1969). For a scholarly and more sobering estimate of the presidential role in shaping the outcome, see Graham T. Allison, *Essence of Decision: Explaining the Cuban Missile Crisis* (Boston: Little, Brown, 1971).

46. Neustadt, *Presidential Power*, 3rd ed., 1976, p. 271.

47. See Paul A. Anderson, "Decision Making by Objection and the Cuban Missile Crisis," *Administrative Science Quarterly* 28 (June 1983): 201-222.

48. Herbert Kaufman, *The Administrative Behavior of Federal Bureau Chiefs* (Washington: The Brookings Institution, 1981), p. 194.

49. In Machiavelli's proverbial wisdom, "Let a prince . . . aim at conquering and maintaining the state, and the means will always be judged honourable and praised by everyone, for the vulgar is always taken by appearances and the issue of the event; and the world consists only of the vulgar, and the few who are not vulgar are isolated when the many have a rallying point in the prince." Niccolo Machiavelli, *The Prince* (New York: Modern Library Edition, 1950), p. 66.

50. Simon, *Administrative Behavior*, pp. 20-44.

51. Ben W. Heineman, Jr., and Curtis A. Hessler, *Memorandum for the President: A Strategic Approach to Domestic Affairs in the 1980s* (New York: Random House, 1980).

52. *Ibid.*, pp. 6-7.

53. *Ibid.*, p. 35.

54. Neustadt, *Presidential Power*, see esp. chap. 7 in the original edition.

55. Reported by Ralph Stogdill and listed in Glenn D. Paige, *The Scientific Study of Political Leadership* (New York: The Free Press, 1977), p. 179.

56. *Ibid.*, p. 66.

57. George and George, *Woodrow Wilson and Colonel House;* in J. D. Barber's typology, such persons are classified as "active-negatives." See his, *Presidential Character.*

58. Greenstein, *The Hidden-Hand Presidency;* on the smaller scale of unifying political party, such traits which are also related to conciliating tendencies seem appropriate as well—the ability to broker factions and to appear as the candidate of the whole. See, in this regard, Nelson W. Polsby and Aaron Wildavsky, *Presidential Elections*, 5th ed. (New York: Charles Scribners' Sons, 1980), pp. 279-286, and James W. Ceaser, *Presidential Selection: Theory and Development* (Princeton, N.J.: Princeton University Press, 1979).

59. Greenstein, *The Hidden-Hand Presidency*, pp. 228-229.

60. The rhetoric of partisanship, John Kessel points out, increases during general election campaigns as the candidates seek to stress selectively those partisan distinctions that run to their advantage. For an analysis of the relationship between political rhetoric and stages of the presidential election process, see John H. Kessel, "The Seasons of Presidential Politics," *Social Science Quarterly* 58 (December 1977), esp. pp. 426-428.

61. John F. Manley, "Presidential Power and White House Lobbying," *Political Science Quarterly* 93 (Summer 1978): 255-275.

62. *Ibid.*, pp. 265-271; also on this point, see Peter W. Sperlich, "Bargaining and Overload: An Essay on Presidential Power," in *Perspectives on the Presidency*, ed. Aaron Wildavsky (Boston: Little, Brown, 1975), pp. 406-430.

63. Manley, "Presidential Power and White House Lobbying," pp. 274-275. Robert Axelrod states the problem raised here for real learning:

> People often interpret a current case as being analogous to a previous case which was in some ways similar. . . . Historical analogies seem to be drawn by selecting the single previous case which provides the satisficing fit to the present case. . . . The more important to the person a previous case was, the more accessible it will be as an analogy for a future case. . . . This dependence of the accessibility of a prior case on its importance is helpful . . . if (but only if) there is actually a correlation between the importance of a case and the likelihood that it will be a useful guide. . . .

See Robert Axelrod, "Schema Theory: An Information Processing Model of Perception and Cognition," *American Political Science Review* 67 (December 1973): 1265.

64. Charles O. Jones, "Presidential Negotiation with Congress," in *Both Ends of the Avenue,* ed. Anthony King (Washington: American Enterprise Institute, 1983), pp. 96-130, esp. pp. 123-127.

65. See, for example, Thomas J. Anton, *Administered Politics: Elite Political Culture in Sweden* (Boston: Martinus Nijhoff, 1980); Harry Eckstein, *Division and Cohesion in Democracy:* A Study of Norway (Princeton, N.J.: Princeton University Press, 1966); and, *inter alia,* Robert B. Kvavik, "Interest Groups in a 'Cooptive' Political System: The Case of Norway," in *Politics in Europe,* ed. Martin O. Heisler (New York: David McKay, 1974), pp. 93-116.

66. Jones, "Presidential Negotiation," p. 111.

67. In this regard, see Larry Berman, *Planning a Tragedy: The Americanization of the War in Vietnam* (New York: W. W. Norton, 1982). Berman emphasizes Johnson's fear of a political challenge from the Right that would halt the Great Society if his administration did not respond to the communist military threat in Vietnam with armed intervention.

68. Greenstein, *The Hidden-Hand Presidency,* pp. 228-248. As Greenstein asserts:

> Eisenhower's leadership style also would have been unsuitable for enacting Johnson's Great Society programs and the 1981 Reaganomics policies. Both of these decision-making sequences were marked by publicized presidential political pressure which was precisely what Eisenhower sought to avoid. (p. 230.)

69. See Robert A. Dahl, *Who Governs?* (New Haven: Yale University Press, 1961) for an accounting of Mayor Lee's exploits. For a study of political entrepreneurship among public authority leaders, see Michael N. Danielson and Jameson W. Doig, *The Politics of Urban Regional Development* (Berkeley: University of California Press, 1982).

70. See George C. Edwards III, *Presidential Influence in Congress* (San Francisco: W. H. Freeman, 1980), pp. 189-202.

71. *Ibid.,* pp. 198-199.

72. Manley, "Presidential Power and White House Lobbying," pp. 271-274.

73. See Berman, *Planning a Tragedy.* For a generally similar view espousing the pivotal role of the president, see Robert J. Art, "Bureaucratic Politics and American Foreign Policy: A Critique," *Policy Sciences* 4 (December 1973): 467-490.

74. Michael Blumenthal, "Candid Reflections of a Businessman in Washington," *Fortune* 99 (January 29, 1979): 36.

75. Richard Rose, "The President: A Chief but Not an Executive," *Presidential Studies Quarterly* 7 (Winter 1977): 5-20.

76. See Herman Nickel, "Can a Managerial Maestro End the White House Cacophony," *Fortune* 100 (October 22, 1979): 58-75.

77. Rose, "The President," pp. 16-18.

78. *Ibid.,* pp. 14-19.

79. See Garry Wills, "The Kennedy Imprisonment," *The Atlantic* 249 (January 1982): 27-40.

80. Berman, *Planning a Tragedy,* p. 142.

81. Wills, "The Kennedy Imprisonment," p. 40.

82. Robert C. Tucker, *Politics as Leadership* (Columbia, Mo.: University of Missouri Press, 1981), p. 45.

83. *Ibid.*, p. 125.

84. See Bert A. Rockman, "Carter's Troubles," *Society* 17 (July/August 1980), esp. pp. 34-35.

85. See Eric B. Herzik and Mary L. Dodson, "The President and Public Expectations: A Research Note," *Presidential Studies Quarterly* 12 (Spring 1982): 168-173. Some conflicting evidence, however, appears from an experiment of Yale undergraduates in several political science classes—a nonscientific sample of a nonrepresentative population, to be sure. Rather than the relative constancy in desired charcteristics found by Herzik and Dodson, the Yale student study found desired characteristics fluctuating (consistent with the argument posed in Chapter 4) based on the undesirable traits of an hypothetical incumbent. See Edward H. Lazarus, "Public Perceptions of Ideal Political Personalities." Paper presented at the 1982 Annual Meeting of the American Political Science Association, Denver, Colorado.

86. Neustadt, *Presidential Power,* 4th ed., 1980, p. 143.

87. *Ibid., p. 243.*

88. *Lewis Edinger, "Where Are the Political Superstars?," Political Science Quarterly* 89 (June 1974): 256.

89. Paige, *The Scientific Study of Political Leadership,* p. 124.

90. Erwin C. Hargrove, "Presidential Personality and Revisionist Views of the Presidency," *American Journal of Political Science* 17 (November 1973): 822.

91. *Ibid.,* p. 819.

92. "ADA Flays Reagan, Pines for Carter," *Washington Post,* June 4, 1982, p. A2.

93. Neustadt, *Presidential Power.*

7

Conclusion: Answers to the Leadership Question

This book began with a set of paradoxical questions: How can governments gain direction yet maintain continuity? How can leadership be exerted yet restrained? How can solutions be devised to long-run problems yet consensus generated on their behalf? As this inquiry concludes, the answers to these questions remain indefinite while the questions themselves remain continuously central.

"The leadership question," indeed, has two principal forms, each with ancillary ones. In one form, the leadership question is descriptive. It asks, what are the impediments to, and opportunities for, direction? More specifically (1) to what extent can direction be had? (2) to what extent can it be sustained? (3) what is its magnitude and depth? and (4) how—through what mix of skills, institutional characteristics, and cultural predispositions—is direction arrived at?

Answers to the first two questions, analysis of the American polity suggests, may be stated respectively as "sporadic" and "not greatly." In fact, however, direction is continually forthcoming but from various sources, and so the question really becomes, to what extent can *central* direction be had, and to what extent can *that* be sustained?[1]

Answering the third question is more controversial and obviously subject to a great deal of judgment. Mancur Olson suggests here, however, that the longer democratic government has had to consolidate, the more powerful are the resistances to central authority and to substantial change. In this view, the magnitude and depth of political change must be increasingly blunted because well-positioned policy clients have vested interests in preventing broad-scale reallocations.[2]

The fourth descriptive part of the leadership question—how is direction arrived at?—is a puzzling one for analysts of government and politics to answer. Although this question is fundamental to political inquiry, the more we inquire of it in any political system, the more our answers seem partial and fragmentary, and not easily susceptible to comprehensive summary judgments. The more we burrow into the question of leadership activities at the microlevel, the more similar these processes look across different contexts and the less indiscriminate are their apparently differentiating features.[3] While a more holistic perspective aids our powers of conceptual discrimination, it also diminishes our ability to test, through reference to concrete empirical processes, ideas about system differences. How leadership is arrived at is a central point of inquiry in answering the three antecedent parts of the leadership question, as well as necessary to the normative elements of the leadership question. To answer it in a conceptually illuminating and explicitly comparative way, however, is a formidable undertaking.

As important as these descriptive elements of the leadership question are, they gain their relevance mainly from the other face of the leadership question—the normative one. Here, the leadership question is especially perplexing. How much leadership is desirable, and to what ends? To what extent can the relentless pursuit of purpose drive out thought, complexity, and proportionality?[4]

Straightforward answers to all of these questions, even when institutional designs appear to provide them, are not apparent. In the bastion of majoritarian party rule, for instance, Richard Rose argues that "Faced with a choice between a government with too much or too little power, the British tradition is to make the first charge upon government maintaining political consent."[5] On the other hand, fragmented or sectorized authority—a more common, if structurally variant, characteristic of Western democracies—does not necessarily paralyze governments from acting. The expression of political will, in short, cannot be determined by institutional design alone, however relevant a factor this is in establishing a point of equilibrium between the autonomy of, and the accountability of, the state and its leaders. This equilibrium, while reached at different points across different political systems, lacks finite stability, and inevitably is subject to pendular shifts. The opportunities for leadership, however, are always constricted by the opportunities provided for effective opposition and these, in turn, are often produced by institutional design. Writing about policy making in West Germany, Fritz Scharpf and his associates bring to bear a dilemma likely to sound familiar to American ears:

> Everything considered, the opportunities for consensus building in support of central policy controls . . . appear to be quite limited in German federalism. . . .
> The general tendency toward policymaking by conflict avoidance will continue to block reform strategies aiming at major societal, economic, or institutional transformations. If . . . problem loads should increase much beyond present levels, political processes in the Federal Republic are more likely to be immobilized . . . than . . . in political systems with either less need for consensus or greater consensus building capacity.[6]

The imperatives of generating direction, however, are not easily stilled. In the United States this task is perceived as preponderantly the president's. Because of this modern vision of where political leadership in America is arched, my analysis has focused on the leadership role of the American presidency and its incumbents. It is a leadership role that in recent times has been subject to wide swings in senti- ment, having been called both "imperial" and "imperiled." Such swings in senti- ment are perhaps an indication of the tensions in the American system that exist between constraints deriving from the institutional framework on the one hand and programs of action and presidentially driven solutions on the other.

In regard to these tensions, the argument presented in this book, in highly dis- tilled form, makes the following claims: (1) Neither institutionally nor culturally is the American system generous in providing resources for central direction; how- ever, (2) from time to time in the long run, and to a much lesser extent but more regularly in the short run, opportunities arise for the provision of substantial presi- dential direction, though such flurries typically are short-lived; nonetheless, (3) these opportunities seem to be trending toward ever briefer duration, an occurrence that seems to be accompanied simultaneously by increased demands on political leadership and diminishing resources available for its support; and, thus, (4) we are led to lean heavily, but with minimal conceptualization and exceeding imprecision, on stressing "skills" which presidents are presumed to possess or, more frequently, thought to be deficient in.

SYSTEM AND STRATEGY

The exercise of leadership is inevitably conditioned by the strategic environ- ment surrounding it. Two important considerations in the formulation of leader- ship strategies are the *level of political aggregation* and the *political culture*. By the concept level of political aggregation, I mean the extent to which demands made on the political system can be filtered to a common point of engagement or not, that is, the extent to which fusion or diffusion (disaggregation) is likely. Fusion is the product of centripetal tendencies, and diffusion the product of centrifugal ones. Thus, a centralized governmental system has the possibility of producing cen- tripetal forms of aggregation—in other words, a common point of engagement. Conversely, the more places through which policy can be formed, the more places at which it can be influenced; in other words, the more likely that there is disaggre- gation and that centrifugal forces are developed.

The level of aggregation is related to formal governmental structure but not exclusively determined by it. Federal systems, naturally, tend to have more dis- persed centers of policy making than unitary systems. There is, however, substan- tial variation within each system and, also, some overlap across them. Disciplined political parties, for instance, in the Federal Republic of Germany and in Canada help to create a basis for "national" decision making (at some severe cost, of course, in the otherwise centrifugal Canadian system). Their absence in the United States reinforces both localism and small group politics (bureaucratic clientelism). In Germany, the idea of the state as an enduring expression of the communal interest provides yet further binding that is lacking in both Canada and the United States, despite the fact that all three are federal systems.

Unitary systems, similarly, are not homogenously centristic, and none are as centrist in behavior as they are in the blueprints.[7] They differ informally, too, in the real structure of authority. Party factionalism, localized patronage, and diversities in regional development may effectively disperse that which in theory is united—the power to exercise influence.[8] In brief, formal structure is a very important, but not singular, predictor to the character of political aggregation.

Let us turn now to the second dimension, that of political culture. While political culture is a very complex concept, my focus here is on one aspect of it; namely the extent to which *adversarial* or *accommodative* relations among elites prevail. Enthusiasm for conflict, the expression of rights, and the staking of positions are characteristic of an adversarial political culture, whereas the explicit seeking of agreement across affected interests and an obsession with consensus are characteristic of an accommodative culture.

By intersecting these two dimensions, level of aggregation and political culture, four hypothetical systems emerge. None of these four comprehensively describes any actual system. Indeed, no single, concise description of constitutional polities will fit all their parts or functions.

TABLE 7.1.   Four Types of Political Environment

		Political Culture	
		Adversarial	*Accommodative*
Level of Political Aggregation	*Centripetal*	Majoritarian exclusive e.g., party government	Corporatist inclusive e.g., the European polity model
	Centrifugal	Splintered inclusive e.g., minorities rule	Bureaucratic exclusive e.g., clientelism, sub-governments

As used in Table 7.1, the terms exclusivism and inclusivism refer to the extent to which control over an agenda, whatever its scope, is held by a limited set of authorities, or a more inclusive set. These terms similarly refer to the breadth of participants involved in the disposition of the agenda, again regardless of its scope. The agenda may be broad and goal-oriented as the upper left cell in Table 7.1 suggests or functional and interest oriented as the lower right cell implies. Exclusive control may rest in the hands of a majority party, as depicted in the upper left cell, or it may evolve from the symbiotic relationship between segments of the bureaucracy and clientele groups, as depicted in the bottom right cell. Party government presumably is a reflection of majoritarian exclusivism. (Other parties, thus, are excluded from participation in the government.) While, as Richard Rose remarks, "only in a totalitarian system would one expect party government to reign absolutely. . . . the governing party is unique in its claim to have the right to choose what solutions shall be binding upon the whole of a society."[9]

Strong parties help to channel demands toward the center, but they are at least the product of there being a center to start with. The party government model is thus associated with a centripetal system of aggregation and an adversarial culture. The majority party government situation (an aspiration of many American party reformers) is exclusivist in the sense that almost no cross-walking or bargaining between parties is necessitated.[10] Imparting direction under majority party government, insofar as parliamentary enactments are concerned, is then relatively *mechanistic* (assuming, of course, that the ruling party is neither excessively factionalized nor otherwise unable to put forth a program).

To sustain direction is yet another matter. In the parliamentary setting majoritarian exclusivism is a form of "push-button" leadership. The means by which direction is imparted lie mechanistically in the discipline of majorities. Much like driving a car on the open highway, little subtlety is required. When the highway narrows (a parallel for when majorities also narrow) and the road becomes tortuous, however, more skill is required to keep going. Party politicians also often have difficulties moving from program to implementation. To move from establishing agendas and passing legislation to actually affecting policies administered through the bureaucracy inevitably requires more than pushing buttons; it requires both knowledge and constant maintenance of the wiring itself.[11] And yet, as B. Guy Peters contends, "Breakdowns of implementation represent a fundamental failure. . . . to transform political ideas into effective action."[12]

Bureaucratic exclusivism, common to some extent in all of the industrialized countries, reflects both dispersed authority and a culture of accommodation. The relationship here is between a dominant bureau and a dominant interest group to the effective exclusion of outside parties. In this type, often noted as the model of private government, bureaucratic agencies and interest group relations are mutually protective.[13] The strategic connection between bureau and interest group is symbiotic. Defining issues in the form of technical discretion rather than as value judgments is the key to an exclusive arrangement. Such a strategic environment calls for a leadership based upon maintenance and incremental adjustment. Again, in Guy Peters's words:

> The political life and, to some extent, the values of bureaucratic agencies are tied up in questions of organizational survival. . . . Therefore, to the extent that bureaucracies appear to be gaining in influence over policy and government, a nation will have many governments, but no government.[14]

The proliferation of clientelistic subgovernments is endemic to advanced industrial societies, and while accommodative treaties between affected interest groups and administrative agencies are easily arranged and operative policy often spewed forth, the collective effect on government is often incoherence unless there is a higher level of aggregation.

As developed by Heisler and Kvavik, the "European Polity" model (particularly characteristic of the smaller European states—the Low Countries, Scandinavia, and the small European states), aggregates or "coopts" functional sectors and ethnic segments through the centralizing devices of mixed advisory and administrative bodies. These are "broadly inclusive, segment-linking policy and decision-making structures."[15] The environmental type is accommodative (corporatist) inclusive. It tends to depoliticize policy issues by reducing them to technical questions and agreed upon formulas—in other words, it is a style of problem solving that is based upon deemphasizing symbolic politics and emphasizing the manageability of policy questions.[16] The formula works something like this: syndicate political risk and thus implicate other leaders in initiatives; think broadly (systemwide), but not boldly (rapid or instantaneous change); think small (is it manageable?), not symbolically (is it ideologically appealing?).[17] If there are very few "new beginnings," there are also very few "sudden endings." For such a system to function there must be a clear center, and equally a small number of very large mass-based peak associations. While policy initiatives do not always originate at the center, they must ultimately be consummated there. Syndication is the strategy for developing consensus.

"Splintered Inclusivism" is the label given to an adversarial system but one that disperses the channeling of influence. In the memorable phrase of Robert Dahl, "minorities rule," and "policy seems to be determined by the efforts of relatively small but relatively active minorities."[18] Disaggregation means that many groups will arise; an adversarial culture means that their interests will likely be pursued with great vigor, pushed often by entrepreneurial activists in government. As Dahl claims, a "markedly decentralized system" also provides "a high probability that any active and legitimate group will make itself heard effectively at some stage in the process of decision."[19] Dispersion coupled with an adversarial culture almost ensures that interest groups will be aggressively assertive. In such a system, it is very likely that entrepreneurial skills in articulating symbols and mobilizing constituencies will be prized. Undoubtedly such a system would look much like contemporary America.

In a system possessed of an adversarial culture but lacking a clear center and thus unhinged to any pivotal force, bureaucratic clientelism is an important vehicle for the expression and reinforcement of interests. In part, therefore, splintered inclusivism is a product of many bureaucratically exclusive subsystems, each driven in different directions. Often, therefore, there is energy without coherent direction, movement without resolution, assertiveness without visible means of accommodation.

To repeat, none of these hypothesized types of political environments exists in exclusive form in any actual setting. Parts of each are likely to be found in all systems, and probably bureaucratic exclusiveness is found in all of the advanced industrial societies. Subgovernments are a widespread phenomenon rather than an exclusively American one. What differs across political systems, however, is how and in what form, if at all, subgovernments are assimilated (or forced) into broader national decision-making structures. The European polities model suggests absorption of the lower right cell in Table 7.1 into the upper right cell when cross-sectoral decisions are to be made. The party government model suggests efforts to dominate subgovernments from the center—efforts which have variable but often limited success. The minorities rule model, by virtue of the centrifugal forces at work on this system, suggests the simultaneous occurrence of both types of environments: a world of both highly charged symbolic clashes and ensconced interests, one in which there is both collision and collusion.

Typologies are limited by virtue of their being simply modal characteristics and by their inability to capture dynamism. But two trends affecting leadership in Western societies are relevant to our typology. One is the increased political mobilization of publics through uninstitutionalized protest behavior, and, in general, an increased emphasis upon participatory activity and adversarial relations.[20] The other, a tendency that has been occurring over a longer term, is the bureaucratization of governments and the dependence of specific publics upon the administrative apparatus.[21] The first trend means more conflict. It may imply movement from the upper right cell in Table 7.1 to the lower left cell. Both trends, however, increase propensities for disaggregation, and each threatens the capacity for policy coherence.

Considered as ideal types, nevertheless, each of the four specified systems generates a dominant form of leadership strategy as noted in Table 7.2. Under majoritarian exclusiveness, the key lies in the instrumentation and the design rather than the person—"better tools," as we note in Chapter 1. This exaggerates, of course. A great deal, realistically, depends upon a leader's attractiveness to electorates, experience in party organization, and abilities in reconciling diversities within the party and differences between ministers. Relatively speaking, however, and at least insofar as passage of a legislative agenda is concerned, leadership strategies under party government conditions will be essentially mechanistic.

TABLE 7.2.   The Political Environment and Leadership Strategy

Political Environment	Leadership Strategy
Majoritarian exclusive	Mechanistic direction
Corporatist inclusive	Syndication and bargaining
Splintered inclusive	Entrepreneurial promotion
Bureaucratic exclusive	Maintenance and adjustment

If mechanistic direction is implied by majoritarian exclusivism, then syndication (the sharing of risk) and bargaining are likely strategies in a corporatist inclusive environment. Rather than being imposed from the top, direction results from a synthesis at the center of party programs and the segmented agendas of bureaucratic and peak association interests. Direction arises from moderate but steady breezes rather than from short-lived but powerful gusts. Bargaining skills and moderate appetites are both essential in such a system. The system also requires certainty as to the interests being represented in the bargains that are reached. At the same time, centripetal aggregating mechanisms coopt key interests into both shaping and being committed to broad elements of the government's policy program. Issues, in other words, typically are woven into a patterned fabric, so that each policy matter does not require the *ad hoc* construction of a new coalition.

Entrepreneurship, promotion, and advocacy are leadership strategies consistent with a splintered inclusive environment. The theme is action, and selling ideas and energizing policy agendas are crucial to it.[22] Being unable to count consistently on a stable majority or a highly institutionalized and centralized process of accommodation, leadership rests heavily upon the assertion of grandiose goals and the stirring of activist souls. Since little can be counted on in advance, capturing attention for one's priorities is necessary. This, perhaps, is one reason why American presidents in modern times have had inspiring labels attached to their administrations—at least until Jimmy Carter's ill-starred "New Foundations."

Finally, an environment dominated by bureaucratic exclusivism is essentially a maintaining one characterized by marginal adjustments. Leadership therein is largely aimed at stabilizing commitments made in the past, and fending off threats to them. The permanence of civil servants, their mastery of detail, and their connections to important interest groups are advantages that enable them to resist externally imposed changes to some degree. But they are not absolutely immunized from the sweep of externally imposed change, especially if there is persistent follow through. Conditions of party government obviously enhance the opportunities to impose central direction over bureaucratic fiefdoms, though there are costs in doing so.[23]

In sum, leadership strategies are contingent upon the nature of the political environment. Majoritarian situations have a kind of "push button" quality to them, to the extent that party discipline can be assumed. Corporatist inclusivism, however, requires leaders to syndicate risk taking ("taking hostages," as an observer of the Swedish system has called it),[24] so that arrangements can be made for a lengthy voyage. On the other hand, a less structured environment is faced by leaders under conditions of splintered inclusiveness. The lack of assured stability places a premium on action, promotion, and entrepreneurship. There are numerous opportunities to advance innovative proposals, but the opportunities for their enactment and successful implementation are limited by the kaleidoscopic nature of coalition building—the lack, in other words, of assured stability.[25]

As with opportunities to play tennis, climate makes a difference for how politics is played. On a sunny day, tennis enthusiasts in Pittsburgh should urgently get to the courts. In California, they can bide their time knowing that the opportunity to play is likely to be as attractive tomorrow as it is today. In quite different ways, the conditions for leadership under both party government and corporatist inclusivism are more like California weather, reasonably predictable. Those under splintered inclusiveness, however, are more like the sun in Pittsburgh, best to be taken advantage of on rare appearances.

GOVERNING FORMULAS

Throughout, I have emphasized more the systemic constraints on presidential leadership in the American system than the opportunities available for its exercise. But I hope equally to have stressed that these direction-providing opportunities are in no setting automatically attained. Moreover, the really central issue is not whether presidents have more or less power at their disposal but, rather, whether adaptive yet accepted directions can be effectively pursued. What, in other words, is a responsible governing formula? Any such question needs to be spiced with much skepticism for at least two reasons: (1) most such formulas are highly idealized, and (2) when such formulas are transferred from one environment to another, their workings are unpredictable. Americans bent on reform often have looked abroad for models of how government can be made to work better. The seemingly pristine features of the British "party government" (majoritarian exclusive) model seem still to be favored, though challenged in recent times by the more placid, accommodative (and seemingly effective) features of the governing styles (corporatist and accommodative) identified with the Scandinavian countries and Japan.

While the structure of party rule in the British case has remained relatively constant, the willingness to embark upon and sustain a course of action has not. Until the election of the Conservative Thatcher government, this exertion of political will had been a missing ingredient for a long time in British politics, perhaps since the reformist flurry of the Atlee Labor government. Thatcher's determination could be sustained by a healthy (now healthier) majority in Parliament, a condition missing in Britain for much of the period in question; it could be sustained also by the profound weakness of the opposition, and a growing willingness of elements of the majority to seek long-term "solutions" to the battered British economy at the cost of much short-run pain. Above all, in the presence of these conditions it has been sustained by a leader of fierce determination and conviction and by a party moving ever closer toward its leader's outlook. Most recently, this determination has been sustained by an electoral system that produces decisive parliamentary majorities from plurality election results. Margaret Thatcher can do what Ronald Reagan cannot do as deeply largely because of political institutions. But Margaret Thatcher can do what François Mitterand in France cannot do, not because of institutions but because of her determination and his relative irresolution in the face of broad and powerful socioeconomic forces—forces, however, that adversely affect his agenda more than hers. Temporarily, economic conditions and the logic behind public sector growth have granted reforms from the Right more leeway than those coming from the Left. Accordingly, the formal power of the French president is mocked by the more compelling economic forces dictating a retreat from his program. In Britain, on the other hand, determination is emphatic and the government is now especially well positioned to sustain the course of austerity on which it has embarked. Thus, although institutions alone cannot create the conditions for generating direction, they can enable vigorous exploitation of these opportunities.

A potential danger posed by institutions that are biased toward the director model of governing, however, is that the leadership may be susceptible to pushing too far with too little support, a critique already offered of Thatcher's plans. Reflecting especially on the dangers of the "director" model of governing implied by party government (and, implicitly, also that of French presidentialism), a student of U.S. legislative processes argues on behalf of the congressional "obstacle" to leadership that

> Where and when there has been national consensus, Congress has acted reasonably quickly and reasonably well—at least as well as any parliament in a comparable situation. . . .
>
> In the absence of consensus, Congress either does not act or prevents the executive from acting. In a vital policy area, this can and does cause delays and problems. But over the long run, it is not necessarily better for either the process

of policy formation or the quality of policy outcomes to have a system in which a legal consensus can be imposed where no public consensus exists.[26]

If the need to gain societal consensus is to temper direction, through what mechanisms can government achieve direction and satisfy social acceptance? Another formula emphasizes mechanisms based on centralized bargaining and accommodation with equally centralized interest groups. This formula is what we call "Corporatist inclusivism." Why does this system seen so desirable? The reason, concludes Philippe Schmitter, is because "in advanced capitalist, highly industrialized societies, there is a strong positive relationship between a societal corporatist mode of interest intermediation and relative governability. . . ."[27]

The virtues of the corporatist model, however, are also its liabilities. Social peace, political stability, gradualism and finely tuned policy making are virtues that help make government a more effective if less dramatic actor. Yet the purchase of social stability and policy effectiveness through corporatist mechanisms diminishes the role of the individual, limits new sources of social and organizational change, and lowers responsiveness to signals for political representation from sources that are not highly organized.

But what does such a model of governance require? The British party government model and even the French presidentialist system require changes that, as far reaching as they are, encompass only the political system. They represent, in other words, systems designed to expedite the "legal" consensus presumably in the hope that doing so will induce a "social" consensus. The corporatist formula, however, requires not merely a retooled political system. It also requires a revamped social order and interest structure, and undoubtedly a great deal of cultural change to go along with that.

This asks a great deal. First, membership in economic interest groups in the United States, for instance, is low by the standards of advanced industrial societies. Second, a unified state with a unified government also is missing. Third, a shift in culture from exuberant and aggressive individualism to deferential collectivism would be necessitated. Fourth, essential agreement on an activist steering role for government would be required—an issue of the greatest controversy in the United States. Given these conditions, it may be a moot question to ask whether such a formula could work in the very large and very heterogeneous American society.[28]

The corporatist design is a formula for a conservative society and an activist government. Precisely the opposite obtains in the United States. To strengthen authority and the mediating bonds between the governors and the governed, of course, is a conservative thing to do. But to do that runs so deeply against the grain of the very nonconservative American society and culture that it essentially calls for their re-creation.

That there are no magical formulas is amply illustrated in the Netherlands, a country billed as featuring a "politics of accommodation."[29] There, within the span of the last decade, the length of time taken to form governments has threatened to match the durability of the governments themselves. Moreover, this process of lengthy negotiation has given disproportionate weight to the political sector that is most rapidly fading in the popular vote, the confessional (religious) parties.

Then, too, the influence of personality and faction and, therefore, of interpersonal and factional conflicts is a fact of life in most political environments. Even the Japanese system (which combines features of majoritarian exclusivism and corporatism), highly regarded for its government's role in the country's economic performance, is not immune from the highly personalized politics that is so much a part of the American political scene. A complaint often voiced about the nature of American politics is echoed by an aide to a former Japanese prime minister who ponders in regard to the prime ministerial succession: "There's not much to choose between these candidates in terms of policy. What counts is the personalities, and personalities are everything in the ruling party."[30] The trivializing elements of politics also are noticeable. Until a recent shift in the scheme for electing members to the Japanese House of Councillors (the upper chamber of the Diet), "members of Japan's upper house of Parliament [were] picked as candidates not as much for their legislative skills as for their vote-catching appeal. Over the years, few countries have turned to celebrities for high office as consistently as Japan—not even the United States. . . ."[31]

The lesson if short is by this time also very clear. There are no unequivocal formulas to improve simultaneously the prospects of generating direction, achieving effectiveness, and securing acceptance. Indeed, there turn out to be none even for the first of these tasks. Panaceas are in short supply. If this is an obvious truth, it is also not meant to deny the unique qualities of the American system of governance. For while the leadership question is everywhere problematic, the American system does stand out in important respects.

First, the separation of powers system combined with weak parties and district elections provides for distinctively different electoral incentives. While the president and members of Congress share powers, they do not necessarily share electoral fates, and in that fact inevitably lies an important conflict of interests. Under stress, therefore, the "troops" often lack discipline. Members of the legislature are driven to do what they can to maximize their electoral safety, and presidents are driven to get what they want quickly. Second, the tangled lines of accountability in the American system and the individualistic culture make for a high level of entrepreneurship and self-promotion. Fortified by omnipresent media coverage, this tends to produce a high propensity for political theatre—a style conducive to, and nurtured by, conflict. Third, the incentives offered by the system of constituency representation and by the system of congressional committees and subcommittees emphasize localistic and pressure group particularism contributing (for better or worse) to an unusually high level of unstructured diversity. Neither the maximizing style of the elite nor the incentives and culture that promote this behavior are very conducive to quiet cooperation or responsibility—which, however, is not to say that these are never achieved.

There are, of course, countervailing tendencies. Yet even these have their ironies. The budget process that the Congress legislated to goad itself into some measure of fiscal discipline as a result of the challenges of the Nixon era has produced a reasonable amount of cooperation and responsibility, provided for a centralizing thrust in the Congress where there had been none, and developed a staff apparatus (the Congressional Budget Office) of apparently greater political independence than its executive counterpart (OMB). Ironically, however, the better the congressional process of budget making and reconciliation works, the more presidents may see it as a threat, unless, of course, Congress adopts their budget proposals. What makes Congress more responsible as a corporate body, therefore, also can make it a more powerful adversary of the president's.

Most definably, however, the American system stands out for its fluid and particularized responsiveness rather than for its capacity to broadly organize constituencies. It stands out too for the inherent and intended conflict promoted within the government by the system of separate institutions sharing power. And, not least of all, it stands out for its culture of individualistic promotion and antistatism. In this culture, individualistic promotion influences the style of the elite while antistatism constrains the range of definable "solutions" to problems.

DIRECTION, EFFECTIVENESS, ACCEPTANCE: A TENUOUS TRIANGLE

In its most simple form, the leadership question inquires only into the means for generating political will, that is, providing direction. Since this has been our chief concern, we can see that even this relatively simple question is abundantly complex. When we add the additional elements of effectiveness and acceptance, we make the leadership question appropriately rich but also seemingly insoluble.

Although in democratic systems direction that lacks legitimacy will normally be foiled, a more complex formulation of the leadership problem is shown below:

$$\text{political will (direction)} \neq \text{quality solutions (effectiveness)} \neq \text{acceptance (legitimacy)}$$

There is, in short, no simple equivalence across these concepts, and also no single agreed criterion behind any of them. Evaluating the linkages among them is, therefore, problematic.

The issue of quality solutions (effectiveness) is particularly troubling because we often have very different ideas of what this should mean. To appropriate the language of economics, the reason for this is that we have no general welfare function. In the more familiar lexicon of political science, there is no common definition of "the public interest," and even if such a definition existed, would we have operational guides to transmit the general line to the firing line?

While "quality solutions" ultimately remain subjective, there is some, if hardly conclusive, evidence that countries significantly characterized by the corporatist inclusive model (through which syndication and bargaining are the mechanisms of governance) have experienced the greatest effectiveness in basic performance. In one study, for example, an index of corporatist characteristics and one of fiscal ineffectiveness is correlated at -.63.[32] Another study emphasizes the link between corporatism and legitimacy, finding that systems with corporatist structures have the least negative resistance to the growth of the welfare state and its accompanying growth in taxation.[33] Correlations are not causes, however. Thus, even if the structures associated with the corporatist model were causal agents for these results, the evolution of such structures is deeply tied to the nature of social development, an inhibitor even to artful schemes of sociopolitical engineering.

In considering the three variables—direction, effectiveness, and legitimacy—the last has been viewed as the leading value of the American political system. Indeed, Samuel Huntington has argued that precisely because of the legitimacy of the political order and the resources of the society, the United States has had a lesser need for governmental intervention. Its incapacity to generate much political will, therefore, was not historically a deep liability.[34] At least since the Great Depression, however, this apparent consensus has changed. Activist government previously seemed to necessitate activist governors. Now, however, activist governors are (perhaps especially) necessary even for those who wish government to be less active. Because the products of government intervention are firmly in place, the generation of considerable political will, ironically, is required to alter them and to uproot their supporting political structures.

MORE PRESIDENTIALISM?

Behind many proposed institutional reforms in the United States is the anticipation that they will increase the capability of government to act in coherent and responsible ways, an outlook that nearly always means enhancing the president's ability to govern on behalf of his goals. By implication at least, many of these reforms or the basic assumptions underlying them are discussed in prior chapters, especially the first. These include reforms to strengthen the political parties as collective agents by reducing the role of single purpose groups and eliminating direct popular selection of nominees; reforms to enable the president to strengthen his ability to give direction to his administration; reforms to strengthen central leadership and policy-making processes in the Congress; constitutional reforms (such as the four-year congressional term) to press the members of the president's party in

Congress to face electoral forces similar to those the president faces; and, finally, reforms to depoliticize the presidency (the single six-year term) in the hope that it will enhance the legitimacy and purposefulness of the officeholder.

The specific effects of changes requiring constitutional consent in order to be passed are probably less important than the sentiments that would be responsible for bringing them to that point. It is exceedingly hard, however, to imagine such legal changes occurring—either to depoliticize the presidency, to give presidents line-item veto authority, to have congressional and presidential terms run concurrently, or especially, to alter the design of the system altogether to a parliamentary one. Aside from a few modest stirrings, such proposals have had no serious political support, much less the overwhelming support that would be required to amend the Constitution. To this point no amendment has effectively altered the institutional balance put forth in the Constitution.[35]

Perhaps the parties can be strengthened as collective agents by less profound legal change—statutory laws and internal rules. But such changes are likely to be marginal or unpredictable. Legal reforms cannot create unity and organizational strength where there is an exhaustion of ideas. And, alas, some efforts to condense the seemingly endless electoral process in the United States may have had just the opposite effect. The effort (a quite modest one) by the Democratic party's Hunt Commission to condense the proliferation of presidential primaries into a three-month period has spawned new straw polls and candidate "beauty contests" occurring over a year and a half before the general election. Ceaseless contestation seems to be the outcome even when that is no longer the intention.[36]

To a considerable degree, an area in which there has been some measure of increased central control has been in the president's direction of his administration. But that direction has been an imposed and asymmetric one, and it may be relevant only to a program of contraction. In his book, *A Government of Strangers,* Hugh Heclo correctly identifies a key problem in the executive as the need to combine direction (the political impetus) with knowledge (the civil servant's know-how to make things work).[37] The administrative presidency, first proclaimed under Nixon and greatly amplified under Reagan, however, is not the reciprocal relationship urged by Heclo. Instead, it is an imposed set of controls (personnel and organizational) deriving from the White House designed to deny, rather than make use of, the skills and experience of the career civil service.[38] This situation has arisen in part from White House desires to shut out of the administrative sphere, as far as possible, congressional influences and clientele pressures, and to weaken the resistances of the bureaucracy to change; that is, to alter an environment of bureaucratic exclusivism and, to some extent, splintered inclusivism, to one of majoritarian exclusivism. The Civil Service Reform Act of 1978 (CSRA) by setting up a Senior Executive Service (SES) additionally made possible further politicization of the bureaucracy and weakening of the civil service.

The Congress—its organization and operation—continues to be very relevant to a president's programmatic fate. As we have earlier noted, both centralizing and decentralizing tendencies have developed within the legislative institution. The decentralizing tendencies weaken those presidential plans that are based on a linked set of proposals. But the centralizing tendencies can make an effective Congress both a powerful adversary and an ally of the president. The budgetary process (a centralizing tendency) as employed in Congress between 1981 and 1983 illustrates how the same mechanism alternately can affect presidential plans positively and negatively. The reconciliation process when employed in 1981 helped to put President Reagan's program in place, but when employed more recently has instead helped put it in its place. Still, even if substantially caused by the prominence of budgetary matters and accompanied by a sizeable reduction of legislative ones, these centralizing tendencies in Congress do enhance the potential for effective bargaining between institutions at a very broad-scoped level of policy making.

In brief, it seems to be that those "reforms" designed to most strengthen the political power of the president require changes that are obviously politically unattainable, whereas those that are attainable lack unequivocal effects. Even the strengthening of the administrative hand of the president is partly illusory because inattentiveness to the perspectives of career personnel jeopardizes effectiveness in government, unless the operational definition of effectiveness is government by presidential fiat.

The key issue, in any event, remains not merely the president's exercise of political will, but the molding together of direction, effectiveness, and legitimacy in government however that can be achieved—if it can. The insecurities endemic to the Washington environment, the fragile support base available to presidents, and the need to "make a record" while the "making" can be done are factors contributing to an effort to politicize and control whatever possible, and, thus, to the creation of the administrative presidency. The briefness of political openings and the maximizing climate are conducive to acting fast and often in an impromptu way; continuity, thought, independent advice, and problem solving are discouraged in this hyperpoliticized ambience.

A resort to more presidentialism without a sufficient concern for making the whole of government more effective hardly seems an appropriate prescription. Refitting the presidency with more powerful tools of governance, of course, poses risks from the standpoint of legitimacy because it grants more authority to a single central source. If by granting more tools, however, we also provide for more certainty and a commensurate need for less politicization, the possibility of matching an increased political will with effectiveness may be correspondingly enlarged. But no one can say for sure how different presidents would behave under conditions granting enlarged prerogatives. Institutions have their limits. Edward Heath and Margaret Thatcher, Charles de Gaulle and François Mitterand, Willy Brandt and Helmut Kohl presiding over the same institutional apparatus nonetheless have operated in different ways—some pressing their advantage, some creating a new agenda, others reversing field or mediating political pressures. No leadership style is guaranteed by institutional features alone as this passage regarding British party government astutely illustrates:

Only in war-time have the British been responsive to energetic or mobilising leaders. British prime ministers are hardly popular figures. . . . Since 1945, only Mac-Millan and Wilson have maintained the support of more than half of the electorate for two years or more. . . .

Assertions of a national destiny by Joseph Chamberlain or Oswald Mosley, a national identity by Enoch Powell, and the Dunkirk spirit by Wilson in 1967 or Heath in 1974 all fall on deaf ears in peace time. The "State of England" literature, with its call for directive leadership implicitly, though mistakenly, suggests that things were different in the past. In view of this disjunction between the institutions and the culture it is more understandable why the diaries and autobiographies of recent ministers convey a sense of governments being hemmed in, of trying to cope, rather than adhering to an overall strategy.[39]

Despite the powerful mobilizing tools provided British government, those of centristic party government and of a highly centralized bureaucracy, and despite the calls for both strong political leadership and more authority in governmental institutions, neither effectiveness nor acceptance has been the recent hallmark of governance in Britain. At least until Thatcher reasserted the vitality of party government, one British analyst argued that the thrust of reforms in governance in recent years in Britain has been away "from the one-party centralised, hierarchical form of government we have known since 1945."[40] And what may produce effective leadership? Let us listen carefully to his conclusion:

An alternative is that maintaining consent and coping with complexity require more power-sharing. The greater the number of decision-points and decision-makers the greater the need for agreement. Effective leadership may now depend on a modern version of John Calhoun's doctrine of concurrent majorities among big groups. . . .[41]

Everywhere that concern exists about ineffective drift, there is a search for answers to the leadership question. The status quo, Richard Rose reminds us, is after all not static.[42] The fact that the leadership question, if posed in somewhat different forms, is universally asked should lead us to move away from the parochialism of our own American dilemma—indeed, from the constraining characteristics of single country analysis and from a singular focus on the presidency. Simply to get the descriptive elements of the question right, we need to look at the problem of how governing actually is done in an explicitly comparative way. What styles of elite and mass behavior are the norm, and why? What bargains, deals, assumptions, and expectations enter in to the process of policy making? How are outcomes affected? In what ways is knowledge used (or abused)? Where are interests pressed? How much variability exists across policy areas and how can these sensibly be characterized? And how, above all, is direction arrived at?

That the leadership question is universally asked also should lead us to think about the temporal functions attached to generating direction. To what extent is direction inevitably episodic? To what extent is it inevitably eroded over time as the impetus for change winds down? To what extent do governments eventually get energized only when attending to crises? To what extent are we investing unrealistic aspirations in the capacities of governments and of leaders to be effective in identifying problems whose symptoms are not currently salient?

Studies of policy making suggest that effective leadership derives not from a single source, but usually from complementary sources. In order for leadership to be both effective and legitimate, central leaders (chief executives) need to heighten their awareness of this without at the same time succumbing to an excess of particularistic payoffs. In the American system it is just possible that appreciation for this need has diminished while the propensity for feeding particularistic excesses has been reinforced. For our system has spawned a disunited state and a myriad of narrow-gauged interests. To compensate, we have created a mystique of presidential leadership to provide for a centralized source of policy making, relying largely upon the personal qualities of the president to overcome the obstacles engendered by this disunity and by the weak aggregating capacities of the intermediary organizations in American political life. The mystique is part illusion, of course. Regardless of the fabled sign on Harry Truman's desk, "the buck" need not (in part because it often cannot) "stop" there. The sign (which leaders now display as evidence of their leadership) contributes to the illusion that presidents are the government as well as the sum of leadership in the system.

The enterprise of governing is a great deal more complex than the mythology of presidential command or, for that matter, party government. The American system expresses this complexity through the convolutedness of its governing structure. Is it possible for presidents to get a handle on government under these conditions? The answer depends on how we (and the president) conceptualize the presidential role in the system. If we expect presidents to command and to have government respond to their bidding, then the answer, with rare exceptions, is probably not. If we expect them, however, to be influential participants in the process, making use of those resources often thought to be obstacles (the career bureaucracy and congressional perspectives), they have a chance not only to make their impact felt but, above all, to lay a foundation of trust in a system built on its opposite. The balance between coherence and compromise is always brittle, but if the former is a desired goal and the latter a preferred means, then habits and outlooks will be of special importance.

Herein, the importance of institutions lies in the change of outlook they may induce and the habits they may help form but in no way can guarantee. Yet, our habits and outlooks also influence the way our institutions operate. The streak of populism and evangelical expectation that courses through our history and, to some extent, is spread across nearly all tendencies in the U.S. political spectrum creates a style of politics that discourages respect for governance and government, and, too often, for the virtues of quiet cooperation. Indeed, this suggests that more presidentialism—the belief that presidents are the sole directors of the system and can be thought to have their success measured through "scorecards"—is a corrosive the system can do without. In a system that breeds insecurities, disunity, and hyperpoliticization, is it possible to generate in the elite a sense of confidence in itself and a belief in the value of cooperative processes?

How may we induce change likely to promote a greater degree of elite unity and accommodation without also insulating it from changes occurring in society? The question I pose is no universal solvent, to be sure. After all, it implies limits to the idea of abrupt change and of the malleability of public problems to clear-cut formulations. It implies also that the politicization of more and more of government threatens the balance between direction and competence. In short, my question will inevitably be viewed as a conservative one that denies the essence and the virtues of adversarial politics, virtues that presumably result when issues and interests clash sharply. Such criticisms, I think, are fair. Moreover, the answers to my question are nowhere apparent.

Yet, if politics fundamentally is about conflict and government about cooperation, then the issue is not whether one or the other should dominate but rather the nature of the equilibrium that obtains between the elements. No doubt, how one judges the question I pose will depend greatly on how this equilibrium is perceived.

"The rule of governmental action," asserts Woodrow Wilson (whose words are better heeded than his behavior), "is necessary cooperation. The method of political development is conservative adaptation, shaping old habits into new ones, modifying old means to accomplish new ends." In this, "The histories of other peoples may furnish us with light, but they cannot furnish us with conditions of action. Every nation must constantly keep in touch with its past; it cannot run towards its ends around sharp corners."[43]

The final irony in these words of Woodrow Wilson is that in the United States "conservative adaptation" in political style operates against a conservative solution to the leadership question. To reconstitute political institutions is one thing; to reconstitute a society and its culture quite another. The first seems unattainable while the second seems inconceivable. Thus, that which lies within ourselves also cuts against our grain—ensuring, I suspect, that the leadership question will remain both centrally important and only rarely answered.

NOTES

1. As put by Richard Rose, "To state that there is no single objective pervasively guiding government activities at a given moment, or that there is no single set of relatively clear and coordinated objectives directing government in a given four-year period is but to say that there is no single central individual or institution giving direction to American government." Richard Rose, *Managing Presidential Objectives* (New York: The Free Press, 1976), pp. 6-7.

2. See Mancur Olson, *The Rise and Decline of Nations: Economic Growth, Stagflation, and Social Rigidities* (New Haven, Conn.: Yale University Press, 1982). A somewhat different perspective

simply suggests that the policy space is finite, and once policies have been generated the available space for large changes in them is reduced. See, here, Brian Hogwood and B. Guy Peters, *Policy Dynamics* (New York: St. Martin's Press, 1983), esp. pp. 2-3.

3. See on this point Andrew S. McFarland, *Power and Leadership in Pluralist Systems* (Stanford, Calif.: Stanford University Press, 1969); and Bert A. Rockman, "Conclusion: Elites and Social Inquiry," in *Elite Studies and Communist Politics: Essays in Memory of Carl Beck,* ed. Ronald H. Linden and Bert A. Rockman (Pittsburgh: UCIS, 1984).

4. On the last point particularly, see Albert Camus, *The Rebel: An Essay on Man in Revolt* (New York: Vintage, 1956).

5. Richard Rose, *Do Parties Make a Difference?* (Chatham, N.J.: Chatham House, 1980), p. 161.

6. Fritz W. Scharpf, Bernd Reissert, and Fritz Schnabel, "Policy Effectiveness and Conflict Avoidance in Intergovernmental Policy Formation," Discussion Paper Series, International Institute of Management, Wissenschaftszentrum, Berlin (December 1977), pp. 67, 69.

7. Jerome Milch, "Influence as Power: French Local Government Reconsidered," *British Journal of Political Science* 4 (Spring 1974): 139-162.

8. See, for instance, Alberta Sbragia, "Not All Roads Lead to Rome: Local Housing Policy in the Unitary Italian State," *British Journal of Political Science* 9 (April 1979): 315-339.

9. Richard Rose, "The Variability of Party Government: A Theoretical and Empirical Critique," *Political Studies* 17 (December 1969): 414.

10. Anthony King notes, for instance, that there is very little cross-party contact in the clear majoritarian situations prevailing in Britain and France, but more of such contact in the coalitional West German Bundestag. See his "Modes of Executive-Legislative Interaction: Great Britain, France, and West Germany," *Legislative Studies Quarterly* (February 1976): 11-36.

11. See, for instance, Dennis Kavanagh, "Party Politics in Question," in *New Trends in British Politics: Issues for Research,* ed. Dennis Kavanagh and Richard Rose (London: Sage Publications, 1977), pp. 191-220; Michael R. Gordon, "Civil Servants, Politicians, and Parties: Shortcomings in the British Policy Process," *Comparative Politics* 4 (October 1971): 29-58; and Rose, "The Variability of Party Government."

12. B. Guy Peters, "The Problem of Bureaucratic Government," *Journal of Politics* 43 (February 1981): 81.

13. For example, see Grant McConnell, *Private Power and American Democracy* (New York: Alfred A. Knopf, 1967); and Theodore J. Lowi, *The End of Liberalism: The Second Republic of the United States,* 2nd ed. (New York: W. W. Norton, 1979).

14. Peters, "The Problem of Bureaucratic Government," p. 82.

15. Martin O. Heisler with Robert B. Kvavik, "Patterns of European Politics: The 'European Polity' Model," in *Politics in Europe: Structures and Processes in Some Postindustrial Democracies,* ed. Martin O. Heisler (New York: David McKay, 1974), p. 74.

16. *Ibid.* Also see Thomas J. Anton, *Administered Politics* (Boston: Martinus Nijhoff, 1980); and Johan P. Olsen, "Governing Norway," in *Presidents and Prime Ministers,* ed. Richard Rose and Ezra N. Suleiman (Washington, D.C.: American Enterprise Institute, 1980), esp. pp. 248-255.

17. Anton, *Administered Politics,* pp. 158-178.

18. Robert A. Dahl, *A Preface to Democratic Theory* (Chicago: Phoenix Books, 1963), pp. 131-132.

19. *Ibid.,* p. 150.

20. See, for instance, Samuel P. Huntington, "Postindustrial Politics: How Benign Will It Be?" *Comparative Politics* 6 (January 1974): 163-192. For reflections on empirical evidence derived from a cross-national survey, see Max Kaase and Samuel Barnes, "In Conclusion: The Future of Political Protest in Western Democracies," in *Political Action: Mass Participation in Five Western Democracies,* ed. Samuel H. Barnes and Max Kaase (Beverly Hills: Sage Publications, 1979), pp. 523-536.

21. For documentation of the growth of bureaucratic activity, see Joel D. Aberbach, Robert D. Putnam, and Bert A. Rockman, *Bureaucrats and Politicians in Western Democracies* (Cambridge, Mass.: Harvard University Press, 1981), pp. 2-3.

22. For supporting evidence of the entrepreneurial style of leadership in America—a system which most closely approximates the attributes of a splintered inclusive environment—see Jack L. Walker, "Setting the Agenda of the U.S. Senate: A Theory of Problem Selection," *British Journal of Political Science* 7 (July 1977): 423-445; Charles O. Jones, *Clean Air: The Policies and Politics of Pollution Control* (Pittsburgh: University of Pittsburgh Press, 1975); Lennart Lundqvist, *The Hare and the Tortoise: Clean Air Policies in the United States and Sweden* (Ann Arbor: The University of Michigan Press, 1980).

23. The persistence necessary for following through and the attention to detail required for gaining direction are indeed significant costs. Note here Richard Rose, "The President: A Chief but Not an Executive," *Presidential Studies Quarterly* 7 (Winter 1977): 5-26.

24. Anton, *Administered Politics*, pp. 163-165.

25. See, especially, here, Anthony Downs, "Up and Down with Ecology: The Issue-Attention Cycle," *The Public Interest* 28 (Summer 1972): 38-50, and Charles O. Jones, "Speculative Augmentation in Federal Air Pollution Policy-Making," *Journal of Politics* 36 (May 1974): 438-464. The dilemma is that while aroused public attentiveness creates possibilities for innovative action and makes movement attractive, it also creates conditions that make implementation difficult and continually subject to negotiation.

26. Norman J. Ornstein, "The House and the Senate in a New Congress," in *The New Congress,* ed. Thomas E. Mann and Norman J. Ornstein (Washington, D.C.: American Enterprise Institute, 1981), pp. 382-383.

27. Philippe C. Schmitter, "Interest Intermediation and Regime Governability in Contemporary Western Europe and North America," in *Organizing Interests in Western Europe,* ed. Suzanne D. Berger (Cambridge, England: Cambridge University Press, 1981), p. 313.

28. See, for example, the analyses of Graham K. Wilson, "Why Is There No Corporatism in the United States?," in *Patterns of Corporatist Policy-Making,* ed. Gerhard Lehmbruch and Philippe C. Schmitter (London: Sage, 1982), pp. 219-236; and Robert H. Salisbury, "Why No Corporatism in America?," in *Trends Toward Corporatist Intermediation* (Beverly Hills: Sage, 1979), pp. 213-230.

29. Arend Lijphart, *The Politics of Accommodation: Pluralism and Democracy in the Netherlands,* 2nd ed. (Berkeley: University of California Press, 1975).

30. Henry Scott-Stokes, "4 Enter Contest to Be Japanese Premier," *New York Times,* October 17, 1982, p. A3.

31. Clyde Haberman, "Stars in Japan's Politics Have Lost the Limelight," *New York Times,* June 23, 1983, p. A4.

32. Schmitter, "Interest Intermediation," p. 313.

33. Harold L. Wilensky, *The 'New Corporatism,' Centralization, and the Welfare State* (London: Sage, 1976), esp. pp. 34-47.

34. Samuel P. Huntington, *Political Order in Changing Societies* (New Haven: Yale University Press, 1968). See his essay, "Political Modernization: America vs. Europe," pp. 93-139, esp. the discussion, pp. 134-139.

35. I include, in this regard, the Twenty-second Amendment limiting the president to two elected terms since no president before FDR ever served more than two elected terms, and no president since, except Eisenhower, has served two full elected terms. In short, I believe the effects of this amendment are inconsequential.

36. I am indebted to my colleague Michael Johnston for this insight.

37. Hugh Heclo, *A Government of Strangers: Executive Politics in Washington* (Washington: The Brookings Institution, 1977), esp. pp. 6-8.

38. For a description of the processes employed, see Richard P. Nathan, *The Administrative Presidency* (New York: John Wiley, 1983).

39. Dennis Kavanagh, "From Gentlemen to Players: Changes in Political Leadership," in *Britain: Progress and Decline,* Tulane Studies in Political Science, vol. 17, ed. William L. Gwyn and Richard Rose (New Orleans: Tulane University, 1980), p. 90.

40. *Ibid.,* p. 91.

41. *Ibid.*

42. Richard Rose, *Understanding Big Government,* forthcoming.

43. Woodrow Wilson, *The State* (Boston: D. C. Heath, 1903), p. 639.

Index

About the Author

BERT A. ROCKMAN is Professor of Political Science at the University of Pittsburgh. He is coauthor of *Bureaucrats and Politicians in Western Democracies* and coeditor of *Elite Studies and Communist Politics: Essays in Memory of Carl Beck*. He has contributed articles to leading scholarly journals in the United States and abroad, and to several anthologies.

He has served on the editorial boards of the *American Political Science Review* and the *Policy Studies Journal* and on the steering committee of the Presidency Research Group.